University of Wisconsin
Center for Southeast Asian Studies

Monograph Number 8

RECALLING THE REVOLUTION

Center for Southeast Asian Studies
University of Wisconsin
Monograph Series

Publications Committee

RECALLING THE REVOLUTION

MEMOIRS OF A FILIPINO GENERAL

by

Santiago V. Alvarez

translation by Paula Carolina S. Malay

introduction by Ruby R. Paredes

published in cooperation with
Ateneo de Manila University Press

University of Wisconsin
Center for Southeast Asian Studies

1992

This manuscript has been translated from a Tagalog typescript of a text that appeared in the Tagalog weekly *Sampagita* from July 1927 to April 1928 under the title *Ang katipunan at Paghihimagsik* [The Katipunan and the Revolution] .

Cover Photo: Courtesy of the Library of Congress.

Library of Congress Card No. 92-71216

ISBN: 1-881261-04-2 (cloth)
ISBN: 1-881261-05-0 (paper)

Published by the

Center for Southeast Asia Studies
University of Wisconsin-Madison
Madison, WI 53706
USA

Telephone: (608) 263-1755
FAX: (608) 262-2150

Asian Edition with original Tagalog text and English translation published by Ateneo de Manila University Press, P.O. Box 154, 1099 Manila, Philippines.

Table of Contents

Maps

TRANSLATOR'S NOTE

Paula Carolina S. Malay

The Philippine Revolution of 1896 aimed to bring an end to Spanish colonial rule in the country. Inspired by the movement led by lawyer Marcelo H. del Pilar and physician Jose Rizal, which exposed the oppressive character of the regime, Andres Bonifacio organized a secret society, the Katipunan—a brotherhood of "sons of the people"—to become the vehicle for the expulsion of the hated Spanish rule. The revolutionary movement quickly spread from Manila to the Tagalog regions north and south of the city.

In Cavite province south of Manila, two factions emerged: the Magdiwang and the Magdalo. The author of this memoir, Santiago V. Alvarez, was a general of the army of the Magdiwang. Emilio Aguinaldo became the acclaimed leader of the Magdalo after spectacular victories in battle against the Spanish forces in his Cavite stronghold.

As the Katipunan's "Supremo," Bonifacio visited Cavite at the invitation of his Magdiwang supporters to drum up support for the revolution. He received an enthusiastic welcome from the Magdiwang-dominated areas, but was rebuffed by the Magdalo group which wanted him replaced as head of the Katipunan. The latter wanted new leadership in the revolutionary government, and their choice was Aguinaldo, the fast-rising, home-grown Cavite militarist. Aguinaldo was in his twenties when elected head of the new government at an assembly called in Magdalo territory.

The assembly, composed mainly of Magdalo partisans, humiliated Bonifacio, saying that because of his lack of formal education, he did not deserve the position of head of the revolutionary government. The Katipunan Supremo was deposed and executed on orders of the new leadership.

These events are the highlights of this memoir written by a participant-eyewitness of the 1896 Philippine Revolution. More important than the highlights, however, are the insights into the day-to-day happenings that give flesh to the historical account and add a human dimension to the Revolution.

The present memoir, Santiago V. Alvarez's *Ang Katipunan at Paghihimagsik* [The Katipunan and the Revolution] was originally published in serial form in 36 installments in *Sampagita*, a Manila weekly magazine, from July 1927 to April 1928. Historian Leandro H. Fernandez had the memoir copied in typescript. Pedro B. Ayuda, like myself a member at the time of the Philippine Booklovers Society, owned a carbon copy of the typescript. I borrowed this for this translation, undertaken under the auspices of the Translation Project Group, Association of Asian Studies.

After I finished the translation, I returned the copy of the memoir to Mr. Ayuda. Subsequently, I learned that he sold this document to Dr. Nicanor Tiongson, currently artistic director of the Cultural Center of the Philippines. I owe to Dr. Tiongson the information about the provenance of the typescript of the Alvarez memoir.

The memoir was written in Tagalog, now called Filipino. Although this is the language we speak at home, General Alvarez's written Tagalog posed some problems for this translator. While his style is clear and often engaging, he wrote as he would presumeably speak—spontaneously, as in oral narrative—with little regard for punctuation. For greater lucidity, I have broken his overly long sentences into shorter statements. I have also avoided literal renderings, striving for simple, straightforward English.

Although this is my first attempt at translation, the task has given me much pleasure. For the first time, I have seen the human side of the Philippine Revolution. I have seen action and drama, as in a good play or novel. The action is gripping, sometimes gory; the narration is graphic but always insightful.

Finally, I wish to acknowledge the emoluments paid by the Translation Project Group of the Association of Asian Studies, which made this project possible.

Quezon City
February 1991

INTRODUCTION

THE REVOLUTIONARY AS HISTORIAN

Ruby R. Paredes

Drawn from fragments of memory and fragile perception, a people's history is more than a recollection of its shared past. Pulled by the currents of cultural change, each generation recasts the past to serve the imperatives of its present, often selecting a central event in the national pageant as the focus for reinterpretation. Since the Revolution of 1896 is the seminal event in the emergence of the modern Philippines, three succeeding generations of Filipinos have written and rewritten its history over the past sixty years.

The leaders of the revolution, educated in Spanish and inspired by the liberal European nationalism of the late nineteenth century, began writing their memoirs in the 1920s, nearly a quarter century after its defeat. Like General Santiago Alvarez, several prominent revolutionaries wrote to make a record of their era for the *sajones* or "Anglo-Saxons," the younger generation of English-speaking professionals whose education in American colonial schools was alienating them from the struggles and sensibilities of the 1890s. Concerned that the youth of the 1920s might forget, these aging revolutionaries combined history and autobiography to create straightforward chronicles of battles and leaders. The revolution's commander, General Emilio Aguinaldo, produced memoirs seeking to vindicate his leadership and secure his place in history, which were widely read as the authoritative account, despite their apparent personal and factional bias. Other histories, including General Alvarez's more critical memoir, attracted little attention and soon sank into obscurity.

In the years following the trauma and destruction of World War II, a generation of academic historians, notably Teodoro A. Agoncillo, began writing textbook histories of the revolution for the children of a newly independent Republic. Although written with the tools of a professional researcher, Agoncillo's two major studies[1] had a larger didactic aim—to create proper heroes to inspire the young citizens of a new nation. Drawing upon General Aguinaldo's memoirs, Agoncillo's account glorified both the revolution and its commander.

During the 1970s, a younger generation of academic historians, in particular Reynaldo C. Ileto and Milagros C. Guerrero, produced revisionist accounts of the revolution for the "martial law babies" of the Marcos era.[2] No longer able to share Agoncillo's implied assumption that nationalism and independence could solve the nation's problems, these historians applied more critical analyses to the class and factional conflicts that had troubled the revolution.

Although each generation has written and rewritten the revolution's history for the youth of its day, there is, nonetheless, an informal dialogue across these generations. Writing with a less heroic view of the revolution in the 1970s, Guerrero and Ileto have, in effect, gone beyond Agoncillo or General Aguinaldo and returned to the empirical evidence and critical perspective that first appeared in General Alvarez's memoirs during the 1920s. While the first generation of writers had tried to create a pantheon of national heroes, more recent historians have sought the human dimensions of that nationalist pageant to recover a more immediate sense of people and events. The rediscovery of the Alvarez account by contemporary historians indicates that it is time for him to emerge from the footnotes and speak directly to the modern generation of Filipinos and Philippine historians.

Publication History

In July 1927, the popular Tagalog weekly *Sampagita* began publication of a 36-part serial by General Santiago V. Alvarez titled *Ang Katipunan at Ang Paghihimagsik* [The Katipunan and the Revolution], his memoirs of the 1896 revolution against Spain. Working from notes taken during the

---

[1] *The Revolt of the Masses: The Story of Bonifacio and the Katipunan* (Quezon City: University of the Philippines, 1956) and *Malolos: The Crisis of the Republic* (Quezon City: University of the Philippines, 1960).

[2] Begun as doctoral research projects at U.S. universities, both studies have since been published. See Reynaldo C. Ileto, *Pasyon and Revolution* (Manila: Ateneo de Manila University Press, 1979) and Milagros C. Guerrero, "The Provincial and Municipal Elites of Luzon During the Revolution, 1898-1902," in *Philippine Social History*, ed. A. W. McCoy and E. de Jesus (Manila: Ateneo de Manila University Press, 1981), 155-190.

years of war and internecine struggle, General Alvarez produced an extensive history containing what one modern Filipino historian has called "immensely useful information about the Katipunan."[3]

Although published in a major Manila weekly over sixty years ago, the Alvarez memoir is known to only a few academic specialists on the period. Available only in manuscript form at the Philippine National Library and a few private Manila libraries, and in serial form at the Ateneo de Manila and the University of Wisconsin Southeast Asia library collection, it has remained beyond the reach of most Filipino and foreign students of the revolution. General Alvarez wrote in the hope that his memoir would educate a younger generation of Filipinos about their national revolution, but the work's subsequent obscurity until now has defeated its author's intentions.

Fortuitously, the Association for Asian Studies (AAS) formed the Translations Project Group (TPG) in 1968 to promote the publication of translations of book-length manuscripts. Financed by a grant from the Ford Foundation, the TPG (through its chair Paul van der Veur and board member C. O. Houston) commissioned a Filipino author, Paula Carolina Malay, to translate three works vital for Philippine historical studies.[4] Drawing on her wide knowledge of sources for the revolutionary period, Mrs. Malay offered to translate the Alvarez memoir from the original Tagalog. Starting work on the Alvarez manuscript by June 1973, Mrs. Malay completed the translation and annotation three years later. Although her translation of the Alvarez memoirs, now titled *Recalling the Revolution,* reached the Translations Project Group in January 1977, a series of editorial delays over the next thirteen years prevented its publication.

After sixty years of obscurity, General Alvarez's memoir is once again appearing in print, in a form that will make it more accessible than the original serialization in *Sampagita.* For a new generation of Filipinos and Philippine scholars, his memoir will shed new light and insight on the

---

[3]The assessment is current, not contemporaneous. See Ileto, *Pasyon and Revolution*, 333-334.

[4]The other manuscripts were Miguel Lucio Bustamante's *Si Tandang Basiong Macunat* (orig. Spanish, 1888) and Jacinto Manahan's *Tagumpay at Kasawian ng Himagsikan* (orig., Tagalog). As part of their involvement in Philippine historical studies, Mrs. Malay's husband, Dean Armando J. Malay, had already translated the memoirs of revolutionary general Artemio Ricarte a decade before Mrs. Malay began work on the Alvarez account.

events of the revolution. To understand its contribution to our understanding of the revolution, we must place the Alvarez memoir in the context of the literature on the revolution as it has developed over the span of three generations.

Generational Context

Serious historical research on the Philippine revolution began in 1924. Writing in Spanish, Teodoro M. Kalaw, the first among this early generation of Philippine historians, published his chronicle of the revolution and soon followed it with his own English translation of the same work.[5] Although he cited works by Aguinaldo, Ricarte and other revolutionaries as his sources,[6] Kalaw still regretted that his history "could not be more comprehensive...."[7] He anticipated additions and corrections to future editions and urged "each province and each general [to] write its or his own memoirs" about the revolution.[8]

In the years that followed publication of Kalaw's chronicle, three prominent revolutionary generals—Ricarte, Alvarez, and Aguinaldo—began work on their own memoirs. A few months before Alvarez began serializing his memoirs in 1927, Ricarte, then exiled in Yokohama, published his *Himagsikan Nang Manga Filipino Laban sa Kastila* [The Revolt of the Filipinos against the Spanish], first as a book and then serially in the pages of *Sampagita*.[9] The following year, General Emilio Aguinaldo, former

---

[5]Teodoro M. Kalaw, *The Philippine Revolution* (Mandaluyong, Rizal: Jorge B. Vargas Filipiniana Foundation, Reprint Series 1, 1969), vii. The published work of other Filipino historians, including Epifanio de los Santos on Andres Bonifacio in 1917 and Emilio Jacinto in 1918, were for the most part biographical monographs. See Epifanio de los Santos, *The Revolutionists: Aguinaldo, Bonifacio, Jacinto* (Manila: National Historical Commission, 1973).

[6]*Resena Veridica de la Revolucion Filipina* (1899) and Ricarte's *Apuntes Historicos de la Insurreccion por los Asociados al Katipunan* (no date); see "Bibliography" in Kalaw, *The Philippine Revolution*, 318.

[7]"[Author's] Preface to the First English Edition" dated Manila, May 14, 1925, in Kalaw, *The Philippine Revolution*, vii.

[8]Ibid., viii.

[9]The English version was published by the National Heroes Commission in 1963 to celebrate Andres Bonifacio's centenary. See Armando J. Malay, "Introduction," in *Memoirs of General Artemio Ricarte* (Manila: National Heroes Commission, 1963).

president of the revolutionary Republic, began reconstructing his memoirs from a diary and documents in his possession.[10]

Whether or not Alvarez and the others wrote in response to Kalaw's call is not known.[11] In the introduction to his work, Alvarez makes it clear that his purpose, like Kalaw's, was to address the younger generation of American-educated Filipinos who were born in the years since the last battles had been lost and thus had no personal memory of the revolution. Noting with approval that the youth of his old age were "discerning and discriminating as regards the competence of ... anyone who dares to write a history of the people," Alvarez makes oblique and dismissive references to some questionable works on the revolution. He is confident that youth will "look for motivations for such writings and inquire about their sources." As an "eyewitness and an active participant" in the revolution, Alvarez seemed sure that his own motivations could withstand such close scrutiny. Indeed, his credentials as a credible witness to history now seem, after close examination by several generations of historians, beyond dispute.

But as leader of one of the two factions that struggled for power during the revolution's first phase, General Alvarez's objectivity was, at the time he first published his memoirs, open to challenge. In the factional strife that characterized the Katipunan's internal politics during 1896-1897, internecine rivalries between the Magdiwang Council of Noveleta and the Magdalo Council of Kawit in the insurgent heartland of Cavite Province south of Manila had grown fierce and would ultimately become deadly. Alvarez belonged to the Magdiwang faction, of which his father Mariano[12] and cousin Pascual were president and secretary, respectively. The Alvarezes were unwavering in their support of Bonifacio and were rumored to be

---

[10]Felisa P. Diokno, Aguinaldo's private secretary, claims, "The original [memoir] in Tagalog was prepared by the General in his own handwriting between 1928 and 1946. See, "Introduction" in Emilio F. Aguinaldo, *My Memoirs*, trans. by Luz Colendrino-Bucu (Manila: Cristina Aguinaldo Suntay, 1967), xii.

[11]In the foreword to his account, Alvarez acknowledges the encouragement of nationalist writer Lope K. Santos, whose own work was crucial in the development of a Philippine national language.

[12]His father, Mariano, was a municipal captain of the town of Noveleta, in Cavite, who had been imprisoned and tortured in the wave of reprisals against Filipino liberals that followed the Cavite mutiny of 1872. For more biographical information on Mariano Alvarez, see E. Arsenio Manuel, *Dictionary of Philippine Biography*, Vol. II (Quezon City: Filipiniana Publications, 1970), 23-25.

related by blood to Bonifacio's wife, Gregoria de Jesus.[13] Apparently denying such a simple bias, General Alvarez proclaimed his close familial ties to the rival faction's leader, Emilio Aguinaldo, who was his brother-in-law. Moreover, Alvarez recalls that it was he who recruited Aguinaldo into the Katipunan and was present at his ritual induction by the society's Supremo Andres Bonifacio.

As these minor discrepancies indicate, Alvarez's generation of historians faced the basic problem of simple factual recall—establishing an accurate record of the names, dates, and sequence of events. Thus, these memorialists expended great energy over such mundane issues as the date and place of the first "cry of the revolution."

Moving beyond the array of simple facts required an exploration of more complex historiographic questions—the causes underlying the revolt, the social composition and varying motivations of the revolutionary forces, and the circumstances of their ultimate defeat. Tracing these events, from the origins of Bonifacio's revolutionary Katipunan in 1893 to its final defeat by the new American regime in 1902, involved Alvarez and this first generation of historians in questions of causation.

How did the movement, which began with such idealism under Bonifacio in the *arrabales* of Manila, descend into bitter factional rivalry between the Alvarezes' Magdiwang Council and the Aguinaldos' Magdalo after it spread to rural Cavite? Since there were similar councils based in other localities, why did the revolutionary struggle come down to an internal dispute between the Magdalo and Magdiwang? Why was Bonifacio ousted from leadership and later executed by the dominant Magdalo faction?

Although many of the details of Bonifacio's death were already known when Alvarez began writing, General Aguinaldo's precise role in giving the orders was still controversial. Since only a quarter century separated these writers from the humiliation of defeat and passionate debates among Katipunan veterans still raged over various versions of events, truth and objectivity became the overriding issues for this first generation of historians.

Seeking to meet the most "discerning and discriminating" standards for his history of the revolution, Alvarez explained his "motivations for such writing." He was, he explained, writing in the "interest of honorable truth."

---

[13]Teodoro A. Agoncillo makes the assertion, but cites no authority. See *Revolt of the Masses*, 178.

Like the other historians of his day, General Alvarez saw himself as a chronicler of memory, preserving the facts that he had witnessed as a record for a younger generation whose experience under American colonialism separated it from an understanding of the Spanish era's harsh realities.

New Historiography

In 1948, a full generation after the publication of the Alvarez memoir, Teodoro A. Agoncillo won first prize in a historical competition for his work on the revolutionary period. Published in 1956 as *The Revolt of the Masses*,[14] Agoncillo's work became the authoritative study of Bonifacio and the revolution of 1896 for a new, postwar generation coming of age under an independent Republic.

Pleading scarcity of biographical data, Agoncillo approached the political biography of Bonifacio through a study of his revolutionary secret society. To portray the Katipunan as embodiment of its founder, Agoncillo quoted extensively from contemporaneous documents and sources. Significantly, he drew what he calls his "most important data"[15] from his own interviews with General Emilio Aguinaldo—the Magdalo faction's leader who had seized control of the revolution from Bonifacio and then ordered his Supremo's execution on charges of treason. Significantly, Agoncillo does not make a single reference to the Alvarez memoir, the chief account of the rival Magdiwang faction that had remained loyal to Bonifacio.

Of equal importance, Agoncillo's analysis relies upon sweeping statements about the class character of the revolution. Arguing that the revolution was mass-based, Agoncillo referred to the Katipunan as "a distinctively plebeian society"[16] and insisted that: "None of its charter members were of the middle or aristocratic class."[17] Drawing upon this simplistic portrayal of Filipino society, Agoncillo characterized the middle class as "always ... opposed [to] the position taken by the mass of the people." With the same broad strokes, he caricatured the masses as "not accustomed to the intricacies of the rational processes ... [so that they] are moved by the impact of feeling and passion and refuse to see, if reminded by their intellectual betters, the probable effects of their planned action."[18]

---

[14]For bibliographical data, see Agoncillo, *Revolt of the Masses*.

[15]Prefatory note to "Bibliography," *Revolt of the Masses*, 369.

[16]Ibid., 1.

[17]Ibid., 45.

[18]Ibid., 99.

Despite their central importance to his argument, Agoncillo does not offer a precise definition of such terms as "plebeian," "mass," "middle class," or "elite" in the context of nineteenth-century Philippine society. He emphasizes "the ever-widening cleavage" between the Filipino classes and excoriates the middle class and intelligentsia for denying "the unlettered masses ... the privileges of their respectable group."[19] Thus, the full force of Agoncillo's condemnation of the Filipino elite—particularly for what he sees as their self-interested usurpation of leadership during the revolution's second phase in 1899—is juxtaposed with a hagiographic view of the Filipino masses and their heroism. The result is a sanitized, indeed idealized, view of the Philippine revolution.

In sharp contrast to "other social upheavals of mighty proportions," Agoncillo saw the Philippine revolution as "tame and carried on with due regard for individual life and property." While conceding some "excesses" and "apparent mistakes," Agoncillo nonetheless contends that: "There was no mob violence on a large scale; there was no useless destruction of property motivated by racial or class hatred; there were few, if any, instances of abuse of authority and arbitrary employment of new-found power."[20] In his insistence upon the positive, Agoncillo echoes his main source, General Aguinaldo, who described the town of Imus during the revolution as an idyllic community, a place of "love and cooperation ... [of] perfect peace and order ...," where there were "no untoward incidents ... nor were rape, banditry, or any other crime committed."[21]

History of the People

A careful review of the Alvarez memoir might have saved Agoncillo from such an idealized characterization. Portraying neither titans nor heroes, but Filipino men and women, Alvarez's account is textured with ordinary lives lived in an extraordinary time. Allowing the "sons of the people"[22]

---

[19]Ibid., 106.

[20]Ibid., 277.

[21]Aguinaldo, *My Memoirs*, 83.

[22]Laden with nationalist meaning and free of gender bias, the Tagalog term *Anak ng Bayan*, was part of the full title of the revolutionary society, i.e., *Kataas-taasang Kagalanggalang na Katipunan ng mga Anak ng Bayan*. Used as an honorific, the term connoted respect for the revolutionaries and was used interchangeably with *katipunero*.

both a voice and presence in his narrative, Alvarez transforms his memoir into history by adding accounts of the revolution from below.

Instead of Agoncillo's vague evocation of the "masses," General Alvarez offers us a detailed description of their actual participation in the revolution. In fact, sections of Alvarez's memoir were written by other named authors who were, without question, "of the masses." Speaking through the Alvarez memoir, Katipunero Juan Maibay, for example, recalls his almost overwhelming fear at the outbreak of the revolution. Caught unprepared and unsure by the exposure of the revolutionary Katipunan, this son of the people suddenly faced the enormity of the decision to fight the Spanish colonial state:

> I began shaking all over and my lips trembled so that I could not speak. My joints faltered and suddenly I felt very weak thinking of the dreadful fate I was sure was in store for me.

Even in the face of such trepidation, Maibay recalls that:

> I forced myself to gather courage and to face up to whatever was going to happen. I realized that my redemption lay nowhere else but with the looming struggle.

In spare prose devoid of hyperbole, Alvarez builds a dramatic intensity through his day-by-day chronicle of the revolution's history in all its complexity and contradictions. With an almost inadvertent candor, he reveals appalling scarcities of arms and food. The revolution's soldiers were unfamiliar with firearms, and, at one critical juncture, a former member of the Spanish *guardia civil* turned revolutionary had to show them how to use a captured Mauser rifle. Moving quickly for strategic advantage, the sons of the people lacked any sort of logistics and eased their hunger by collecting money from the ranks to buy food from stores in the town.

Yet their will to fight was fierce. Using *bolos* when firearms were not available, the Katipuneros were inspired by the speeches of their commanders. Urging his men toward total sacrifice, Magdiwang President Mariano Alvarez said:

> [T]he Revolution cannot be stopped.... Do not lose faith; pray for our victory and give us as much as you can bear to give for the needs of our Motherland.

Exhorting, cajoling, even threatening, the revolutionaries swept people into the movement. And when human encouragement proved insufficient, some fighters sought the efficacy of *anting-anting* [amulets], finding through these magical objects the courage they needed to charge into enemy rifle volleys.

Unlike many military memoirs, including those of Aguinaldo and Ricarte, the Alvarez account does not conceal the abuses that accompanied the mobilization of men for battle. Without coloring his experience, Alvarez does not hesitate to present both sides of the revolutionary experience. He recalls with clarity the commitment of the people to their vision of freedom, glimpsed in such utopian communities as Kakarong. With equal force, Alvarez captures the mix of courage and cruelty that accompanied revolutionary warfare. Alongside men and women who served with inspiring selflessness were craven dissemblers who betrayed their comrades and abused unarmed civilians. Some officers broke under the stress of combat and descended into cowardice and gross carnality, abandoning a post or raping women, including the daughter of a comrade-in-arms. Some of Alvarez's *Katipunan* leaders reflected the machismo of the day and were quick to anger, drawing pistols and threatening each other with death. Similarly, personal and regional antipathies seethed beneath a barely mustered unity.

Alvarez's account deplores the cruelties and abuse, but provides neither exculpation nor justification. The memoir affirms the Filipino national identity, but becomes neither a simplistic celebration of the revolution's triumphs nor a deification of its leaders. Writing "in the interest of noble truth" to reveal success as well as failings, bravery as well as human brutality, Alvarez has given generations of Filipinos the raw material they need to create and recreate this aspect of their past. Now translated and published in English, his memoir will serve as a partial redress of Harry Benda's complaint that Southeast Asian voices have been excluded from the drama of their own history:

> The *dramatis personae* ... as often as not accompanied by ... their ill-fated if heroic defiance, disappear from the stage, to make room for the bloodless, bureaucratic administrators of modern colonial regimes. The history of modern Southeast Asia then ...

becomes [a] history ... from which Southeast Asians ... get progressively drained.[23]

No longer among these lost Southeast Asian voices, General Alvarez now speaks with renewed resonance. Providing the densest and most detailed first-person account of the revolution, he offers us a way to skip over the dated biases of an intervening generation and gain a closer approach to the revolution's actual events. Adumbrating the revisionist work by such current generation Filipino historians as Guerrero and Ileto, General Alvarez's memoir offers a fresh challenge for historical research. Like Ileto, General Alvarez recalls in great detail the lower-class messianism which gave force to the elite's Europeanized nationalism. And like Guerrero, Alvarez records the revolution's excesses towards ordinary Filipinos. Moreover, in his recollections of the internal conflict that often disrupted the revolution's progress, Alvarez offers an approach to faction- and gender-based analysis still not attempted by any contemporary historian.

---

[23]Harry Benda, "The Structure of Southeast Asian History: Some Preliminary Observations," *Journal of Southeast Asian History* 3 (1962), reprinted in *Continuity and Change in Southeast Asia: Collected Journal Articles of Harry J. Benda* (New Haven: Yale University Southeast Asia Studies, 1972), 127.

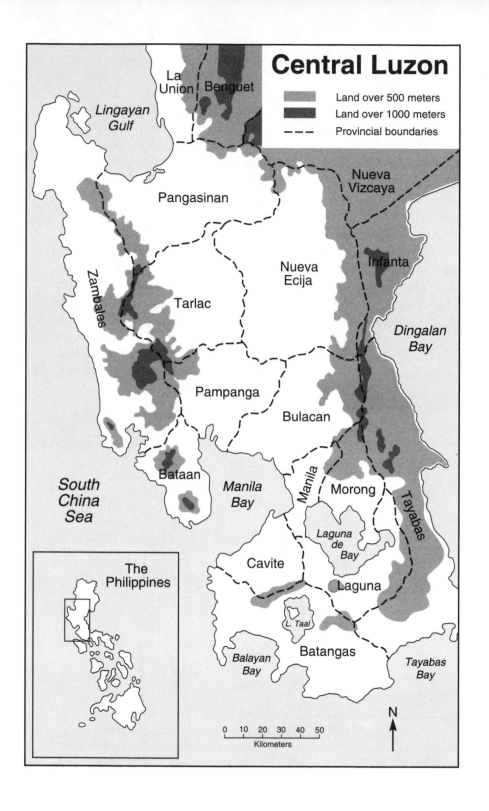

Central Luzon

Land over 500 meters
Land over 1000 meters
- - - Provincial boundaries

La Union
Benguet
Lingayan Gulf
Pangasinan
Nueva Vizcaya
Nueva Ecija
Infanta
Tarlac
Zambales
Dingalan Bay
Pampanga
Bulacan
Bataan
Manila Bay
Manila
Morong
Tayabas
South China Sea
Laguna de Bay
Cavite
Laguna
L. Taal
Balayan Bay
Batangas
Tayabas Bay

The Philippines

0 10 20 30 40 50
Kilometers

N

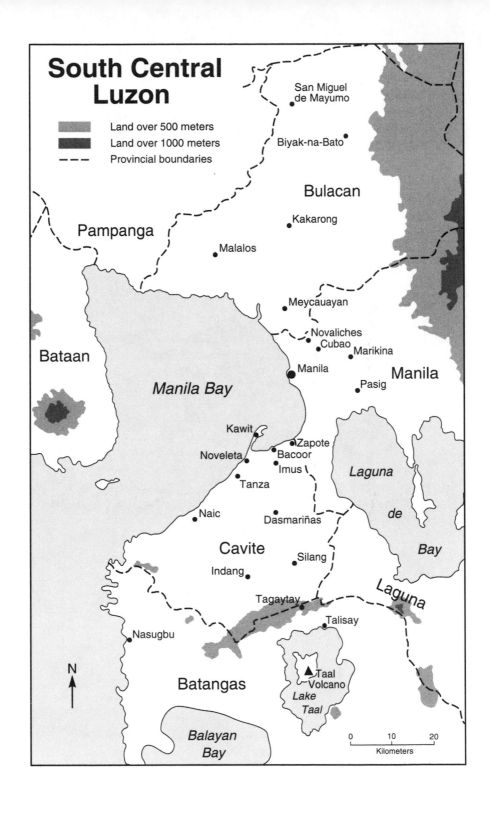

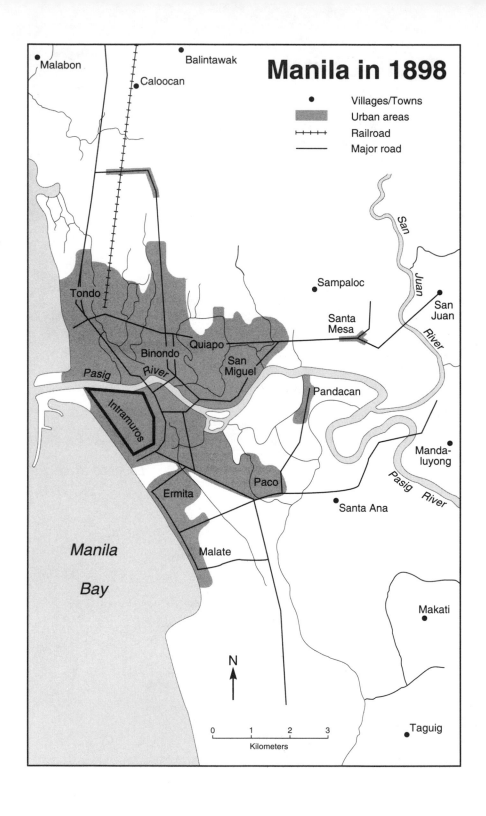

Manila in 1898

- Villages/Towns
- Urban areas
- Railroad
- Major road

Malabon

Balintawak

Caloocan

Tondo

San
Juan
River

Sampaloc

San
Juan

Santa
Mesa

Quiapo

Binondo

San
Miguel

Pasig

River

Pandacan

Intramuros

Mandaluyong

Paco

Pasig River

Ermita

Santa Ana

Manila
Bay

Malate

Makati

N

0 1 2 3
Kilometers

Taguig

Oktubre 2, 1927 — SAMPAGITA

ANG KATIPUNAN AT PAGHIHIMAGSIK

Akdâ ni Santiago V. Alvarez

THE KATIPUNAN
AND THE REVOLUTION

FOREWORD

As the country moves towards change, the youth become more discerning and discriminating regarding the competence of authors, especially those of historical writings. They begin to question the credentials of anyone who dares to write a history of the people or even of mere episodes. They look for motivations for such writings and inquire about their sources.

Before we look into the period of Philippine history concerning the Katipunan and the Revolution that I discuss in the following pages, I wish to say a few things about my humble self. I shall be fifty-five years old on July 25, 1927; I was born in the year 1872 in Noveleta, Cavite. In my early years, I studied under Macario Hernandez at his school located on Camba Street in Manila. Subsequently, I attended San Juan de Letran College and the University of Santo Tomas. After the tumultuous cry for national freedom (the Revolution), I resumed my studies in 1902 at the law school of the Liceo de Manila, and later worked at the law offices of Felipe Buencamino, Sr. and of R. del Rosario. While working in the latter's law office, I earned my law degree.

For five full years, from August 1896 to August 1901, I was one of those who guided the Revolution. But even before the outbreak of the Revolution, I was already active in the Katipunan as a member and as a delegate; as such, I was often in the company of the Supremo, Andres Bonifacio, Dr. Pio Valenzuela, and Mr. Emilio Jacinto. We organized chapters and propagated the movement in general. In the process, I was able to keep some notes about our experiences. As these were written in pencil on ordinary paper, they are now faded with age and have become difficult to read, especially by people other than myself. The following narrative, therefore, is not only of an eyewitness but also of an active participant.

I am greatly indebted to my colleague and friend, Mr. Lope K. Santos, whose nationalist sentiments encouraged me to undertake this project. He prodded me into writing these memoirs by arguing that since I could shed more light on the different facets of the Revolution, I would be doing a service to the youth, whom he saw as the direct beneficiaries of this work. I myself would prefer that I reconstruct those events from my notes now instead of somebody else doing it after my death. My notes would appear disjointed and unclear to anyone other than myself, and any attempt to utilize them to write a historical account of the period would prove of little value.

The events I have related in this account of the Katipunan and the Revolution reverberate with shouts of "Long live our patriots!" and "Death to the enemy!" These were in answer to the enemy's assaults with mausers and cannon, the latter fired from both land and sea.

The Magdiwang Government[1] honored me with an appointment as captain-general, or head of its army. General Artemio Ricarte was lieutenant-general.

I will now attempt to write down what I saw and what I know about the Katipunan and the Revolution. First, I shall narrate the events relating to the Revolution beginning from March 14, 1896; then I shall deal with the organization and activities of the Society of the Sons of the People (full name: *Kamahalmahalan at Kataastaasang Katipunan ng mga Anak ng Bayan*, [The Most Venerable Supreme Society of the Sons of the People]). The Katipunan account is based on records which were entrusted to me by the original founders of the Katipunan.

In the interest of honorable truth, I shall now attempt to write a history of the Katipunan and the Revolution which I hope will be acceptable to all. However, I realize it is inevitable that, in the narration of actual happenings, I shall run the risk of hurting the feelings of contemporaries and comrades-in-arms. I would like to make it clear that I shall try to be as objective as possible and that it is far from my intention to depreciate anyone's patriotism and greatness.

I shall be honored if these memoirs become a worthy addition to what General Artemio Ricarte has already published in this weekly.[2]

Santiago V. Alvarez

---

[1] The Province of Cavite, to the south of Manila, had two Katipunan Councils: the one called Magdalo was based at Kawit and headed by Emilio Aguinaldo; the second called Magdiwang was based at Noveleta, headed by the Alvarez family.

[2] "Memoirs," or *Apuntes*, was written in Tagalog while Ricarte was confined in Bilibid Prison, Manila and first published in *Sampagita*. It was published in book form in Tokyo in 1927 and translated by Armando J. Malay as *Memoirs of General Ricarte* (Manila: National Heroes Commission, 1963). Henceforth, it will be referred to as *Ricarte Memoirs*.

I

On March 14, 1896, a Saturday, I accompanied Emilio F. Aguinaldo and Raymundo Mata to Manila for their initiation into the Katipunan secret society. Messrs. Aguinaldo and Mata were prominent townsmen of Kawit in Cavite, my home province. Reaching Manila at about five in the afternoon, we waited for the appointed time at the quarters of Jacinto Lumbreras, a Katipunan member. He was the caretaker of the central telephone exchange located on San Jacinto Street in Binondo.

At about seven o'clock that evening, a Katipunan director arrived to take us to the Katipunan headquarters. Before leaving Lumbreras' place, my two companions were blindfolded. Then we got into a *calesa* [horsecart] and reached the home of Andres Bonifacio, the Katipunan Supremo, after about an hour's ride. It was a moonlit night and since the street was well-lighted, we could see the house clearly. It was of moderate size, the floor not raised much from the ground; it had wooden walls and a roof thatched with *nipa* [palm leaves]. The house was located on Cervantes Street (now Rizal Avenue) in the San Ygnacio area of Bambang. It was surrounded by many guards, some of them police who were Katipunan members. Directing operations was Gregoria de Jesus, the wife of the Supremo Bonifacio.

We were led into a room in the inner part of the house. On a table covered with black cloth were a skull and crossbones from a human skeleton. Lying beside the skull and crossbones were the following paraphernalia: a new long-bladed weapon, an old revolver, a small knife with a sharp edge, a new pen, a copy of the Katipunan "primer," and a sheet of paper on which were written blood-colored characters. On both sides of the table were Katipuneros blindfolded with black cloth. On the wall behind the skull was a rectangular banner of black cloth on which was the same motif of human skull and crossbones. Above the banner were three letter K's arranged as in a tripod; all were in white paint.

Meanwhile, a woman look-out was heard to say, "Cool!" which was the code word for "all-clear." Shortly later, the guides led the blindfolded into the house. The woman look-out told the guard, "They're all here. Nobody else is coming. Alert your comrades about tighter security."

The ritual trial and examination of the neophytes was held inside the room described above. When Aguinaldo's turn came, the examiners became uneasy because the neophyte was responding in the Masonic manner. Although he denied at the outset that he was a Freemason, in truth Aguinaldo was a member of the Del Pilar Lodge in Imus, Cavite. Thus his cross-examination was prolonged; and it was not until after ten o'clock that night that he and Mata took their oath as Katipunan members. Despite risk of imprisonment or execution, they pledged to destroy oppression by signing their names in their own blood. When the ritual was over, the happy crowd of Katipunan members warmly embraced the neophytes amid shouts of "Brother! Brother!"

Still blindfolded, the neophytes were then escorted down the house and cordially sent off with a repetition of fraternal embraces. I then took over escorting Aguinaldo and Mata. When we had walked some distance from the Supremo's house, I took off their blindfolds. We proceeded to Comrade Jacinto Lumbreras' quarters at the telephone exchange, where we retired for the night. Incidentally, Lumbreras' wife delivered a baby that night, and we were witnesses of that event.

II

Emilio Aguinaldo asked me to accompany him to see the Supremo Bonifacio again to learn more about the Katipunan. We made the trip to Manila on a Monday, April 6, 1896.

In those days, we Cavite folk traveled to and from Manila aboard Spanish vessels called "Ynchausti boats." They bore names like Isabel, Dominga, and others. These vessels were purchased by Mr. Luis Yangco; their operations are now managed by his son, Teodoro.

We left the pier at Cavite at seven in the morning, and an hour later we were in Manila. Aguinaldo went to the port office to attend to some business while I waited outside. When he came out after about ten minutes, he was agitated. His face was flushed and his steps were longer than usual. I asked him what was the matter. He was upset over the superciliousness of one Ramon Padilla, with whom he had exchanged some sharp words. He said that Padilla, who was a functionary in the port office, tried to impress people with superior airs but only succeeded in showing how rude and uncouth he really was.

We talked while walking, and soon we reached Lavezares Street in Binondo where Dr. Pio Valenzuela was living in a rented house. Dr. Valenzuela was then the provisional chairman of the Katipunan. In the house we met the Supremo, Andres Bonifacio, his wife, Gregoria de Jesus, Jose Dizon, and Dr. Valenzuela himself. We were welcomed cordially with fraternal embraces. Before we took the proffered seats, I introduced my companion. They responded most warmly and said that they already knew Mr. Aguinaldo, but they did not recognize him since he had been blindfolded on their first encounter.

After we were all seated, we happily exchanged news and talked about the progress of the Katipunan. Once in a while, Brother Aguinaldo hesitated, which prompted the observant Bonifacio to ask solicitously if anything was bothering him. I volunteered the information that he had had some unpleasant experience with an official at the port office and that was what probably was on his mind.

I had scarcely finished what I was saying when the Supremo's face flushed and his voice shook as he said, "It is necessary to defend the honor of our brother here."

Immediately he sent Dr. Pio Valenzuela and Jose Dizon to the house of Ramon Padilla for redress to the dishonor he had showed to Brother Aguinaldo. In default of an apology, the two emissaries were to be seconds in a duel.

When the emissaries had left, I began teasing Brother Aguinaldo. This I could do because, aside from his being a friend of long standing, he was also my brother-in-law. When I asked him if he would fight, he just looked at me without saying a word. Seeing that he was so pale, I put a hand over his pounding heart. Still he did not say a word, but only smiled back. I made a motion to feel his chest again, but he pushed my hand away and pleaded to be left alone, "If you yourself don't want to sleep, let others who want to, do so." Saying this, he fell asleep.

At two in the afternoon, Dr. Pio Valenzuela and Jose Dizon returned. On entering the house, Dizon blurted out "Peace!", meaning that Padilla had offered an apology to Aguinaldo. With his honor intact, Aguinaldo accepted the apology, and he and I proceeded home to Cavite uneventfully.

III

The Katipunan continued to spread.

It was Good Friday in the month of April, 1896. At nine o'clock in the morning, the Supremo, Andres Bonifacio, accompanied by Dr. Pio Valenzuela, Emilio Jacinto, and Pantaleon Torres, arrived in the town of Noveleta, Cavite province, to establish a provincial council of the Katipunan.

This council came to be known as the Magdiwang. The following were its officers: Mariano Alvarez, President; Pascual Alvarez, Secretary; Dionisio Alvarez, Treasurer; Valentin Salud, Prosecutor; Benito Alix, Sergeant-at-Arms; Nicolas Ricafrente, Adriano Guinto, Emiterio Malia and Valeriano Aquino, Directors.

When the Revolution broke out and succeeded in disabling the enemy, the Magdiwang Council was acknowledged and honored as the supreme organ responsible for the successful campaigns against the enemy. The Magdiwang record of efficiency in organization, planning, and implementation accounted for the growth and strength of the revolutionary forces. Among the leaders of the Council were Mariano Alvarez, President and First General of the army; Pascual Alvarez, Minister of Administration; Diego Mojica, Minister of Finance; Mariano Trias, Minister of Justice; Ariston Villanueva, Minister of War; Emiliano Riego de Dios, Minister of Welfare; Cornelio Magsarili, Minister of the Interior; Santiago V. Alvarez, Captain General; Artemio Ricarte, Lieutenant General.

At five o'clock in the afternoon of that day, the Supremo, Bonifacio, Dr. Valenzuela, Emilio Jacinto, Pantaleon Torres, and I, went to Kawit as secret guests of Emilio Aguinaldo, Baldomero Aguinaldo, and Candido Tirona. Our purpose was to organize another Katipunan Council. This Council, based in Kawit, was to be known as Magdalo [lit., "succor"] after Emilio Aguinaldo's *nom-de-guerre*.[3] The initiation of new members was held in the home of Emilio Aguinaldo. A great number enlisted voluntarily, each one signing the Katipunan oath with his own blood.

The yard of Aguinaldo's house was crowded with volunteers milling around like they were ready to join the Good Friday procession that evening.

---

[3]When Aguinaldo joined the Katipunan, he chose this name in honor of St. Mary Magdalene, the patron saint of his home town, Kawit, (Pedor S. de Achutegui, S. J., and Miguel A. Bernad, *Aguinaldo and the Revolution of 1896: A Documentary History* [Quezon City: Ateneo de Manila University Press: 1972], 5).

Others stood by in shops and other places where their presence was not conspicuous. When the procession started, the recruits crowded into the Aguinaldo house to take the Katipunan oath. Afterwards they quickly and unobtrusively dispersed so that they would not invite the suspicions of those who were not "in the know."

At about eight o'clock that evening, when we were about to begin the initiation ceremonies and while the procession was going on, we heard shouts of "Fire! Fire in Manila!"

We went to the stone bridge to the east of the house to look across the bay to Manila. When we saw the huge conflagration, the Supremo was dismayed and he fell limply against the stone wall. He said that he felt certain that his house and furniture had gone up in flames. Because of his indisposition, we were constrained to go back to Noveleta to rest for the night so that he could take the first boat to Manila at Cavite the next morning.

Two days later, I received a letter from the Supremo saying that his house had indeed burned, along with important Katipunan materials. Subsequently, Baldomero Aguinaldo came to Noveleta to discuss with Mariano Alvarez matters relating to the establishment of their Katipunan Council at Kawit. Alvarez suggested that the new Council should belong to the category of a local community chapter instead of a provincial level, since the Supreme President of the Katipunan gave it no sanction as such.

Not long afterwards, the Magdalo Council was established. Its leader was Emilio Aguinaldo; but because of his responsibilities as municipal captain,[4] he delegated his duties in the Magdalo Council to Baldomero Aguinaldo, who became its President. Benigno Santi was Secretary.

IV

Towards the end of April 1896, I received a letter from the Supremo Bonifacio inviting me to attend a general meeting of the Katipunan to be held in Pasig on the evening of May 3, 1896. He asked me to meet him in

---

[4]Head of the municipal government, elected by the *principalia,* or property-owning class. The title "capitan" replaced that of *gobernadorcillo* during the last years of Spanish rule.

Manila before four o'clock in the afternoon of that day, so that I would know the point of departure and which boat to take.[5]

I went to see Brother Emilio Aguinaldo at his office in the municipal hall of Kawit to notify him about the meeting. After talking about many matters, we agreed to meet in Manila on the scheduled date.

It was Sunday, May 3, 1896. At four in the afternoon, many of us from Cavite province were already waiting at the Quiapo landing of the Pasig River. However, we waited for the sun to set before boarding the boats readied by the Katipunan. We were in a convoy of five boats, one after another, going against the current. The smallest boat carried ten people. We stopped and alighted on the right bank of the Beata River near the residence of Captain Ramon Bernardo. He was our host at a most delectable supper. We marveled how it was that, despite their distance from the sea, they had lots of shrimp and blue crabs for us. However, we ate hastily in the manner of Katipuneros, always on the look-out for the enemy.

We were back on the boats soon after supper; and when we resumed our trip, our flotilla kept on increasing. We were joined by other Katipuneros from Santa Ana, Mandaluyong, San Pedro Makati, Pateros, Taguig, and Pasig. Our advance guards were in boats with peddlers of sweetmeats, a clever ruse, since it was the feast day of the patron saint of Antipolo, a nearby town.[6]

Perhaps it was about nine o'clock that night when we reached the spot called Sapang Nabas. A short distance beyond it, we all disembarked on the left bank at the site of an eating place owned by an old woman named Fausta. Bamboo groves fenced off the area from the river bank; and on the western side, there was a large trellis that supported an *upo* [gourd plant]. We gathered in this yard where the Supremo proposed to hold a meeting. But it was soon evident that we would not be able to do so because of the constant drizzle and the dark clouds threatening to let loose a heavy rain. And since we expected our discussion to last until morning, we would be exposed to the river traffic, especially heavy because of the Antipolo *fiesta*. Moreover, we would risk detection by the *guardia civil* who patrolled in boats. At the suggestion of members from Pasig, the meeting was held at

---

[5] Travel from Manila to the town of Pasig, near Laguna de Bay, was by boat up the Pasig River.

[6] Antipolo attracts pilgrims from the Tagalog areas in the month of May, especially on the feast day of its patron saint, Our Lady of Good Voyage.

another place, in the home of Katipunero Valentin Cruz, located behind the Pasig Catholic Church. Led by a guide, we walked in the dark through orchards and canefields, trying to beat the coming storm.

"Faster! Faster! The storm's coming!" each whispered to the other. In our hurry, some fell in mud puddles, causing laughter and relieving tensions during the difficult trek. The rain fell harder as we approached our destination; those who were ahead were only slightly wet, but those in the rear had to wring their dripping clothes.

The hot coffee and bread, which our host quickly prepared, warmed our chilled bodies. Meanwhile, the rain fell in torrents and made the posting of distant guards unnecessary. As the Supremo prepared to call the meeting to order, many remarked that nature was on our side and that this kind of weather was what we needed to protect us.

The house of Brother Valentin Cruz was a big one. Our great number filled the large reception hall at the top of the stairs. The Supremo Bonifacio stood behind a table at the far end of the room; on his left was Emilio Jacinto, the Secretary, and on his right was Dr. Pio Valenzuela, the prosecutor. The Supremo opened the proceedings by rapping loudly on the table and saying, "Brothers, let us come to order."

The meeting was conducted along secret Katipunan procedures. When the Supremo called the prosecutor to report on "weather conditions" (i.e., security), his reply was, "It's cool, sir," meaning it was safe to proceed with the meeting. In turn, when the guard was asked to report, he said, "I am faithfully doing my duty, sir."

"In that case," the Supremo announced, "in the name of the Motherland and by virtue of my authority as Supremo, which was bestowed upon me by the Highest Council of the Most Venerable Supreme Society of the Sons of the People, I hereby declare this meeting open. Let us all be seated."

"I invited you all to this meeting," the Supremo began, "for the purpose of apprising you of the difficulties with which our Society is beset. We are in a condition as precarious as that of a pregnant woman who is forced by circumstances to deliver before her time is due. We have been exposed. Our enemies know of our existence because of the confession to priests by three women, wives of Katipunan members; two of them are from Tondo and the third is from Santa Ana. Aside from these revelations at the confessional, other happenings have betrayed our secret. Now the Spaniards are closely and secretly watching our every move. If our Society does not make a move to defend ourselves, we shall be forced against the wall and we shall perish. Under the circumstances, to do nothing would be cowardly. If we do not defend the honor of the land of our birth, the enemy will prevail and continue to oppress us. What is your decision? Shall we rise in revolt now?"

"Mr. Chairman," Emilio Aguinaldo volunteered, "I regret to say that it is easy to say that we should rise in revolt, especially if we don't know the actual conditions in all places. I feel that before we do anything too quickly, we must first be assured of victory. Before we undertake something as delicate as that which will involve the giving up of our lives, we must be aware of our limitations. We in the Katipunan are still few in number; and moreover, the only weapons we have are the bolo, the spear, and the bow and arrow. These are inadequate in the face of the superior number and firepower of the guns and cannon of the enemy. For these reasons, I am against rising in arms now while we are not yet prepared to face the enemy."

"Mr. Chairman," seconded Benigno Santi, "our enemy, the Spaniards, have war vessels they can use against us in land and sea operations. If we build fortifications, these can be demolished by their cannon. We shall be forced to flee; otherwise we would be overpowered by their superior arms. Where would be our prospects of victory?"

"My brother," the Supremo answered, "I realize that we are poor in weaponry and material for warfare. But this should not be the only consideration. We should not ignore the fact that the Filipino is by nature brave, especially if he is fighting oppression. We can find no greater cowardice than what Florante[7] called an 'imaginary fear of the enemy'. On this occasion, we are discussing not weaponry, but our will to fight. If we are already up in arms and are in need of better weapons, we shall get these weapons from the enemy."

"Mr. Chairman," I said, "I was entrusted with various and discreet information by Mr. Mariano Alvarez, chairman of the Magdiwang Council. I will now bare to this gathering one of these well-guarded secrets. Mr. Mariano Alvarez was a survivor of the persecution after the Cavite revolt of 1872.[8] He became a marked man because the authorities found in his

---

[7] Florante is the hero of the tale *Florante at Laura*, by Francisco Balagtas. First published in 1888, this allegorical long poem in Tagalog purported to describe the intrigue and corruption in court and society in far-away Albania, but readers saw it as a disguised expose of social conditions of the Filipinos of the time.

[8] The Spaniards maintained a navy yard and fortress in Cavite town, jutting into Manila Bay. During the night of January 20, 1872, some 250 Filipino troops,

possession a picture of Father Jose Burgos with an autographed dedication to him. And we should not forget that at this moment, Dr. Jose Rizal is still languishing in exile at Dapitan.[9] We should take care, so that whatever decisions we make here should not be the cause of much regret in the future. If they result in our freedom, well and good, but if not, the consequences of defeat are terrifying. And should we be defeated, the enemy would make it appear to the uninformed that the Katipunan was indeed a secret tool of the friars. A malicious rumor to this effect is even now being circulated by the friars themselves, who are the enemies of the patriot Dr. Jose Rizal."

"Mr. Chairman," Emilio Aguinaldo asserted, "I believe that what the brother who spoke before me had to say is correct and in consonance with the lofty ideals of the Katipunan. I, therefore, propose to defer any decision until after we have agreed on whether to seek the counsel of Dr. Rizal in Dapitan."

"My brethren," the Chairman announced, "we need a little rest and relaxation of the mind so that we can respond more sensitively to the noble aspirations of the Katipunan."

A brief recess was called. On the wall behind the presidential table was a big clock. It struck two while the meeting was recessed. I made a mental note that it was two o'clock in the morning, Monday, May 4, 1896.

During the recess, the multitude present broke into groups to discuss the issues raised at the meeting. Some smoked, while others chewed betel; some sat on chairs, while others sat on their haunches on the floor; some were joking and laughing; others were sad and deep in thought. But everywhere the whispered consensus was that Dr. Rizal must first be

---

sailors, and workers in the navy yard attacked the fortress and massacred the Spanish troops. The mutiny was quelled; and, in retaliation, the Spanish authorities arrested many Filipinos, who were imprisoned, exiled to the Caroline Islands, or garroted in public (such as the three Filipino priests Jose Burgos, Mariano Gomez, and Jacinto Zamora). Historians point to this event as the beginning of the rise of the nationalist movement in the Philippines.

[9]After the publication in Europe of his two novels—*Noli Me Tangere* (1887) and *El Filibusterismo* (1891)—Rizal, the national hero of the Philippines, became an avowed enemy of the powerful Spanish friars and the civil authorities in the Philippines. These novels, which were smuggled into the country, and the writings of Marcelo H. del Pilar and others in the so-called Propaganda Movement, awakened the people's political awareness and stimulated many to join the Katipunan. When Rizal returned to Manila in 1892, he was arrested and exiled to Dapitan. His exile in this town in Mindanao lasted until shortly before his execution on December 30, 1896.

consulted about the matters discussed before any final decision and concrete action be taken. Others were asserting that if Dr. Rizal were to favor a revolution, they could count on his many influential friends abroad.

After some ten minutes of rest and informal exchange of views, the meeting was again called to order. The Supremo asked, "My brethren, what is your decision? Shall we now rise in arms?"

Everyone wanted to take the floor to say that Dr. Rizal's consent must first be had before approving such a decision. The Supremo abided by the popular will and announced, "Dr. Pio Valenzuela is hereby delegated to confer with Dr. Jose Rizal in Dapitan. He will be accompanied by a man who has lost his eyesight; Mr. Emilio Aguinaldo assures us that he can provide such a person who will pretend to seek the ministrations of Dr. Rizal.[10] In this way, Dr. Valenzuela's mission will not arouse the enemy's suspicion."

The meeting ended at five in the morning, and we left the house hurriedly so that daybreak would not expose us. Some of us went downtown to Pasig, while others returned to our disembarkation place on the river.

It was Monday morning, May 4, 1896. By eight o'clock we were back in our rowboats, sailing dreamily downstream. In one boat were the leaders of the Katipunan. While they were in the vicinity of Sapang Nabas, they convened a secret caucus to organize a confidential body to be known as "Secret Council." Its purpose was to eliminate all the evil elements and enemies of the nationalistic movement. The Council could elect its own members. When the deliberations were over, the Supremo informed those present of the existence and purpose of the newly-formed organ. Many signified their approval by digging into their pockets for revolvers and firing them in the air and shouting, "We approve!"

They rowed on while discussing the issues raised at the meeting. After disembarking they dispersed to go their separate ways.

---

[10]While in Europe, Rizal had specialized in opthalmology in order to cure his mother's failing sight.

V

After the meeting, the apprehension of the Katipuneros about the enemy, the Spaniards, did not abate. The Supremo Andres Bonifacio took even greater precautions for his personal safety because of the threats from the enemy. He made fewer personal appearances, but continued to write circulars boosting the morale and expanding the membership of the Katipunan.

Before the end of May 1896, Dr. Valenzuela visited and interviewed Dr. Rizal at Dapitan. He was accompanied by Raymundo Mata, the eye patient recommended by Emilio Aguinaldo for the mission. However, when he returned, Mr. Mata could not report on anything that had transpired between the two physicians because they had conducted their interview privately. All that he heard from their talk was about the medication prescribed for him. Dr. Valenzuela reported at once to the Supremo, but neither would talk about the result of the interview with Dr. Rizal.

Restless and anxious about their precarious situation, the Katipuneros were eager to know Dr. Rizal's opinion about an armed revolution. Was he for or against; and if against, what should be done to avert the reprisals with which the enemy threatened them? The silence of the Supremo and Dr. Valenzuela about the much-awaited views of Dr. Rizal was interpreted by many as tacit proof of his disapproval of the Revolution. This situation gave rise to a new wave of apprehension among the Katipuneros, for it meant that they could neither rise up in arms nor enjoy peace, and that the only certainty left for many was the firing squad. Thus, like a sick person who is to die anyway despite medication, the Katipuneros opted for the Revolution. The rallying cry was "Better to die fighting!"

In June of the same year, the scope and powers of the secret Council were announced to the general membership of the Katipunan. The Council started functioning when it identified a confirmed enemy of the people in the province of Rizal. After his mysterious disappearance, his wife and children mourned for him.

In the course of time, the surge of the revolutionary movement began to swell and the opposing forces became clearly polarized. A microcosm of the revolutionary situation was concretized in the printing shop of the *Diario de Manila,* where two individuals representing opposing forces found themselves in confrontation. On the one hand was one named Patiño, who was in charge of tools and equipment; on the other, was a certain Apolonio de la Cruz, who was the foreman. Both were earning fourteen pesos a month.

Patiño was a protege of the Spaniard La Font,[11] the general manager of the printing establishment. Apolonio de la Cruz was a Katipunero and Treasurer of the Maghiganti [lit., "to avenge"] chapter in Tondo, Manila. All the other workers in the shop were members of the Katipunan. Consequently, the printing shop had become a keeping place of many Katipunan documents and material, knowledge of which the Katipunero workers tried to keep from the non-Katipunero, Patiño. However, the latter slyly pretended not to see or hear anything.

At five o'clock on Saturday afternoon, July 11, 1896, the Spaniard La Font announced to all the workers in the shop that the management was disposed to increase the pay of one of the two overseers—Patiño or Apolonio. The one who would be favored would receive a monthly pay of twenty instead of the former eighteen.

The announcement generated selfishness and more dissension. All the workers wanted Apolonio to get the pay increase, while Patiño was happily anticipating that he would be the lucky one since he was La Font's favorite. This happening at the printing shop was an unpropitious portent for the success of the Katipunan.

The competition between Patiño and Apolonio for the two-peso bonus added spice to the daily routine in the printing shop. Patiño devised newer means of boosting his stock and courting the favor of La Font. The workers perceived that if they did nothing to denigrate Patiño in the eyes of La Font, their friend Apolonio would lose out to Patiño.

When Apolonio reached a point where he could no longer contain his revulsion for Patiño, he thought of writing a poison letter to La Font. In the letter he said that Patiño was surreptitiously taking out of the shop and selling equipment and supplies such as types, paper, ink, and other materials. He left the letter unsigned and mailed it on his way home that afternoon.

Because they knew about the anonymous letter, the workers were covertly watching the behavior of Patiño and La Font. Nothing seemed to change except that La Font seldom went out of his office, whereas before he often did. Then the tension building up in the shop suddenly surfaced at a little past four in the afternoon of July 18, 1896. Flushed and trembling,

---

[11]The typescript has Lafon.

Patiño barged in among the workers and began shouting angrily, "I am not an evil man. Nobody can prove that I am shameless and a thief. Now we shall know who is evil."

"Be specific. Whom among us are you accusing?" the workers shouted back.

As more angry words were exchanged, the workers nearly mobbed Patiño. La Font averted a scuffle by coming out of his office and intervening. He told the workers to go home, and he made sure that they did so by standing at the door and watching each one take his leave. When the last worker had left, he asked the guard to tidy up the place. Then he locked the door of the shop and left in a horse-drawn cab.

Soon La Font was back in the shop with a Spanish police lieutenant. They went straight to the desk of Apolonio de la Cruz and forced open the drawers. They found Katipunan paraphernalia such as a rubber stamp, a little book, ledgers, membership oaths signed in blood, and the membership roster of the Maghiganti chapter of the Katipunan.

Himself a member of the Maghiganti chapter, the guard in the printing shop became alarmed, especially when the roster was discovered. He had been watching the goings-on from a hiding place, but dashed out as soon as he had a chance. He outwitted two soldiers at the door by telling them that their lieutenant wanted them inside quickly. He jumped into a cab and, after stopping briefly at his house, he went the rounds to warn his fellow members about the raid at the shop.

At ten o'clock that night, the witch hunt began. Guided by the roster they had discovered, the police searched the houses of persons on the list. They arrested some who had stayed in their homes, but missed others who had already fled; these latter became the objects of an intensive hunt. The next day, which was a Sunday (July 19, 1896), was a day of gloom in many households. Weeping and lamentation greeted the morning after the arrests and the flight of those who did not even have a chance to bid goodbye to their parents, brothers and sisters, wives and children. In the case of those who escaped, their families neither knew where they were nor whether they could still return or not.

The first ones who were arrested were tortured and forced to identify other Katipunan members. More went into hiding and had to abandon their means of earning a livelihood, while many others fell into the hands of the enemy. Tighter measures were taken by the metropolitan police of Manila and by the civil guard in the provinces against the subversives. On their part, the Spanish priests extracted confessions from the womenfolk and kept in constant communication with the Spanish civil authorities. Anyone walking abroad ran the risk of being arrested, jailed, and tortured to death. And the only basis for the arrest was that someone, himself being tortured, was forced to name anyone to put an end to his agony.

On Wednesday of that week, which was July 22, the rumor spread that the Supremo Andres Bonifacio and members of the Highest Council of the Katipunan were being intensively grilled by the troops of the Spanish government. In truth, however, they were in Rizal province under the care and protection of the local Katipunan chapter. Another rumor brought about a new wave of terror, causing many to go to confession and seek the protection of the parish priest or other Spanish authorities. This concerned the imposition of the infamous *juez de cuchillo* [judge of the knife] or "kangaroo court," with which the Spanish government intimidated everyone, man or woman, old or young.

As the crisis worsened, more and more Filipinos joined the Katipunan. Chapters in Manila and in the provinces were kept busy enrolling and administering the oath to new members all day and far into the night. One could not say whether this upsurge was a desperate response to the extremely explosive situation or whether it was due to the conviction that, like it or not, one had to get involved and take up arms anyway.

A concomitant of this enthusiasm to join the Katipunan was the desire to meet the Supremo Andres Bonifacio. But since the Supremo was in hiding at the time, many were disappointed; and in their exasperation over the imminent danger, they felt betrayed and came to revile him.

"Where is he now?" they asked. "See what he has done! Why did he take us to the brink of death and now he is nowhere to be found? Impudent and evil one!"

Some of the women whose husbands were arrested began to heap scorn on the Katipunan. "Shameless Katipunan!" they cried, "You tore away from us our protectors and breadwinners and dragged them to the edge of death. We ourselves are now dying of hunger and sorrow. Do you see this youngest one he left behind? He keeps on calling for his father in vain!"

All these rebukes, abuses, and accusations, the Supremo accepted stoically. But he never lost courage. Instead he continued with his task of developing and organizing more Katipunan chapters. And to appease the feelings of the malcontented, he planned to convene a general meeting to discuss a strategy for the Revolution.

VI

The general meeting was called at ten o'clock at night on August 21, 1896, a Friday, at the home of Katipunero Vidal Acab in Caloocan, Rizal. Aided by the Secretary, Emilio Jacinto, and the Prosecutor, Dr. Pio Valenzuela, the Supremo Andres Bonifacio presided over the meeting. Among those who attended were Aguedo del Rosario, Ramon Bernardo, Romualdo Vicencio, Teodoro Plata, Pantaleon Torres, Ariston de Jesus, Jose Dizon, and Silverio Baltazar. The last named was the incumbent municipal captain of Caloocan. Assigned for security were the town *cuadrilleros* [municipal policemen]. Just as the Supremo was calling the meeting to order, the guards shouted, "Halt! Who are you?"

Fear gripped everyone. Some drew their weapons and prepared to fight. Others looked for hiding places and exits to avoid an encounter with the enemy. Captain Silverio Baltazar quickly went down from the house to investigate. After a few minutes, he returned to reassure his comrades that there was no cause for alarm. The guards had stopped a rig in which an Englishman then residing in Caloocan was riding.

Although the incident caused no undue alarm among the rest of the neighborhood, since it was not unusual for the cuadrilleros to stop vehicles and question passengers especially in the night, still many in the group thought it would be more prudent to move out to another place. When the meeting was resumed, Captain Ramon Bernardo found it easy to convince the others about a transfer of their meeting place outside the town to avoid detection and confrontation with the enemy. Thus it was unanimously and quickly decided to reconvene at Kangkong, a village on the outskirts of the municipality of Caloocan.

We started our trek to Kangkong at about eleven that night. We walked through the rain over dark expanses of muddy meadows and fields. Our clothes drenched and our bodies numbed by the cold wind, we plodded wordlessly. It was nearly two in the morning when we reached the house of Brother Apolonio Samson in Kangkong. We crowded into the house to rest and warm ourselves. We were so tired that, after hanging our clothes to dry, we soon fell asleep.

Our host received us warmly. Readily opening his granary, he asked friends and neighbors to unhusk large quantities of rice. He also had a water buffalo butchered for us. The Supremo began assigning guards at five o'clock in the morning of the following day, Saturday, August 22, 1896. He placed a detachment at the Balintawak boundary and another at the backyard to the north of the house where we were gathered. He asked the Secretary, Emilio Jacinto, to write to the chairman of the Katipunan Councils. The following is a sample of that letter:

> Mr. Laureano Gonzales
> Chairman, Makabuhay Council
> Mandaluyong, Rizal
>
> Dear Brother:
>
> On orders of our Honorable Supremo, you are hereby informed that upon receipt of this letter, you and all the heads of chapters under your jurisdiction should as soon as possible come to this village of Kangkong, in the municipality of Caloocan, for the purpose of discussing the measures we should take against the enemy. Take along the treasurers. They should be present because we in the Katipunan can no longer evade incurring expenditures. You are also reminded to take more careful precautions because we are being closely watched.
>
> Receive my loving embrace.
>
> (sgd.) EMILIO JACINTO
> Secretary
>
> August 22, 1896
>
> Seal of the Supreme Council
> KKK

No less than three hundred men assembled at the bidding of the Supremo Andres Bonifacio. Altogether, they carried assorted weapons: bolos, spears, daggers, a dozen small revolvers and a rifle used by its owner, one Lieutenant Manuel, for hunting birds. The Supremo Bonifacio was restless because of fear of a sudden attack by the enemy. He was worried over the thought that any of the couriers carrying the letter sent by Emilio Jacinto could have been intercepted; and in that eventuality, the enemy would surely know their whereabouts and attack them on the sly. He decided that it was better to move to a site called Bahay Toro.

At ten o'clock Sunday morning, August 23, 1896, we arrived at Bahay Toro. Our number had grown to more than 500 and the house, yard, and warehouse of *Cabesang*[12] Melchora was getting crowded with us Katipuneros. The generous hospitality of Cabesang Melchora[13] was no less than that of Apolonio Samson. Like him, she also opened her granary and had plenty of rice pounded and animals slaughtered to feed us.

Coming from different localities, everyone was eager to meet the Supremo and his aides. The Katipuneros were also eager to present their arms to him. On this occasion, the Supremo received 100 bolos [machetes] donated by Lieutenant Apolonio Samson. The bolos were especially crafted in Maykawayan, Bulacan, under the supervision of Arcadio de Jesus.

The following day, Monday, August 24, more Katipuneros came and increased our number to more than a thousand. The Supremo called a meeting at ten o'clock that morning inside Cabesang Melchora's barn. Flanked on both sides of him at the head table were Dr. Pio Valenzuela, Emilio Jacinto, Briccio Pantas, Enrique Pacheco, Ramon Bernardo, Pantaleon Torres, Francisco Carreon, Vicente Fernandez, Teodoro Plata, and others. We were so crowded that some stood outside the barn.

The following matters were approved at the meeting:

1. An uprising to defend the people's freedom was to be started at midnight of Saturday, August 29, 1896.

2. The organization of the revolutionary forces, under the following, who were named brigadier generals: Aguedo del Rosario, Vicente Fernandez, Ramon Bernardo, and Gregorio Coronel. They were given full freedom to choose the necessary army chiefs.

3. The planning of tactics for the taking of Manila at an agreed time by the four brigadier generals.

4. To be in a state of alert so that the Katipunan forces could strike should the situation arise where the enemy was at a disadvantage. Thus the uprising could be started earlier than the agreed time of

---

[12] From the title in Spanish *cabeza de barangay*, or village headman. The title was shared by the headman's wife.

[13] Now more popularly known as *Tandang Sora*.

midnight of August 29, 1896, should a favorable opportunity arise before that date. Everyone should steel himself and be resolute in the struggle that was imminent.

5. The immediate objective was the capture of Manila. Troops of Generals del Rosario, Fernandez, and Bernardo were to make the offensive and converge inside the walled city. General del Rosario was to pass by way of Tondo, General Fernandez by way of San Marcelino and General Bernardo, by way of the rotonda.

After the adjournment of the meeting at twelve noon, there were tumultuous shouts of "Long live the Sons of the People!"

VII

At about two o'clock in the afternoon of Tuesday, August 25, 1896, a sentinel atop a tamarind tree guarding our position at Bahay Toro jumped to the ground and yelled that the enemy was coming. The Sons of the People prepared to fight. They engaged the Spanish troops somewhere between Bahay Toro and Kangkong in Balintawak. Only a few shots were fired in the brief encounter because the enemy soon retreated after sensing that they were outnumbered. The enemy contingent was composed of civil guards and *carabineros* of the national police. A non-combatant youth of about fifteen years who was trying to conceal himself from the combatants was caught in the crossfire and killed.

The next day was a Wednesday, August 26. The Supremo Bonifacio ordered that food be prepared early, both for breakfast and for provision for a journey. After breakfast, he briefed the assembled men about the march to the upper part of Sampalukan. He appointed Old Leon of San Francisco de Malabon to lead the troops. A former bandit, Old Leon, whose real name was Gregorio Tapalla, had bolted jail and joined the Katipunan.

This old man was an alcoholic. Apparently drunk, he accepted the assignment happily and shouted, "Get ready, everyone! In this march, you must all do as I do and say."

Old Leon unsheathed his long knife and raised it with his right hand. Simultaneously, he also raised his left foot. Because of his order to do as he did, many imitated him. Then he commanded,"Santo, Santo Kasis! Santo, Santo Kob! Make the enemy surrender!"

He let fall the upraised hand and foot and then kicked vigorously. The kick landed in a puddle and splattered mud on Dr. Pio Valenzuela, nearly blinding him.

The invocation over, the march began with Old Leon at the head. It was nearly seven that morning when they approached Pasong Tamo. About 200 arms' length away they saw enemy troops. Some of the civil guards with them shouted that they wanted to see the Supremo since they themselves were Katipuneros, too. The Supremo Bonifacio and Dr. Pio Valenzuela quickly obliged and came forward. They asked what the civil guards wanted, and the reply was that they would like an interview.

A melee ensued. Surrounded by the enemy, the Katipunan lines broke and each one tried to defend himself. Many escaped, but those who could not perished. One of those killed was Lieutenant Manuel; his gun was confiscated by the enemy.

In the flurry of escape, the Supremo Bonifacio, who was with some members of the Supreme Council, left a valise containing the flag and funds of the Katipunan. Luckily, this was retrieved by Old Leon, who was close on their heels. To avoid carrying an unwieldy burden, the valise was opened and its contents divided so that each one carried a portion of the funds in his pocket. Suddenly a cannon fusillade exploded from behind them. It hit Old Leon at the back and pierced his neck where he had at the time a large carbuncle. He fell and died instantly while his companions scampered away. The flag was dropped again, but was saved by Katipuneros from Bago Bantay. They concealed it from the others for fear that they would be questioned about the Katipunan money that was kept with it.

At noon, the group of the Supremo Bonifacio rested at a site between Balara and Krus na Ligas. They sent Katipunero Genaro de los Reyes to Mandaluyong to apprise the chapter there of the encounter with the enemy that morning. They also asked him to collect donations of food and clothes, for they were hungry and their clothes were wet from the continuous rain.

It was six in the afternoon when Genaro reached Mandaluyong. At his house was Nicolas de Guzman, who was with him in the march but who had fled when the firing broke out. He had, therefore, already broken the news of the debacle that morning.

After Genaro had conferred with Laureano Gonzales, chairman of the Makabuhay chapter of Mandaluyong, the latter convened a meeting of his constituents. The chapter voted to send the needed help and the members were mobilized to solicit contributions.

A baker named Simeon gave three hundred pieces of bread; two Chinese stores gave two packages of *La Insular* cigarettes, two packages of matches, five cans of sardines, and five pesos cash. A Katipunero by the name of Jose Reyes donated thirty pieces of clothing consisting of underwear, shirts, and jackets. The chapter chairman designated Jose Reyes to help Genaro bring their donations to their brethren in the field. The two left Mandaluyong at nine in the morning of Thursday, August 27, 1896. When they reached the long stretch of road in San Juan del Monte, Jose Reyes fell ill and could not continue with the trip. Genaro proceeded and soon met Katipunero Gregorio Bautista, who donated five pesos. Behind the place called Escombro, he met another Katipunero named Torres, who gave twenty pesos. Torres also gave a telescope sent by Celestino Santos, chairman of the Marikina chapter.

As he walked faster towards the highest point on Cubao, Genaro saw enemy troops about half a kilometer away. Fortunately, he was not noticed. He followed another path which took him to Krus na Ligas, but he found that the Katipuneros had left the place. He was told that when the troops had dispersed, the Supremo went eastward. The village folk warned him about the deployment of the police, civil guard, and Spanish infantry. They were in the fields around the village and were closely watching Katipunan movements.

Genaro continued his search for the Supremo over muddy and slippery paths as the capricious weather alternated between sunshine and rain. Walking quickly despite a heavy load on his back, he slipped and fell on his knees and hands. After noon he met a group of stragglers from his contingent who were also looking for the Supremo. They parted ways somewhere between Krus na Ligas and Balara, after he had given them bread, sardines, and cigarettes.

The wind and the rain grew stronger towards the afternoon, but Genaro persisted in his lonely search. Before sundown he reached a wooded place called Ulat, where he met an old peasant planting rice. Genaro saw an opportunity not only to rest and relax, but also to make inquiries. But first he tried to befriend the old man. He offered cigarettes and then asked casually if he had heard about the Supremo Andres Bonifacio and if he knew his whereabouts. The peasant was cautious; he said that he did not know the Supremo, much less where he was. However, he had heard that the day before the Supremo and some Katipuneros had had an encounter with the enemy. He was getting ready to go on his way when perhaps on impulse or intuition, Genaro made a secret Katipunan signal. The old peasant broke into laughter and exclaimed, "Brother, now I can believe you. I am a sentinel. Come, I'll take you where they are."

Suddenly, Genaro's anxieties vanished. He even forgot the weariness from the long and arduous trip and happily followed the old peasant, who led the way. After walking through a bamboo grove and then a wooded area, they finally came upon a hut concealed by thick stands of banana trees. It was a dilapidated thing that seemed ready to fall apart. The wonder was how such a frail and small structure could have accommodated the some twenty Katipuneros Genaro found resting on the few remaining strips of flooring. At last he found the Supremo and his aides, Dr. Pio Valenzuela and Emilio Jacinto.

The men were eating boiled green bananas, which was their only food since breakfast. The Supremo stood up as soon as Genaro came in and gratefully thanked him for bringing the relief goods they sorely needed. All the others in the group were just as profuse in their thanks. After the men had eaten, changed their wet clothes and tidied up, the Supremo briefed them for a march to Mount Tupasi, where he planned to build a strong fortification for defense in case of encirclement.

Genaro objected to the Supremo's plan because he had been instructed by the Councils to ask the Supremo to come down to Mandaluyong. Thousands were girding for the attack at midnight of Saturday, August 29, 1896, and were looking to the Supremo for leadership. Secretary Jacinto also objected to the Supremo's plan and advised him to go to Mandaluyong instead. Just then, Katipunero Agapito de Leon, Secretary of the Marikina chapter, arrived to inquire about the plans for the scheduled insurrection.

The Supremo agreed to go to Mandaluyong with his men. While walking along a level stretch called Payong, it rained again so that they had to seek shelter inside a sugar mill owned by a certain Cabesang Claro of Malanday, Marikina. It was an unfortunate moment for a poor horse to stray close to where the men were waiting, for despite its skinny condition it could still provide some nourishment to the hungry Katipuneros. They slaughtered the miserable beast and made unsalted soup with green bananas with the better cuts. With this and the bread leftover from the largesse brought by Genaro, they had a nourishing supper, indeed.

As soon as the rain stopped, the satiated men continued their trek, but without Dr. Valenzuela. Exhausted by fatigue, sleeplessness, hunger, and exposure, he was in no condition to join the others. He asked a Katipunero to accompany him to Malanday in Marikina, where he hoped he could rest.

Meanwhile, the Supremo Bonifacio, Emilio Jacinto, Procopio Bonifacio, Genero de los Reyes, Agapito de Leon, and others proceeded to the village of Barangka, Marikina. Lodging at the house of Katipunero Gregorio de la Cruz, they convened the chairmen of Katipunan chapters, who arrived just as the bell of the Roman Catholic church in Marikina town was striking the hour of ten. After a lengthy discussion about the impending Revolution, they decided to hold a final meeting the following day at Mandaluyong. They all then retired for the night.

Mindful of the hardships to which they were exposed, their host was most solicitous of their comfort and well-being. Aside from serving them nourishing and palatable food, he provided them with a change of clothing and shoes to protect their feet pricked with thorns. What a funny looking lot they were after they had put on the clothes which did not belong to them. Some looked like Chinamen, others like Indians; some had shoes too big for them, while others had sleeves too long.

The Supremo Andres Bonifacio woke up early. At three in the morning he roused his companions from their sleep to give them instructions. He said, "You, Brother Genaro, must go to Santolan to organize our brothers there and get ready their available arms. I will be conducted to Bulaklak, a hilly area in Mandaluyong, the house of Chairman Romualdo Vicencio. Before we disperse, I am asking you, Katipuneros from Marikina, to get ready what you will need to keep in close touch with your chapter headquarters so that any communication can easily reach you."

VIII

Before eight in the morning of Friday, August 28, 1896, Genaro was conferring with Chairman Valentin Cruz and Secretary Victoriano of the Santolan chapter at the house of Katipunero Feliciano del Rosario. Santolan was astir with anxiety. Men and women alike were extremely tense over the news of the impending rebellion. All day long multitudes voluntarily enlisted with the Katipunan. Each one donated a peso, and the chapter treasurer collected more than one hundred pesos from morning up to two in the afternoon.

Genaro listed the following arms in the hands of the Santolan Katipuneros: fifteen Remington guns under the custody of the Katipunero caretaker of the municipal water reservoir, one rifle, and one revolver donated by Tomas Encho, the machinist at the water reservoir. Encho joined the Katipunan at the intercession of his assistant, Lorenzo Regino.

At four that afternoon, the courier Genaro arrived at Balabak in the Mandaluyong hills to report to the Supremo Bonifacio and to relay the messages from the Santolan chapter.

That same afternoon, the Supremo convened a final meeting in which they discussed the logistics and methods of communication in the coming struggle. Chairman Laureano Gonzales of the Makabuhay chapter of Mandaluyong was entrusted with the task of dispatching urgent letters to the Manila, Cavite, and Nueva Ecija chapters. Katipunero Sinforoso San Pedro, chapter Secretary, assisted Emilio Jacinto in writing the letters.

All day Santolan was a beehive of activity and excitement. Katipunan delegations from various chapters came and went, making it necessary for the Supremo to hold two meetings, one in the morning and the other in the afternoon. Everyone was very light-hearted. No one seemed to feel any fatigue or fear, nor mind the lack of sleep. The ambience was one of gay anticipation of a grand festival slated for the following day. Beneath the surface gaiety, however, were undertones of grimness as each one primed his personal weapons for the coming struggle.

At nine that night, Chairman Laureano Gonzales informed the Supremo that the enemy had set up a small emplacement at the Pasig River on the Mandaluyong side fronting Santa Ana and that another cannon had been installed on the San Juan del Monte riverbank opposite the water reservoir. He also reported that an artillery detachment with a big cannon had taken position at the reservoir.

It was Saturday, August 29, 1896. While still very early in the morning, the Katipuneros were exceeding themselves in dexterity, preparing arms for the coming battle that night. The Supremo received news that saddened them all. Dr. Pio Valenzuela had been arrested and was being tortured inside the parish house of the Catholic Church in San Mateo.

At past ten that morning, the Supremo Bonifacio instructed Katipunero Genaro to make the rounds of the different Katipunan Councils of Mandaluyong to make sure that all available guns were ready before sunset. Genaro readily did as he was told. He saw that the Sumikat chapter headed by the Katipunero Guillermo Vasquez had, except for one rifle and one Remington gun, only bolos, daggers, and spears. The Liwanag chapter headed by Katipunero Liborio de Guzman likewise had mostly bladed weapons and two Remingtons. The Manalo chapter headed by Katipunero

Adriano Gonzales had only one firelock aside from the usual bladed ones. The Sinukuan chapter under the leadership of Katipunero Nonong had arms no better than the others.

Katipunero Genaro realized that other chapters were as poorly equipped as those he had visited, so he concentrated on ways of procuring additional firearms from the enemy. By three in the afternoon, Katipunero Tomas Arienda Jose had succeeded in smuggling out of the Mandaluyong friar estate house three guns and ammunition, and Juan Capulco procured one firelock, two Remingtons, one rifle, and bullets. These they turned over to Katipunero Genaro.

At five that afternoon, the Supremo Andres Bonifacio with more than 500 Katipuneros went down to the village of Hagdang Bato in Mandaluyong and stopped at the house of Katipunero Felix Sanchez, chairman of the Sapa chapter. Mandaluyong had seventeen Katipunan chapters all under the jurisdiction of the Makabuhay Council headed by Katipunero Laureano Gonzales. All the local chapters prepared food for the Katipunan army in the homes of Simeon Borja, a bakery owner, Pascual Francisco, a former municipal captain, and Katipunero Tranquilino Mendiola.

At seven that evening, more than a thousand men were gathered around the Supremo at Hagdang Bato. He distributed the guns, procured by Genaro, to those competent to handle them. Earlier that day, he had instructed Katipunero Buenaventura Domingo, chairman of the Tala chapter, to keep close surveillance over the Mandaluyong parish house and not allow the parish priest to escape.

So strong was the movement in Mandaluyong that the Katipunan had even infiltrated the local police force. Five *cuadrilleros* [head of a squad of the rural guard] led by Lieutenant Leon Bautista came to Hagdang Bato at eight o'clock that evening to receive instructions. The cuadrilleros were Sergeant Felix Sanchez, Froilan Tatko, Cirilo (alias *Butas*), Luciano Benito (alias *Mulawin*), and Fermin (alias *Matanda*). They were assigned, naturally enough, to the town hall where another Katipunero, Buenaventura Domingo, was holding office as deputy town mayor. As mentioned earlier, Domingo was chairman of the Tala chapter. Sergeant Sanchez and Lieutenant Bautista were also chapter chairmen of the Matunog and the Malanday chapters, respectively.

As part of their strategy, these Katipunan members in the municipal establishment tried to lure the civil guards out of the town hall. When they failed, they asked the Supremo for permission to attack the town hall to capture the civil guards and confiscate their arms. The Supremo approved their plan, but before the offensive started he briefed the troops, under each chapter, so that their movements would be coordinated. Formations were grouped from the following chapters: Sinibulan, Bitin, Ilog San Juan, Malanday, Sapa, Matunog, Sumikat, Magdiwang, and others.

IX

When the Supremo had given the final instructions, everyone broke into shouts of "Long live the Sons of the People!"

The first battle cry of the Katipunan coincided with the pealing of the church bell at nine that fateful night of August 29, 1896. When the last peal died out, the Supremo commanded, in a ringing voice, "Advance!"

The Katipuneros rushed to the town hall and almost at once, half of them entered the building to seize the guns of the civil guards. Those they recognized in the civil guard detachment were Pedro Mercado, Serapio Cabanlan, and Sulpicio Plata. The guards resisted at first and refused to give up their arms, but they were soon overwhelmed by the sheer numerical superiority of the Katipuneros.

"Will you surrender or not?" the Katipuneros asked, brandishing their sharp weapons.

"It's cool!" [Katipunan code phrase], Pedro, one of the civil guards, answered, at the same time making a secret Katipunan signal. His Katipunan brethren rushed forward and embraced him. The other civil guards then willingly gave up and surrendered their arms. However, one of them, S. Plato, was punished for having committed evil deeds against the people. He was captured, executed, and his body was taken to the outskirts of Balara for burial.

To allay suspicions about the intended attack and to keep close surveillance over the movements of the parish priest, the Supremo assigned Chairman Buenaventura Domingo of the Tala chapter to be at his post at the town hall. It will be recalled the Katipunero Buenaventura was deputy town mayor. As soon as the Supremo entered the building, he looked for Buenaventura to inquire about the whereabouts of the curate.

"He escaped, sir!" was the answer.

"Evil brother! Renegade sons of the people!" the Supremo shouted, aiming his revolver at Buenaventura. Chairman Laureano Gonzales pacified the Supremo and pleaded with him to forgive Buenaventura.

The troops under General Ramon Bernardo were divided and organized into three contingents under the leadership of Katipuneros Celestino Manuel, Miguel Resurreccion, and Angel Bulong, respectively. An hour after the siege at Mandaluyong, they attacked the town hall of Pandacan; they took it without resistance and easily confiscated two guns. However, as in Mandaluyong, the parish priest eluded arrest; Father Angel of Pandacan had fled before the Katipuneros came.

After taking Pandacan, General Bernardo next turned his attention to Santa Mesa. At eleven that night he ordered his troops dispatched immediately to Santa Mesa. Deploying them to the east of Sancho Valenzuela's rope factory, he ordered the troop commanders to post those with firearms in front, and those with bolos on the flanks. They were to await the major force coming from San Juan del Monte under the Supremo's command, and at the stroke of twelve midnight, altogether, they were to take Manila.

While all these preparations were going on in the Manila suburbs, the Katipuneros in Cavite were waiting for the cue to strike with no less readiness and excitement. As early as ten that night, armed men were already deployed in the towns of Noveleta and San Francisco de Malabon (now General Trias). The Katipunan leaders *Apoy*, *Vibora* and *Labong*[14] kept vigil in the open fields between the above-mentioned towns watching for signals, either balloons to be let loose or cannon fire from Manila. They watched for these signals, to synchronize their attack against the civil guard garrisons in the towns of San Francisco de Malabon and Noveleta with that of the Supremo's plan to take Manila.

At eleven that night, after the siege at Mandaluyong, the Supremo Bonifacio and his troops proceeded to San Juan del Monte. With the Supremo were the leaders of the advance detachments, Genaro de los Reyes (alias *Bato-Balani*) and Vicente Leyba (alias *Kalentong*). They were intercepted at the San Juan Bridge by Feliciano Ibañez who was then the *capitan* [mayor of the town]. Ibañez begged them to put off the attack on the water reservoir for another day. He told them that the reservoir had become a formidable fortress, with more than a hundred troops ready to defend it, and that they were equipped with a big cannon so powerful it could mow down hundreds of people at a time.

---

[14]*Apoy, Vibora, and Labong* were the *noms de guerre* of, respectively, Santiago V. Alvarez, Artemio Ricarte, and Mariano Closas Trias. See *Ricarte Memoirs*, 8.

"Shut up! And woe to you if the Supremo hears you. You can only redeem yourself if you come and join us, " the leaders of the advance detachment remonstrated. The Katipuneros brushed aside Ibañez's misgivings and continued their march. When they were passing in front of the house of Vicente Tagle, they heard a loud, "Who goes there?"

They were sure it was the civil guards, for when they answered "Sons of the people!" two shots were fired at them at once. The Katipuneros returned the gunfire and charged with their bolos, killing one civil guard. Because they outnumbered the enemy, the Katipuneros easily routed them. They found the other civil guards hiding in the food pantry in the house of one Francisco Angeles (alias *Kikong Bakle*, lit., Francisco the Broken).

The Katipuneros resumed their march towards the Catholic church in town, but they were soon halted by the enemy near the place called Kaseta. They were ordered to identify themselves, and when they answered, "Sons of the People!", surprisingly they were not fired upon. So they moved closer and saw that they had only a sergeant and a civil guard to contend with. They overpowered and killed the two and confiscated their guns and daggers. On their part, the Katipunan lost two men, one named Teong (alias *Kapampangan*) and the other, a certain Juan (alias *Apog*). They suspected that the two were killed because another Katipunero, one named Luciano, fired at the enemy from behind them and accidentally hit their own comrades.

After these two successful skirmishes with the civil guards, the Supremo was preoccupied with the arrival of a 300-man contingent from Santolan. Led by their chapter chairman Valentin Cruz, who was armed with a revolver, they had seventeen other guns distributed among their rank and file. Their leader immediately put himself and his army under the command of the Supremo. The latter enthusiastically welcomed the newcomers, whom he integrated with his own troops.

With all these goings-on far into the night, and the talk and elation over their victories, the Katipuneros felt that they had to take a respite before the big offensive at midnight. They had scarcely rested when the Supremo pulled out his watch to look at the time.

Imagine the Supremo's dismay when he saw that it was four o'clock, four hours past the deadline of midnight, August 29. It was too late to release balloons or fire a cannonade to signal the beginning of a coordinated uprising. If they did so at that late hour, they might confuse other Katipunan groups who were anxiously waiting for the signals. The

Supremo decided that, considering the circumstances, they had better retreat to Balara, to rest and recover their strength, and carry out the aborted attack on Manila the following night.

They took the road leading to Balara; and when they reached Cubao they met five infantrymen, in the service of the enemy, but who were Katipunan members. The five surrendered their arms to the Supremo and defected to his army.

X

After waiting in readiness since eleven o'clock the previous night, the troops under General Ramon Bernardo continued their vigil until early morning of the following day, Sunday, August 30, 1896. Their high spirits did not leave them despite the watch in the night that was in vain. From the gunshots they heard in the distance, they surmised that the Supremo's forces had been delayed by some skirmishes. General Bernardo saw to it that his troops ate early that morning so that they would be ready for any contingency. While they were gulping down the steaming soup of their chicken *tinola* [ginger-pepper soup], they were fired upon by enemy troops who had been furtively watching them and were waiting for an opportune moment to attack. Composed of combined elements from the municipal police, infantrymen, and carabineers, the enemy at first succeeded in dispersing them.

On orders of their chief, the Katipuneros ducked, then regrouped and charged, fearlessly shooting and brandishing their bolos. The enemy eluded their attempt at encirclement by fleeing as fast as they could on their mounts and on foot. Unfazed, the Katipuneros gave chase.

The chase led them near the Santa Mesa River, where unexpected reinforcements joined in the pursuit. On the opposite banks of the river were a group of Katipuneros, under the leadership of Ricardo Losada. With the only gun in their band, Losada tried to intercept the fleeing enemy troops, but just then a large detachment of Spanish infantry and cavalry came to the rescue of their beleaguered comrades. The Spanish reinforcements occupied both sides of the river and began firing away furiously, not only with their guns but also with a mountain cannon they brought with them.

In the face of this onslaught, the Katipuneros were on the verge of dispersing when they heard the rallying cry of their leader, "Charge, my brethren!"

The battle came to a fever pitch with General Bernardo's troops fighting like Moros turned *juramentado*.[15] With their dead and wounded lying everywhere, the enemy could do nothing but retreat. It was wonderful, however, to see them fall in formation immediately after a single bugle call and then flee in an orderly manner. This battle ended at about eight that morning.

After the enemy left, General Bernardo realized that only about thirty of his troops remained. Puzzled about what had happened to the majority of his men, he decided to march towards San Francisco del Monte, where he intended to regroup his army. The stragglers passed by way of Santol, Barong Pipa, Kailokohan, and Matalahib.

It will be recalled that the Supremo Bonifacio had decided to lead his troops to Balara for a rest, after the *faux pas* about the signals. They had not yet reached their destination when he stopped his men to tell them that he had a hunch that the gunshots they had been hearing came from Santa Mesa, where General Bernardo's army must have had an encounter with the enemy. Then and there he decided to go back to reinforce General Bernardo's troops. To intimidate the enemy, he thought of a ruse to make it appear that all his men had guns. He ordered those without firearms to carry a cudgel on their shoulders to simulate a gun. Then to avoid detection by the enemy, he placed these men at the rear, behind those who had real firearms. Finally, he gathered all those with revolvers around him, and together they led the march to aid General Bernardo's forces.

At about seven-thirty that morning, they reached the village called Ermitaño. Suddenly they were fired upon from inside the water reservoir compound located at the place called Vista Alegre. Despite the fusillade, they continued to advance towards the enemy stronghold that they knew contained a powder cache. The Supremo was organizing a squad to capture the powder cache when his plans were thwarted by the arrival of the Spanish infantry and cavalry troops, who had been driven back by General Bernardo's army at Santa Mesa. The Supremo was counting on the cooperation of their Katipunan brethren who were infantrymen of the Spanish army, inside the compound. He knew of their presence in the enemy camp because they made discreet signals which helped them in the siege, and when they were ordered to fire, they either fired upwards in the air or at the Spaniards.

---

[15]Moros are Muslim Filipinos, living in the southern islands of Mindanao, Sulu, and Palawan. When sufficiently provoked, they were said to run amok, hacking at everyone, especially Christians. The "amok" was called *juramentado*.

But the arrival of the Spanish cavalry and infantry units caught them by surprise, and they were easily encircled. Among those killed were Hermogenes Losada, Apolonio Ordino, Anastasio Reyes, Venancio Binangunan, Francisco Vicencio, and Jose Magno.

The survivors managed to regroup at about ten that morning. The Supremo decided that they should retreat to Balara for reorganization and preparation for new encounters. He ordered the commanders Genaro, Lucino and Kalentong to account for the dead and wounded in the last battle and to retrieve the missing firearms. They were to report immediately to Balara after they had accomplished these tasks. Then they parted ways. With the Supremo were fifty men, seven of whom had firearms. This number did not include those who had revolvers.

XI

The following are some sidelights to the stirring events narrated above:

On the eventful night of August 29, 1896, Katipunero Bernabe Sunga was preparing his unit to join the Supremo's forces, who were then on their way from Mandaluyong to San Juan del Monte. His wife, Francisca Angeles, slung a bolo on her waist and insisted that she, too, was joining the Revolution. It took a lot of persuasion before she resigned herself to give up the idea and stay at home instead.

The Supremo and his men arrived to take along Katipunero Bernabe's band for support in the siege of San Juan del Monte.

"Here we are, ready to fight, sir," Katipunero Bernabe presented his men to the Supremo. "But all we have are bolos and other bladed weapons. Where do we get the firearms we shall need?"

The Supremo did not answer him immediately; instead he looked at Bernabe with an amused expression. Finally he said, "Brother, wherever there is mortar, there is also a pestle. It is up to you to decide which weapon to use."

"What do you mean by that, sir?"

"There is no place for indecision," the Supremo replied. "As long as the blood with which we signed our oaths runs in our veins, true love for the motherland will prevail."

Then they all marched together to meet the enemy.

* * * * *

The following is another story about Francisca Angeles, Katipunero Bernabe Sunga's high-minded wife:

The Supremo was in her parents' home, where she also was at the time. A panicky civil guard fleeing from the Supremo's men sought refuge in this house, little realizing that he was running right into lioness's den, so to speak. For as soon as she saw him come in, this resolute woman snatched a gun, ordered the civil guard into the food closet, shut the door tight, and handed the gun to the Supremo. Then she led him to the prisoner whom she had locked in.

* * * * *

Andres Soriano. This mention is made lest his services in the revolutionary army be overlooked.

* * * * *

It will be recalled that at the battle of Santa Mesa, General Ramon Bernardo's troops were nearly decimated because of the enemy's superior arms. How frustrating it must have been for them to confront the Spanish troops with their puny knives when the latter had guns, a mountain cannon, and a cavalry besides. But the height of frustration and shame must have been when his own soldiers called out to their chief, General Bernardo: "Run, sir! Run, general, run!" For a general to be told to run away—what a bitter taunt!

XII

Let us leave for a time the army of the Supremo Andres Bonifacio as it recuperates from the rigors of the encounters just ended.

In the earlier part of the narrative, I overlooked mentioning that a *nom-de-guerre* was adopted by each Katipunan neophyte. Examples are *Mainam* (Fine) for Mariano Alvarez; *Magdalo* (in honor of Mary Magdalene) for Emilio Aguinaldo; *Apoy* (Fire) for Santiago V. Alvarez; *Labong* (Cane shoot) for Mariano C. Trias; *Mabini* (Modest) for Pascual Alvarez; *Vibora*, (Viper) for Artemio Ricarte; *Kugon* (Tall grass) for Aquilino Monton; *Lunas* (Relief) for Candido T. Tirona; etc. The Katipunan Councils also adopted names like *Magdiwang* (To Celebrate) for Noveleta; *Mapagtiis* (Forebearance) for San Francisco de Malabon, now General Trias;

Magdalo—Kawit, etc. All the above-mentioned Councils were in the province of Cavite.

Let us now turn our attention to the activities of the Magdiwang, Mapagtiis, and Magdalo Councils. The Magdalo leadership, it will be recalled, protested against the launching of a revolution at a large mass meeting of the Katipunan, held at Pasig in May 1896. In his memoirs,[16] General Vibora confirmed the objection by the Magdalo faction to an uprising.

At the meeting in Pasig, it will be recalled, it was agreed to start the rebellion at midnight of Saturday, August 29, 1896. That evening, the partisans of the Magdiwang and Mapagtiis chapters gathered and ate an early supper in anticipation of the scheduled uprising. Afterwards, their leaders, Katipuneros Apoy, Labong, Vibora, and Kugon conferred far into the night, under an areca palm grove in the middle of an open space, as the mass members, all armed, milled around in groups waiting to join other Katipunan units that were to attack Manila. They were awaiting the signals—either balloons to be released in the air or the firing of a cannon.

However, the tense and eager Katipuneros were disappointed when the whole night passed without the awaited signals. Nor were they aware of the encounters at Santa Mesa and San Juan del Monte; had they known about these, the sting of disappointment over the aborted strike would have been assuaged somewhat. In their anxiety, the fever of the Revolution rose higher, so that the next day they wanted to start the uprising with or without the participation of the Manila Katipuneros. But they were cautioned by Commander Mainam, who said, "Let us not make haste. We know that this struggle is inevitable, but let us be circumspect. Let us wait for the opportune time to strike. Since we have already shed blood and risked life itself, we should strike only when we are sure of victory. This we must do to attain freedom for our Motherland."

XIII

Now I shall set aside my own narration and attend to interviews with old Katipuneros and revolutionaries about their experiences during those crucial times. I shall let them tell their stories themselves.

---

[16]*Ricarte Memoirs*, 7.

Juan Maibay

I am Juan Maibay, a native and resident of Noveleta, in Cavite Province. Today, June 25, 1927, I have just completed my eighty-first year, since I was born on June 24, 1846. Although my eyesight is not as it used to be, my mind is still alert and my body is still vigorous. I still have the strength to go about my usual vocation of healing with herbs.

I remember those days very well—it is as if 1896 were only yesterday. I recall that I was *alguacil mayor* [chief constable] in the town hall of Noveleta, and our municipal captain was Mr. Mariano Alvarez when I joined the Katipunan of the Sons of the People. I assumed the name *Makabuhay*, "To Give Life."

I remember clearly that at about two in the afternoon of Friday, August 28, 1896, Mr. Mariano Alvarez instructed Katipunero Talahib, Nazario Caldejon, as follows:

"Go to Parang and contact the well-known outlaw brothers Hipolito and Hermogenes Sakilayan. Tell them to enlist men and collect more weapons. Tell them that I shall be waiting for them tonight to talk things over."

Katipunero Talahib left immediately to relay the message.

From eight o'clock in the evening of Saturday, August 29, to the following morning, groups of armed Katipuneros and peasants stayed up everywhere in the town of Noveleta and its environs, awaiting orders from their superiors. The leaders, in turn, were watching for the awaited signals. In their frustration, they would have gone ahead with the attack on the Spanish garrison, with or without action from the Manila Katipunan. But they were counseled against precipitous conduct by Commander Mainam.

All day that Sunday, August 30, Commander Mainam was besieged by endless delegations wanting to begin the uprising. But he persuaded them to abide by the decision of a coordinated rebellion. He counseled, "Let us wait. Maybe the situation which impeded us from action last night will be resolved, and the plan to attack Manila will be carried out."

When Monday, August 31, came and still there did not seem to be any prospect of an imminent uprising, we who were raring for action could hardly contain our impatience. We did not hear or see any of the expected signals; neither did we know of the skirmishes on the outskirts of the city which would have triggered the synchronized attack on Manila.

Very early that morning, Katipunero Vibora arrived in Noveleta from San Francisco de Malabon to confer with Katipuneros Mainam, Apoy, and

Mabini on what to do about the awaited insurrection. At the suggestion of President Mainam,[17] they decided to start the revolt at two o'clock in the afternoon of the same day. All steps would be taken to insure victory, including a close surveillance of the Magdalo group. It will be recalled that they did not approve of an uprising. In the event that they might choose not to join the insurgency, the enemy would encounter little resistance on the way to our territory, and that would lead to the ruination of our Magdiwang and Mapagtiis contingents.

After the decision was announced, Katipunero Vibora bade us a cheerful goodbye. He was eager to relay the welcome news to the impatient and frustrated Katipuneros seething to rise up in arms.

Not long after Vibora left, President Mainam received a flash bulletin saying that a lieutenant of the Spanish civil guard and one soldier were coming to Noveleta from San Francisco de Malabon, and that the people were planning to waylay the two. Chairman Mainam's advice was to refrain from carrying out the ambush, and, instead, to let the enemy reach the Noveleta garrison and there trap and capture them.

I was overcome with trepidation when I heard the announcement about starting the rebellion that afternoon, and my fear was compounded with the certainty of an encounter with the civil guards coming to town. And to make matters worse, we were not sure of the cooperation of the Magdalo people; their support was crucial to us since their territory was adjacent to ours. Moreover, we had no knowledge of what was happening to the Katipunan in Manila. Why was the coordinated attack not carried out? What were the chances if the Magdalo did not join forces with the few of us in the Magdiwang and the Mapagtiis? Because of these doubts and misgivings, I ran a fever but my feet and fists were chilled. I became restless and I could neither sleep nor sit still. I was hungry but could not eat. But in the face of all my comrades who were happy and enthusiastic, I became ashamed of myself. I forced myself to overcome my fear by thinking of my hatred and contempt for the Spaniards. I determined to join my brethren in the defense of the Motherland.

Still early in the day, the house of Katipunero Malimlim (Emiterio Malia) was in readiness with an abundance of food for the armed groups who came and went. The streets were full of men in battle gear. This joyful-sad

---

[17]He was concurrently municipal executive or town mayor. At the time the memoirs were written, the title was "president," but in its context in the 1890s, it was *capitan.*

ambience must have moved Mr. Catalino Angkiko and Mrs. Hilaria Caldejon to implore Chairman Mainam to put a stop to the planned uprising. On bended knees and with tears in their eyes they pleaded with him saying:

"You know very well that, contrary to our expectations, other Katipunan chapters will not come to our aid. The fact that the Magdalo is against the rebellion places our security in jeopardy. The Spanish authorities will send troops to annihilate us, and when we are defeated they will send their infamous *juez de cuchillo* and spill our blood and take the lives of all they can reach, young and old alike. We should not forget the 1872 Revolution.[18] You yourself, you were one of those arrested and tortured by the Spaniards. You should be grateful that they spared your life. We are afraid that what happened in 1872 will happen again."

"Please understand that I appreciate your concern, but you must realize that this moment is the opportune time for us to throw off the Spanish yoke. Whether we like it or not, the Revolution cannot be stopped anymore, and no one has the power to stop it. Do not lose faith; pray for our victory and give us as much as you can bear to give for the needs of our Motherland."

Having thus spoken, President Mainam then ordered Hipolito and Hermogenes Sakilayan to notify their followers to ambush the Spanish lieutenant and his aide and not to let them return to San Francisco de Malabon.

It was nearly eleven that morning when Katipunero Kugon (Aquilino Monton) came rushing from San Francisco de Malabon. With his sleeves and trouser cuffs rolled up, he was brandishing in one hand a knife commonly used for cutting betel nuts and in the other a bamboo pole with a sharpened tip. Excitedly, he reported to President Mainam that the Mapagtiis Katipuneros were already attacking the enemy.

The awed audience had barely recovered their wits from the shock of hearing that news when they heard shouts of "Ambush! Ambush!"

Then they saw the terrified Spanish lieutenant and civil guard running back towards the Noveleta garrison and later intercepted by the vanguards lying in wait for them at the confluence of two rivers, in the village of Dos Rocas between Noveleta and San Francisco de Malabon.

---

[18]That is, the Cavite Mutiny of 1872, which resulted in the execution by garrote of three Filipino nationalist priests and the arrest and exile of those others implicated in the revolt.

When the excitement from the spectacle had subsided somewhat, the three Alvarezes—Mariano, Pascual and Santiago (Mainam, Mabini, and Apoy)—quickly organized and assigned troops at street corners and at the town hall. They instructed the men not to attack unless provoked. They should let the enemy penetrate the town unmolested and then close in on them with the firing of the first shot.

Perhaps due to my faint-heartedness, I began shaking all over and my lips trembled so that I could not speak. My joints faltered and suddenly I felt very weak thinking of the dreadful fate I was sure was in store for me. The chairman saw through my timorousness and scolded me. He told me to grip my bolo tightly and to prepare myself for the struggle that had become inevitable.

At about noon, a Katipunan courier suddenly appeared to tell the chairman that a large detachment of civil guard led by a captain and a lieutenant were on their way and were arriving very soon.

"Jesus! Mary! Joseph![19] And now their brand of justice is here!" I exclaimed. I forced myself to gather courage and to face up to whatever was going to happen. I realized that my redemption lay nowhere else but with the looming struggle.

As soon as the civil guards arrived, they stood, abreast a yard apart, in front of the town hall. There were only four civil guards and two Spanish officers, a captain and a lieutenant. The officers went up the town hall and were met at the stairs by President Mainam who extended a hand in greeting to the captain. The latter disdained the proffered hand and, together with the lieutenant, strode haughtily up the stairs. On reaching the reception hall, he angrily shouted to ask for the *directorcillo* (municipal clerk).

Then he confronted President Mainam. The latter aimed his revolver at the captain, but when he pulled the trigger, it did not fire. The bewildered captain could only exclaim, "Ay! ..."

The captain went to the window to summon his troops downstairs to come to his aid. Just then Katipunero Apoy fired three shots at the captain. Three lead bullets the size of *kalumbibit* seed[20] hit the captain on the right side of the head, causing him to fall prostrate.

After the shots, the people's troops pounced on the civil guards to seize their arms and to strip them of their uniforms. Meanwhile, the lieutenant

---

[19] A common interjection among Christianized Filipinos.
[20] Grey niker seed or Molucca bean, used as marbles by Filipino children.

continued the combat against the three Alvarezes. When his saber broke, he grabbed an old broken-down gun fixed with a rusty bayonet from the gunrack and began brandishing it.

Mainam's revolver would not fire, no matter how many times he pulled the trigger. Apoy dared not shoot with his rifle for fear that he might hit a comrade. Finally Katipunero Mabini subdued the lieutenant by grabbing him from behind. Then he plunged his dagger into the Spaniard's chest. After motioning his uncle Mariano to keep out of the way, he pulled out the dagger and shoved the lieutenant, causing the latter to fall on his face. The Spaniard managed some last dying gasps before he expired.

Just then Katipunero Francisco de Castro came up the hall. Upon seeing the gasping officer, he asked, "Is this cur still alive?" He unsheathed his machete and bashed the Spaniard's skull above the nape.

After the Alvarezes had said their private prayers for the souls of those who died in the combat, they ordered that the bodies be buried in the sandbank of the river to the east of the big bridge in town. Then they had the blood-stained hall cleaned up. I myself supervised the job.

Shortly afterwards, a melee broke out at the junction of the road to Cavite and Salinas, which was some forty paces from the town hall. When we went to investigate, we saw some Katipuneros capturing two civil guards. With the guards were two prisoners, whose elbows were bound with rope behind their backs. The civil guards had come from their garrison at Naic and were on their way to the garrison at Noveleta, where the prisoners were to be subjected anew to interrogation and torture, until they were forced to admit culpability. The prisoners were set free, while their tormentors were stripped of their arms and uniforms.

This done, President Mainam gave orders for the wives, children, and other members of the households of the civil guards, living near the Noveleta garrison, to be brought out. It was nearing four in the afternoon when the families of the civil guards were gathered and ranged in front of a squad of seven gun-bearing Katipuneros; behind them were other Katipuneros armed with bladed weapons. Marching ahead of the whole formation was Mr. Epifanio Malia, who carried a white flag.

Meanwhile, the civil guards inside the garrison were girding for retaliation, for they already had received news that their captain and lieutenant had been killed and that their comrades who were with these officers had been captured.

President Mainam and his party cautiously approached the garrison and stopped when they were within shouting distance. The one bearing the white flag ran towards the garrison and announced:

"President Mariano Alvarez, who is our general, wants to make peace with you. You must surrender. What we need is freedom for our Motherland. Don't kill yourselves in defense of the Spaniards and their country in the manner of your captain and lieutenant. If you do not surrender and if you insist on fighting, the first ones to suffer and be killed will be your wives and children who are now held hostage in front of our gun-bearing troops. They will be the first targets both from your side and ours. And if you choose to kill me, one shot would be enough. But you can be sure that my comrades will make certain that you and your families will pay the debt in kind. What is your answer? Our President Mainam wants your answer now!"

"Go back while we discuss the matter," was the reply of some.

Epifanio Malia did as he was told. He went to report the reply of the civil guards to his superior.

Meanwhile the women began crying desperately and calling out their husbands' names, "Pio!" "Gajonera!" "Lakap!," etc., as the children whimpered, "Father! Father!"

In their state of extreme danger, the civil guards, whose families were held hostage, appealed to the others to give up. Everyone then agreed that the prudent thing to do under the circumstances was to surrender without a fight. They walked down single file to a corner where they laid down their arms. Then they waved to the People's troops to come in.

The Katipuneros entered the garrison without any resistance. And because they were eager to try the firearms, they grabbed at the guns and bullets collected at the corner of the room. One of the guns was not unloaded, and because it was handled improperly, it suddenly went off. The bullet plowed through the right leg of the maid-servant of the dead captain's wife. It tore a big gaping wound, which, however, later healed and did not incapacitate the woman.

The Katipunan captured a total of twenty-eight guns that day. The garrison was placed under the command of Katipunero Apoy. He reorganized the troops led by the brothers Hipolito and Hermogenes Sakilayan and assigned them to take charge of the prisoners. The dead captain's widow, with her children and servant, were transferred to the house of Ariston Villanueva.

We should not forget to mention here that after the town hall encounter, the troop commandant Katipunero Agap (lit., "Diligent")—Bernabe Diaz was ordered by President Mainam to see Katipunero Magdalo (Emilio Aguinaldo) to apprise him of the Magdiwang victories over the civil guards and to urge the Magdalo to like action.

The following was the lucid report rendered by Commandant Agap:

"I arrived at Kawit at about two o'clock in the afternoon following our battle with the civil guards in the town hall of Noveleta. As soon as I arrived in Kawit, I inquired if I could meet the municipal captain, Mr. Emilio Aguinaldo, at his office in the town hall. When I was assured that I could, I hurriedly climbed up the stairs paying no attention to two enemy civil guards I passed. As soon as I was up the building, Brother Magdalo saw me and beckoned me to go to his private room. There I told him the news about the death of a captain and a lieutenant of the civil guards and of the captain of the troops under them. Also, I relayed to him the message from President Mainam (Mariano Alvarez) that they, too, should rise up in arms. He became silent when he heard this statement, so I said, 'Well, do as you please!'

"I returned to Noveleta to report to my superior about the outcome of the interview. I reached Noveleta town after the People's troops had taken the civil guard garrison.

"I prepared this account today, July 21, 1927, when my mind is still alert and my body still zestful despite my eighty-seven years of age, for I was born on the 17th of August in the year 1840."

* * * * *

When Katipunero Agap arrived from Magdalo, we were demolishing what was called the Calero Bridge in Dalahikan. After demolishing the bridge, we cut off the telegraph wires. That same afternoon, President Mainam assigned Messrs. Antonio Virata and Romualdo Mata as commanders of the People's forces in the town of Salinas (now Rosario). On Tuesday, September 1, 1896, President Mainam appointed Katipunero Salasa (Esteban Alvarez) as his deputy to negotiate with the Magdalo Council regarding the urgent matter of joining the revolution. Esteban mounted a swift horse and quickly reached Kawit. At the townhall he met Katipunero Lunas (Candido Tirona) who informed him that Katipunero Magdalo (Emilio Aguinaldo) had gone to Cavite to ask the governor for six

Spanish soldiers to help in securing the town of Kawit, purportedly against the intended attack of the outlaw San Mateo.

Katipunero Salasa was not pleased with this information. On seeing two civil guards in the building, he convinced Katipunero Lunas to capture them. For this job, they enlisted the help of a cuadrillero. They seized the guns and ammunition of the civil guards and stripped them of their uniforms.

The news of the capture of the two civil guards inside the townhall spread quickly throughout the town of Kawit. Everyone became anxious and apprehensive because they believed that certain reprisal from the Spaniards would be forthcoming. But, they concluded that the only way out for everyone was to join in a common resistance. Katipunero Lunas was worried about Katipunero Magdalo's return with the reinforcement of Spanish troops he had requested. With utmost caution, he organized a secret detachment of his troops to intercept the enemy.

However, Aguinaldo returned alone because his request had been turned down. When he learned of the capture of the civil guards while he was away, the municipal executive was taken aback, and he began to reflect seriously. Finally, he ordered the preparation of the People's Army to attack that very night the civil guard garrison, the parish house, and the Imus estate house of the friars.

Meanwhile at Noveleta, the People's Army had had a very busy afternoon. They took the civil guard garrison in town, destroyed a bridge, and cut the telegraph wires. They started building three emplacements at the site called Dalahikan, in anticipation of the enemy assault they expected from Cavite, the provincial capital, and against the bombardments from the Spanish battleships ranged along the shore. Three hundred men worked all night to build the defenses, to which many troops were assigned. Their arms consisted of arrows, arquebuses, spears, bolos, daggers, and an ordnance-like contrivance with a wide diameter fashioned out of bamboo and coarse wire. They concentrated their best weapons in the emplacement mounted on the demolished Calero Bridge. The emplacement was equipped with thirteen Remington guns and one big iron tube improvised as a mountain cannon. Commandant Pio Baluyot was in charge of the gunners while Captain Gahasa (Epifanio Malia) was the leader of the cannon squad.

Although it was already about midnight of the same date, the leaders of the Revolution decided to call a mass meeting of the Sons of the People. The purpose was to consolidate the People's forces and organize them under one stable and strong leadership that would give direction to a revolution that had become inevitable. Among those who attended were those of us who had led the attack earlier in the day and leaders of the movement in the neighboring towns. We unanimously approved the following:

1. The Magdiwang Council was to be the highest organ to direct the Revolution.

2. The following Council officers were chosen:

President:	Mr. Mariano Alvarez, concurrently Secretary of Noveleta Municipality
Secretary of the Treasury:	Mr. Diego Mojica
Secretary of Justice:	Mr. Mariano C. Trias
Secretary of War:	Mr. Ariston Villanueva
Secretary of Welfare:	Mr. Emiliano Riego de Dios
Secretary of Interior:	Mr. Cornelio Magsarili
Captain-General: (Commander-in-Chief)	Mr. Santiago V. Alvarez
Lieutenant-General: (Deputy Commander-in-Chief)	Mr. Artemio Ricarte

3. The Council was invested with powers to appoint capable and deserving individuals to positions needed by the government.

The above-mentioned election was held openly. Some of those elected were not present but were duly notified afterwards. Mr. Pascual Alvarez recorded all proceedings and gave one copy to Mr. Cornelio Magsarili. But because of the lack of time and the need to attend to more urgent matters, it was decided to postpone the preparation of a constitution that was to bear our signature. We adjourned the meeting at this point.

[Sgd.] Juan Maibay

XIV

Additional Statements of Juan Maibay:

Unwittingly, I found myself compromised in a difficult situation. I found it strange that I was chief constable of the Spanish government at the town hall and, at the same time, chief constable also for the new People's Government. I had to be always at the side of Mr. Mariano Alvarez, my captain in the Spanish government and my chief in the Revolutionary Government. He would often consult me about the latest news and developments.

Because I had to run errands for him, I was here, there, and everywhere. My friends came to call me "Twenty-fourth of June."[21] By this they meant that I was everywhere and about all the time, as if it was St. John's Day every single day, no matter if the tide was high or low.

We have seen that early in the morning of Monday, August 31, 1896, the People's Army of Mapagtiis (San Francisco de Malabon) headed by Messrs. Artemio Ricarte, Mariano Trias, and Diego Mojica, started the rebellion. The Magdiwang troops led by the three Alvarezes—Mariano, Pascual, and Santiago—started mobilizing at noon of the same day. The Magdalo of Kawit, under the three Aguinaldos—Crispulo, Baldomero, and Emilio—and Candido Tirona, followed suit in the afternoon of the next day, Tuesday, September 1, 1896. On that day, the Magdalo troops encircled and attacked the parish house, the friar estate house, and the civil guard garrison at Mayhaligi in Imus, Cavite.

On Wednesday, September 2, 1896, the Magdiwang towns were filled with activity; one would have thought it was New Year's Eve. There was beating of tin cans and shouts rising above the din. When it was nearing twelve midnight, shooting broke out at Salinas and spread towards Noveleta. The shots were aimed at the townspeople who were aiding the confused and cornered Spanish lieutenant and two civil guards from Naic. On their part, the civil guards fired at anyone they saw.

Earlier, Salinas Council members Antonio Virata and Romualdo Mata had received intelligence reports from their vanguards, who ranged as far as Timalan village in Naic, that a Spanish lieutenant of the civil guard and two troops were leaving Naic to go to Salinas. Alerted, the People's troops and

---

[21]The feast day of St. John the Baptist, Juan's patron saint and namesake.

townspeople of Salinas lay in wait for the civil guards, but the latter eluded their would-be captors by shooting it out and fleeing.

On learning of this incident, General Apoy correctly anticipated that the enemy would seek the aid of the Noveleta garrison which, unknown to the Spanish officer, had already been captured by the Magdiwang. General Apoy assigned Captain Hipolito Sakilayan to lead an ambush party of ten men, all armed with guns, and deployed them along the friar road leading to the Noveleta garrison. At the approach of their enemy, they opened fire, but noticed that one of the civil guards, whose name was Apolonio Esguerra, was shooting upwards, unlike the other one, Caballero by name, who imitated his lieutenant in firing shots so low that the bullets flew just above the ground. After a few token shots, it did not take long for Apolonio to defect to the Magdiwang side.

In an attempt to avoid bloodshed, General Apoy tried to negotiate peacefully by waving a white handkerchief to the Spanish lieutenant. He made three such attempts despite strong objections from his comrades. However, the Spaniard ignored his overtures and, instead, continued firing and egging on his soldier to do likewise, by tapping his shoulder and saying, "Go ahead, fire, valiant gentleman!"

From their concealment behind thick foliage of swamp vegetation, the Noveleta People's troops watched the enemy advance toward them. Presently, General Apoy fired his revolver and Captain Hipolito shouted the order to fire. The troops fired and then and there felled the Spanish lieutenant.

Seeing that his officer had fallen dead, Caballero, the poor misguided but brave Filipino, staggered, but continued to fight. The chief of the engineer corps, Mr. Basilio Salud, tried to save Caballero. He tried to subdue Caballero in order to make him surrender and later to dress his wound, but the latter fired at him instead. Luckily, Caballero missed, for in his weakened condition he could hardly lift the nose of his gun from the ground. Probably taken aback and acting instinctively in self-defense, Mr. Salud unsheathed his sharp-bladed curved machete and with all his might whacked at Caballero. The blow fell on the neck and instantly severed the head. What a horrible sight it was!

XV

More of Juan Maibay's Memoirs:

The leaders of the Revolutionary Government did not have a moment of rest. They attended to many needs such as the procurement of goods and weapons and responding to requests and queries from the different towns joining the revolution. And everything had to be done quickly. In the face of such awesome responsibilities, President Mainam (Mr. Mariano Alvarez) strained his physical endurance to the limit. He had bags under his eyes, his voice was so hoarse that he could only speak in whispers, but, despite a fever, his morale remained high.

The Spaniards mounted an offensive against Noveleta on Friday, September 4, 1896. At past ten that morning, some fifty troops of the Spanish marine infantry from Cavite, the provincial capital, tried to penetrate the town via the usual highway. But the demolished Calero bridge was impassable, and the battery emplacements of the Katipunan loomed formidable; so they followed the trail, over the large fishpond dikes, until they eventually reached the front of the headquarters defended by the People's troops. They started shooting in earnest.

General Apoy was prepared for the contingency. Dividing his troops, he deployed half in the yard of their headquarters and the other half inside the building. They successfully repulsed the enemy, who fled with their dead and wounded in their arms.

But the Spaniards did not give up. After their retreat, they positioned a small vessel mounted with cannon on the bay across from the Noveleta People's Army headquarters and bombarded it from about two to four that afternoon. A casualty on the Magdiwang side was Katipunero Marcos Torres. After the bombardment, his body was found inside the water tank on the flat roof of the building. A bullet had hit him on the brow and pierced his skull through the back. Found beside him was a little gun he had used against the enemy.

On the enemy side, the Katipuneros saw trails of copious blood over the fishpond dikes where they passed in retreat. They collected an abandoned Mauser gun and some ammunition.

In the history of the Revolution, some events Magdiwang folk would always remember were the death of Marcos Torres, the first casualty from their ranks, their seizure of the first Mauser gun from the enemy, and the misfiring of his revolver the first time President Mainam pulled the trigger.

The above-mentioned Mauser taken from the enemy became an object of curiosity among many brethren who were not used to handling firearms. Not one of us knew how to use the new-style gun, neither did anyone know how to load and unload it. We handled it gingerly and cautiously. The arrival of a former civil guard, Pio Baluyot, saved the day; he soon solved the puzzle of how to use the Mauser.

The battle just ended convinced the leaders of the Revolution about the urgent necessity for good, strong, and well-planned fortifications. It was demonstrated that the low and broad emplacement they had built all night long barely served its purpose and obviously could not stand heavy enemy attack. For this reason, President Mainam ordered the building of stronger and better fortifications as quickly as possible. When the fort was finished, the new wall, which was higher and wider than the previous one, afforded a strong position for concealment and defense. From it, they could espy the enemy as far as the eye could see and shoot away without fear of being spotted. Built on the Dalahikan road, this fortification was constructed under the direction of the chief of engineer corps, Mr. Basilio Salud. It was the object of much admiration because of its durability.

From then on, Noveleta, which was the seat of the Magdiwang Revolutionary Council, was daily subjected to heavy bombardments from various types of enemy vessels firing from the sea. But despite the barrage of bullets, the people became more determined to resist.

XVI

[*Translator's Note*: The following section points out some purported errors in the memoirs of General Artemio Ricarte about the Philippine Revolution of 1896. Like the present work, the Ricarte memoirs first appeared in serialized form in the Tagalog weekly *Sampagita*.]

Perhaps due to the haste in writing about the events or to typographical errors, some inaccuracies appeared in General Artemio Ricarte's account regarding the Mapagtiis Council of the Katipunan in the town of San Francisco de Malabon in Cavite. In one instance, it appeared that: "One of the civil guards who was unarmed came to see the schoolteacher [i.e., General Ricarte himself] in front of the townhall of Noveleta." The townhall referred to should be that of San Francisco de Malabon, not of Noveleta; General Ricarte was in charge of the revolutionary forces in the latter town, not of the former. In another instance he wrote: "The officer they allowed to escape was later killed when he refused to surrender to a Katipunan detachment in the town of Rosario." However, it should be remembered that this Spanish lieutenant was killed not in Rosario, but in the townhall of Noveleta. In still another case, he wrote about the Spanish sergeant who refused to surrender and in the face of certain death kept shouting, "Long live Spain! Long live my beloved country!" This did not happen in the town of Salinas or Rosario, as it appeared in the account, but in the village of Dos Rocas.

* * * * *

The following is about the beginning of the armed struggle by the Magdalo army in the town of Imus. They marched into the town on the night of Tuesday, September 1, 1896, and captured two civil guards in front of the parish house. They killed one, but the other escaped and alerted his garrison.

The civil guards under a Spanish officer returned in full force and confronted the Magdalo forces who were standing by in front of the townhall. The officer asked the men who they were, and they answered that they were the civilian night patrol; this was on instructions of their leader Emilio Aguinaldo. By this ruse, Aguinaldo hoped that the civil guards would come nearer so that they could encircle them. But the civil guards were not convinced, so they started shooting. They hit Regino Kahulis in the leg.

To avoid more casualties, Aguinaldo ordered his men to take shelter. Meanwhile, the enemy entered the church and parish house and began shooting from the church belfry. Confusion reigned among the Sons of the People, especially since the enemy was shooting from an elevated position. Finally, Aguinaldo ordered a retreat so that all could rest and resume the attack on the next day.

Very early in the morning the following day, Wednesday, September 2, the townsfolk were awakened by a reveille from a cornet; and when they looked out, they saw a great number of armed men. The civil guards, who were holed up inside the church and parish house, began to panic. At first, they did not know what to do or where to go, but finally they all fled and took refuge at the friar estate house in Imus. Leading them in their flight was their Spanish officer, whose blood-drained face betrayed his terror.

The Katipunan pursued and surrounded them, but it took two days before they could subdue the enemy. The battle ended with the death of the priest in charge of the estate house. Coming out in the open with a rifle and a revolver, he engaged Celestino (alias *Taga*) and Igmeng (alias *Medisyon*) in a shooting bout. The priest fell dead on a paddy dike.

Before the end of September that year, the Sons of the People in Cavite had captured all the civil guard garrisons in the province, except a small one called *polvorista*, in the village of Binakayan in Kawit.

Meanwhile, the enemy confined its operations along the offshore area bordering the Magdiwang territory. From vessels moored on the bayshore, they bombarded the area with various shapes and sizes of ammunition, which, however, did not intimidate the people. Instead, a happy and carefree spirit prevailed. They had abundant food because the prices were cheap. There were no roughnecks, bandits, robbers, or pickpockets. With the Katipunan principle of brotherhood dominating their behavior, they loved and cherished each other. There was a holiday air everywhere as people freely indulged in various diversions. They only regarded with amused detachment the sight and sound of cannon balls flying overhead. No one had any fear of death because they believed that God was on their side and would protect them. The municipal councils under the Revolutionary Government freely made decisions for the common good; they cooperated with other councils to build defense fortifications along the path of the enemy, should it venture to make an overland offensive.

The first important decision of the (Magdiwang) leadership was to elevate the Magdiwang Council to a higher organ, separate from the revolutionary municipal council. This was to free the Council from local government affairs and to enable it to concentrate on the delicate problems of the Revolution. In line with this decision, they elected a new municipal council composed of Nicolas Ricafrente, President; Andres Diaz, Secretary; Emiterio Malia, Treasurer; Benito Alix, Prosecutor; and Adriano Guinto, Judge. The new municipal council immediately concurred with the local revolutionary leaders in elevating the Magdiwang to a supreme organ to direct the Revolution.

The proceedings of the organization of this Supreme Council appeared in the first installment of General Vibora's memoirs, published in *Sampagita*, Vol. 1, No. 45. However, he made some errors, as when he failed to mention Cornelio Magsarili as Secretary of Interior and when he said that he, Artemio Ricarte (alias *Vibora*) was designated Brigadier General, when his appointment was that of Lieutenant General.

The people recognized and respected this Supreme Revolutionary Council headed by Mr. Mariano Alvarez, who was concurrently the first General of its army. Less than a month later, the Magdalo Council also created a similar higher revolutionary organ composed of Baldomero Aguinaldo, President; Candido Tirona, Secretary of War; Edilberto Evangelista, Lieutenant General; and other generals and colonels from the ranks of the Magdalo Council.

The existence of two revolutionary councils, the Magdalo and the Magdiwang, was taken for granted by the people, who regarded the two groups not as rivals, but as allies, with the same sacred and righteous aspirations. Indeed, they thought it was an advantage to have more than one organization, as long as all were working towards one common goal— national independence. Thus, there was rejoicing everywhere, especially since the enemy dared not meet the revolutionary forces head-on. There were minor skirmishes between the two factions, but only because they mistook each other for the enemy, as so often happened in the early mornings and late afternoons. However, all would end well, with laughter breaking out from both sides when each would find out who the other group was. There still was cannon fire overhead, but no one minded it anymore; people learned to regard it like fireworks in a celebration. All day and all night long, young ladies kept their refreshment booths open. There was singing, dancing, and feasting under the trees; and in every corner, there was cockfighting and gambling. These were the distractions by which they sought to forget for the moment that, inevitably, they had to offer their blood and life sooner or later.

But all that was needed to drop all the merriment was a single call for attack. As women, children, and the weak retreated to places of safety, the men immediately grabbed their weapons and went to battle proudly and without hesitation. Among the first casualties were Juan, Marcos, and Pedro, but news of their death, instead of instilling fear, only invited reverence for them who, in their own words, had already "fulfilled their sacred mission." Participation in the struggle became more meaningful as a means to avenge the lives of their comrades.

Both factions regarded their unity of purpose as a strong and priceless bond binding them together in defense of the country's freedom. But it remained to be seen whether the bond would break.

XVII

The Katipunan position in Binakayan was in a shaky state because the enemy had succeeded in packing their small garrison there with reinforcements. They attempted to take the garrison several times, but all they could do was to isolate the enemy so that they would not be able to attack the Magdalo territory of Kawit. They built a defense position not far from the house of Baldomero Aguinaldo, and it was in this fortification that the joint leadership of the Magdiwang and the Magdalo often met to plot their tactics. General Apoy, whose assignment was to lead the defense of the Dalahikan beach, often conferred with the Magdalo leaders Baldomero and Emilio Aguinaldo, in spite of his reluctance to leave his troops who were keeping the enemy at bay. These meetings were happy occasions because they afforded temporary relaxation from the rigors of battle, aside from giving the leaders a chance to exchange views in furtherance of the Revolution.

The Magdiwang army defended the territory that included the eastern shores of Dagatan and Dalahikan and the wide expanse of open fields to the boundary of Cavite and Batangas. The Dalahikan position was strategic because it connected the interior of Cavite province to the sea, where enemy war vessels were deployed. The Magdalo army's territory stretched from the lower part of Dagatan towards the east as far as the Rizal-Cavite border.

The two armies were as one in their adherence to the great and sacred principles of the Katipunan. Each one cooperated with and complemented the other, boosting each other's morale. Rallying under the Katipunan black and white banner, which signified Death or Freedom, they rejoiced over each other's victory with shouts of "Long live the people!"

On September 17, 1896, which was a Thursday, Colonel Arcadio Arrieta of the Magdiwang army reported to his chief, General Apoy, that the Magdalo troops were noticeably lacking in their usual respect for Magdiwang officers and that, to get even, the Magdiwang troops were likewise getting disrespectful to Magdalo officers. He attributed this change in behavior as originating from a quarrel between two lieutenants from each side. The hostility had spread to the ranks until it reached the situation where they refused to give due respect to the superiors of the other army. This development jeopardized not only the unity of the armies but also the Revolution itself.

General Apoy instructed the colonel to communicate the information to General Vibora so that the latter could take steps to restore amicable relations between the two armies. Two days after Colonel Ariata's visit, General Apoy went to see the Magdalo leaders as was his habit. He met only President Baldomero Aguinaldo and Secretary of War Candido Tirona, since, at the time, General Magdalo was inspecting troops and fortifications among the Zapote River shoreline. They discussed mutual problems about strengthening fortifications and the preparation of artillery and ammunition at first, but, inevitably, talk veered towards the unseemly behavior of Magdalo troops towards the Magdiwang. This was a matter that needed to be resolved at once, especially since there was a lull in the enemy attacks. In his wish to patch up differences and head off disunity and disaffection for the common struggle, General Apoy broached the subject. This was Secretary of War Candido Tirona's rejoinder:

"There are two reasons for a possible break between us. The first would be if we do things without the knowledge of the other. The other has to do with the behavior of some of our officers; they pretend to be brave when they neither have the ability nor the right to be officers. However, I concede that their audacity could arise from a need to make quick decisions. Meanwhile, our armies do not yet have a common code of discipline. We can deal with the problem in either of two ways: by compromise and soothing ruffled feelings, or by execution."

President Baldomero Aguinaldo was more conciliatory. He said, "Precisely because of these matters, I have been wanting to discuss with and present to you a model of insignias by which we could identify our officers. This has already approved by us in the Magdalo Council; we are hoping you would adopt it too in the Magdiwang. If you also use the same insignias, our troops will not be confused, because we each will use a different color and style in our uniforms."

The following day Captain General Apoy presented to the Magdiwang High Council the Magdalo model for rank symbols and asked that it be adopted by the Magdiwang as well. The plan was unanimously approved, as was the Magdiwang uniform of black shirt and red trousers.[22]

The rank insignias were to be worn on the cuffs of the shirt sleeves in the manner of the Magdalo army. The stripes were in red and were defined by black cording, as in the following illustrations:

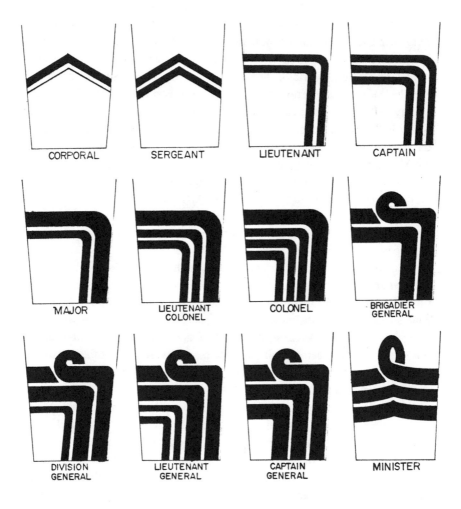

CORPORAL   SERGEANT   LIEUTENANT   CAPTAIN

MAJOR   LIEUTENANT COLONEL   COLONEL   BRIGADIER GENERAL

DIVISION GENERAL   LIEUTENANT GENERAL   CAPTAIN GENERAL   MINISTER

[22]The Magdalo uniform, on the other hand, was a white and blue-grey pin-striped *rayadillo* suit, still worn by surviving veterans of the Revolution on ceremonial occasions.

XVIII

While both Councils approved their respective regulation uniforms, with a common set of rank insignias, very few were able to comply because of unsettling events coming one after the other.

On Saturday, September 26, 1896, Captain General Apoy and General Vibora prepared to go to the field to inspect the fortifications to the west along the Cavite-Batangas border, which were under the command of Brigadier General Eleuterio Marasigan and Colonel Luciano San Miguel. But before the two generals could leave, the commander of the troops defending Dalahikan, Major Aklan, came to the war ministry to report that they had sighted the enemy fortifying the narrowest neck of Dalahikan. The enemy activity, which had started in the night, included the massing of Spanish troops. What they saw at night was subsequently confirmed in the daylight when they saw troops busy building new fortifications. This was clearly a threat to the People's Army, so Major Aklan wanted to prepare for an attack. He had already informed his immediate superior, Colonel Santos Nocon, about his plan, but the latter and General Mariano Riego de Dios had not yet acted on his proposal. Captain General Apoy advised him to study the situation very carefully before he launched an offensive, even after his superior officers gave the go-signal.

Generals Apoy and Vibora returned from their inspection of the western defense line on Wednesday, September 30. They were very pleased about the good job of the army command in that area under General Eleuterio Marasigan and Colonel Luciano San Miguel. They also brought with them the news that Major Aklan's plan of attack and encirclement, to be carried out at night on the enemy position at the narrowest section of the Dalahikan road, had been approved. Secretary of War Ariston Villanueva approved the carefully sketched plan presented to him by Major Aklan.

The attack was set for Monday, September 28, at eight at night. Major Aklan and his troops were aided by guerrillas, who first surrounded the enemy detachment with some thirty men. Then they attacked in full force with their guns and bolos, but a few of the enemy managed to escape their encirclement. They pursued those who fled, little realizing that they were being led to a trap. The enemy fortification to which they were lured was surrounded by a barbed wire wall the height of a man, which was not visible to them in the dark. The result was that those in the vanguard ran smack against the barbed wire wall and injured themselves. Some managed to climb over and enter the enclosure and began hacking and stabbing the enemy with their bolos. Others fell on their bellies outside the barbed wire wall and began shooting.

The enemy reinforcements suddenly arrived from a war vessel anchored along the beach on the lower side of the fort. At the same time, the warship opened fire on the Sons of the People, killing and wounding many of them. Among the wounded was Major Aklan himself, who was hit on the right wrist at pulse point, causing blood to spout. Within three hours, the following were among those counted dead on the premises: Calixto Colorina of Malabon (San Francisco de Malabon) died in the front yard; Jose (alias *Mainit*), twenty-three years old, native of Naic, was one of those who had climbed up the top of the fort and was shot in that very vulnerable position; Sergeant Clemente Diaz, twenty-four years old, of Noveleta, was one of the dead found inside the building.

A story of this battle was that of the Katipunan squad leader known as Naro, from Noveleta. He was crouched on his belly outside the barbed wire wall when the enemy began shooting. He decided to flee, but he could not stand for fear of being an easy target, so for about two hours he kept rolling like a log over the sand stretch between the battlefield at Dalahikan to the village of Liktong in Salinas. Only upon reaching this place did he stand to continue his flight on foot. But all the while he was rolling on sand he kept muttering, "Jesus, Mary, Joseph! God save me now and I promise never to go to battle again. I did not know it would be so terrible; even if I wanted to quit, they wouldn't let me. Please, virgins, help me!"

After this battle, Magdalo troops attacked the civil guard garrison at Carmen, otherwise known as Puting Kahoy, located between Silang in Cavite and Santa Rosa in Laguna province. They attacked this garrison repeatedly, but they never succeeded in capturing it. The encounters between the Katipunan and Spanish troops became an almost daily occurrence, and the outcome of each encounter was reminiscent of the battle at Dalahikan between the Magdiwang and Spanish soldiers.

XIX

At about eight in the morning of Saturday, October 3, 1896, small fishing boats in the offshore areas of Noveleta and Salinas began scampering ashore. They were escaping the range of cannon fire from a small war vessel grounded on the beach beyond the Roman Catholic church of Salinas. With thirty Spanish troops aboard, it was left high and dry by the tide. At first, the People's forces thought of attacking the vessel from a shielded boat, but the plan was abandoned because they realized that there was no shield they could put up that could protect them from cannon fire. In their search for a way by which they could capture the vessel, Generals Apoy and Vibora inched their way and hid behind a bamboo grove within visual distance of the ship. The enemy sighted them and bombarded their position for about two hours. The two, who returned the fire without fear of death, miraculously escaped unscathed.

Two days after this devastating experience, Captain General Apoy, the Magdiwang commander-in-chief, received a letter from General Eleuterio Marasigan of the Batangas command, asking him to appoint a deputy to aid him in his planned attack on the garrison at Balayan, Batangas. His own deputy, Colonel Luciano San Miguel, could not help him since he was, at the time, on a critical task of defending the shorelines. General Apoy thought that a suitable one was Mr. Severino Caoibis, a prominent citizen of Balayan, so he forthwith wrote a letter to Mr. Caoibis requesting him to serve in General Marasigan's brigade.

In the siege of Balayan, General Marasigan was accompanied by Secretary of Justice Mariano Trias, Major Domingo Dones, Rafael Sotto and other leaders, and a detachment led by Major Dones. The battle unexpectedly lasted three days, during which they ran out of ammunition when they were encircled by enemy reinforcements from surrounding towns. They were unfazed by the encirclement, but what broke their morale was hunger and running out of ammunition. So great was their hunger that even Secretary Trias was forced to join in the scramble for anything edible, fruit or even leaves, like those of *kamias*. Finally they decided to gather their dead and wounded, carry those they could, and retreat.

Sunday, October 11, 1896, was a black day for the people of Nasugbu, Batangas. At eight that morning, while the townspeople filled the church for the usual Sunday Mass, a ship full of Spanish troops anchored at the quay. After disembarking on the beach, the troops fell in formation, and at the sound of a bugle call they marched forward and surrounded the whole town of Nasugbu. They fired mercilessly at all living things, people and beasts alike, including the women, the old and the young. And when they were done with their murderous deed, they next burned the town. Everything was razed to the ground: the church, townhall, houses, and corpses.

The news about the massacre and burning of Nasugbu reached Colonel Luciano San Miguel at his defense post while the enemy was still on the rampage. Immediately he pulled out troops from the fortification to rush to the defense of the hapless people of Nasugbu. But they had not been gone two minutes when they were frustrated by guerrilla units of the enemy. They were surrounded, and in the ensuing hand-to-hand fight they used bolos and daggers rather than guns. All his men perished. Colonel San Miguel was the only lucky survivor in that encounter.

On returning to base to gather fresh troops to halt the enemy's advance, Colonel San Miguel was promoted to brigadier general. This was in recognition of his heroism in the last battle. Besides, the Magdiwang army was in need of a new general since General Marasigan had failed to communicate, much less report, to headquarters about the outcome of the battle at Balayan.

Captain General Apoy, disappointed over the defeats of his army, decided that a study of the terrain of the Magdiwang territory was needed in order to turn defeats into victory. For this purpose, and to promote the cause of the Revolutionary Government, he instructed the colonel on his staff, Atty. Jose del Rosario, to make a survey of the western front, to find out the extent of the territory they would need for the successful prosecution of the revolutionary effort. Colonel del Rosario contacted the new Brigadier General in charge of the area, General Luciano San Miguel, and the two returned together to report to Captain General Apoy. General San Miguel recommended an attack on the Lian garrison, since he had already made a careful study of the lay-out of the garrison, the possible routes the enemy reinforcements could take, the sites for building fortifications, and the routes of entry, and bivouac sites for the Sons of the People.

The siege of Lian was set for Friday, October 11. Captain General Apoy and Brigadier General M. Riego de Dios led the Magdiwang forces in the march to Lian. They collected additional guns on the way. Left behind to man headquarters was Lieutenant General Vibora. The army marched in the following order:

First group: The cavalry led by Major Jose Mojica. With him were a captain, the lieutenants, and a standard bearer with the red Katipunan flag.

Second group: Captain General Apoy, Brigadier General Mariano Riego de Dios, staff Colonel Jose del Rosario, Colonels Pablo Mojica, Juan Cailles, Arcadio Arrieta, and other officers.

Third group: Brass band of the Magwagi troops of Maragondon, Cavite.

Fourth group: The artillery led by Majors Alvaro (alias *Baro*) and Damaso Fojas.

Fifth group: The bladed weapons detachment by Bernabe Diaz and Pantaleon Granados.

Sixth group: The mass of townspeople.

This expeditionary force arrived at General Luciano San Miguel's headquarters at nearly two o'clock in the afternoon. From there it preceded to the town of Nasugbu that, as we have seen, had been devastated by the Spaniards. They found some corpses still littering the streets, while others were rotting at the bottom of wells; and so great was the stench that no one dared to go near and look in. Near the church was an old cannon with a barrel measuring about one and a half yards long. Some people could be seen on the outskirts of the town, but so great was their fear of strangers that at the sight of them they quickly hid themselves inside thick sugar cane stands. General Apoy instructed his troops to deal with the fear-stricken people with sympathy. They should persuade those in hiding to come out and talk, and under no circumstances should they use their weapons to harm or intimidate them.

A man, with a woman and three little children in tow, gingerly approached Captain General Apoy. He was holding in his left hand the rim of a rice cooking pot. The Captain General wondered what he had in his hand, and so he asked what it was. The man answered that it was a pot of rice they were keeping for the children; he dared not leave it behind for fear that the precious rice would be lost. The Captain General burst out laughing. Pointing to what the man had in his hand, he said, "Look! With what are you going to feed your children?"

The man looked, and when he saw that what he had was only the rim of the clay pot, he was so embarrassed that he quickly dropped it. He explained, "There was a little rice left in the pot. We were keeping it for the children. I was not aware that the pot broke and that all that I had in my hand was the rim."

Everyone had a hearty laugh, easing the tension all around. The relaxed atmosphere lifted the sagging morale of the destitute family as well as of the many others hiding inside the canefield. The latter came out of hiding and readily volunteered to serve with the Sons of the People.

Heady with new enthusiasm, the army continued their march until they reached the site called Kugunan, across the river from the town of Lian. They rested in a ruined house and in a warehouse with a rice mill and posted guards in the vicinity and inside the town to look out for traitorous enemy attacks. A make-shift kitchen and mess were set up with Captain Juancho Luna in charge. In one corner, first aid medicines were arranged under the direction of the old herb healer Major Juan Maibay. And while the troops were engrossed in such preparations, the brass band played lively, pleasing martial music until nine at night when the bugle sounded the signal for retiring.

However, there was no rest for an artillery detachment led by Colonel Pule of Magallanes. The men labored all night to assemble and load a captured cannon on a two-wheeled cart. They encircled it with wide strips of sheet iron they had stripped from a broken cauldron and then lined the insides with carabao hide. Then for improvised ammunition, they prepared iron strips of various shapes and sizes that could easily be slipped into the mouth of the cannon.

XX

At four in the morning of Saturday, October 17, 1896, the bugle sounded the reveille for the expeditionary force to Lian. The Sons of the People woke up in high spirits. Their morale got a further boost from the gay tunes the brass band played as they began to eat their breakfast at five that morning. At six, they fell in formation for a parade. All those who had only bolos were made to carry either a bludgeon or a pipe on their shoulders and were interspersed with those with real guns. With the brass band at the rear end, they marched round and round their camp to impress and intimidate the enemy.

By eight that morning, the contingent was ready to attack. Captain General Apoy deployed the troops in different positions. Colonel Arcadio Arrieta and Major Dalmasio Fojas were to guard the lower and western parts of Lian town, while Colonel Juan Cailles and Major Baro were to do likewise in the upper and eastern parts. Colonel Pablo Mojica and Major Mojica were to accompany Brigadier General Mariano Riego de Dios and Captain General Apoy in the attack, while Colonel Pule of the artillery was to take charge of the cannon that was to shell the parish house where the enemy was entrenched. Major Bernabe Diaz and his bolo detachment were to build a fortification for the war headquarters. This fortification should be in front of the enemy position and should be within shouting distance from it. Everyone went to his post with alacrity. Colonel Cailles and Major Baro located the highest point in the site called Talipusngo and fortified it, for it was the only passage through which the enemy could come in or escape from the town. Colonel Arrieta and Major Fojas busied themselves building the fortification assigned to them, while the two Mojicas, the colonel and the major, entered the town. The enemy inside the town closed tightly all doors and windows when they saw the Katipunan troops slowly making headway into town. Colonel Pule ordered that the cart bearing the cannon be placed in front of the parish house. About two hundred troops armed with bolos pushed and hauled it in position. Another detachment with guns covered this entourage until they reached that part of the wide road in town which was some 100 arms' length away from the parish house.

Suddenly the enemy opened fire. In only three seconds (winks), they felled some sixty People's troops. Captain General Apoy wept; but despite the hail of bullets, he helped gather the dead and the wounded. Then he ordered the bugler to sound the signal for the guns and cannons to return the fire.

Everyone on the general staff fought the enemy to the best of his ability. Colonel Pule of the artillery tried his utmost to deliver cannon fire across the lines, but the enemy retaliated with machine gun fire. From their position at the staff headquarters not far from the enemy concentration, Captain General Apoy, General Riego de Dios, and Colonel Mojica issued instructions that were communicated by means of the bugle.

The Captain General ordered the troops under Captain Sagasa and Lieutenant Araro to position themselves in the big house belonging to Mr. Espiridion (alias *Piryon*). From this house, they were to besiege the enemy holed up in the nearby parish house. The ambience in this house, during the battle, was a melange of gaiety and sadness. Inside the house was a piano that the Katipuneros played, even as furious firing came from both sides. By such insouciance, they infuriated the enemy. But this was not all; they also exasperated the Spaniards by shouting "Buenas dias, señor!" ("Good morning, sir!") any time of day or night.

This battle began in the morning of October 17, 1896, and ended at noon two days later. The following are the events leading to the unfortunate end of this encounter:

While the Sons of the People were increasingly optimistic about their eventual victory, the enemy was already showing signs of waning strength. For example, two Filipino soldiers in their ranks escaped by slipping out of a window in the dark of the night. They were apprehended by the Sons of the People, who had wanted to shoot them; but the Captain General prevailed upon the latter not to harm, but, instead, to exact information from them.

The prisoners cooperated and said that the Spaniards were at the end of their rope—they were sleepless, weary, hungry and frightened. Inside the parish house there were already corpses and among the wounded were many in serious condition. The last few shots that came from them were fired by Filipino soldiers on instructions by their Spanish superiors, but they fired aimlessly, for they were already weak and dazed from hunger. Their rations were very meager because of anxiety over dwindling provisions. They were told to leave so that they could ask for food and reinforcements. However, it was dangerous to get into the parish house because they had a reserve force that was still strong. Of the more than 500 troops inside, most were foot soldiers and a few were civil guards. After two more days they would be ready to surrender, for by then only about ten would be strong enough to fight.

After the interrogation, the Captain General sent the prisoners to the Kugunan army, with instructions to feed them and treat them well. But they were to be held prisoners for the duration of the war.

With victory as their goal, the Sons of the People fought with delirious courage. They defied all dangers and approached the enemy position fearlessly.

But something happened that turned the tide for the Spaniards on Monday, October 19. At about ten in the morning, the enemy, holed up in the parish house, began to be animated and they started firing with new vigor. Moreover, the bullets that flew thick and fast seemed to come from all directions. At the Captain General's headquarters inside the town, a bullet hit the nape of a lieutenant who was arm-in-arm with Colonel Mojica. The bullet pierced the neck and blood spurted, but before he breathed his last, the lieutenant was able to exclaim, "Jesus! Mary! Joseph!"

Among those wounded was Mateo Reyes, Captain General Apoy's bugler, who was hit in the arm. The Captain General was telling Colonel Mojica to find out the cause of the sudden enemy activity when General Riego de Dios came in. The latter, who was in charge of the combat troops, informed the Captain General that they were in grave danger; they had been encircled by enemy reinforcements who had been able to penetrate the town, because they had passed the Talipusngo position without any resistance.

Bedlam broke loose when the People's troops learned about their encirclement. They fled in confusion, spilling blood and littering the streets with corpses. In less than an hour the shooting stopped, but was replaced by hand-to-hand combat. Bayonets, daggers, and bolos were wielded with abandon by both sides.

General Riego de Dios rallied some seven soldiers who would have thrown themselves against the multitude of enemy reinforcements, but he was prevailed upon by the Captain General from making such a futile plunge. Out of about thirty men they had, only two survived that battle. They swam across a river even while being pursued by enemy bullets. They easily negotiated the deep portions of the river, but ironically it was in the shallow portions where they swam into trouble. Swimming as fast as they could, they did not realize quickly enough that they were heading into the portion of the riverbed which was only ankle deep. Then all at once their eyes, noses, mouths, ears and heads were buried in the sand.

The brass band continued playing lively music throughout the enemy attack; and when the firing subsided somewhat, the musicians relaxed by lying flat on their backs. Still they continued playing, and those with big instruments, like the bass drum and the bass horn, played with their instruments on their bellies. Thus relaxed, they played even more loudly than before. But when the enemy's bullets began flying low over the ground, the musicians took to their heels and fled for their lives.

The weary survivors among the Sons of the People regrouped at the Kugunan station. They also brought with them the many wounded who were given first aid by the chief healer, Mr. Juan Maibay. Captain General Apoy would have wanted to ask Colonel Juan Cailles to explain why the enemy succeeded in penetrating their lines. But the colonel was not present, so he interrogated Major Baro instead. Colonel Cailles was the only army officer who was absent at their retreat in Kugunan. Captain General Apoy wanted to find out why the enemy was able to get past the Talipusngo defenses without a fight, and why no on warned them of the enemy approach, thus exposing them to encirclement and unexpected attack. The following was Major Baro's deposition:

"When Colonel Cailles saw the approaching enemy horde, sir, he did not give me the order to fight. Even when the enemy was already near, he did not allow any gun to be fired; he said that since we were outnumbered, any attempt to stop the enemy would be futile. Moreover, he said, we would all die if we did. When the enemy approached and it was opportune to begin shooting, Colonel Cailles ordered us to put away our cannon and our rifles and leave the fortification. He himself fled ahead of us; we only followed his example.

"The troops asked me why we did not fight. I told them the colonel did not want us to fight because it was futile to do so," Major Baro replied in answer to the Captain General's interrogation.

The Captain General did not say a word; he mulled and kept his thoughts to himself. General Riego de Dios reacted sharply—he reddened quickly but also kept silent.

After giving instructions to the officers assigned to the defense of the Batangas border to exercise extreme vigilance, General Apoy prepared the army for retreat to Magdiwang. There they intended to rest and plan for a new attack. On the way, they met a detachment of troops led by the Magdiwang Secretary of State, Mr. Emiliano Riego de Dios. He was carrying a bundle of vines of a wild root with which he was intending to poison the enemy's source of drinking water while they were holed up inside the parish house. However, he changed his mind and gave up his scheme and, instead, joined the army in its retreat to Magdiwang.

XXI

To make a fuller account of the events previously narrated, let us turn our attention from the home trek of the Magdiwang army to other matters—for example, criticism about the name of the Katipunan, an outline of the account of the heated battle in the municipal hall of Noveleta on August 31, 1896, and then to the siege of Imus the following night.

It has been previously mentioned that General Pascual Alvarez was called by the Katipunan "Mabini," but General Artemio Ricarte referred to him as "Bagong Buhay" in his memoirs. This is by no means contradictory, for even individuals carried more than one pseudonym; for example, General Ricarte himself had one symbolic name for the Katipunan and another for Masonry. In this case, Mabini and Bagong Buhay were alternatively used by the Magdiwang head, Mr. Pascual Alvarez, as personal pseudonyms, and like Magdalo in the case of Emilio Aguinaldo, he also bestowed the symbolic names to the organization he headed. Incidentally, General Ricarte joined Masonry in September 1896 through the sponsorship of the Venerable (Master) Pedro Camus.

The next is a clarification of the account written by Major Juan Maibay about the Battle of Noveleta on August 31, 1896.[23] The following paragraph was inadvertently omitted:

"General Pascual Alvarez bent and blunted the sword of the Spanish lieutenant of the civil guard when he parried the latter's attack. However, he was wounded when the severed tip of the sword hit his brow. Also, he complained of a chronic pain in the right shoulder (which recurred) as a result of the battle."

Regarding what was written in the same report about President Mainam, the following quotation from him should be added: "I did not know that the taste of blood is salty and fishy. Blood spattered my lips when you, Pascual, pulled out the dagger with which you stabbed the Spanish lieutenant in the chest."

Regarding the siege of Imus that the Magdalo originally had planned for the night of September 1, 1896, it was actually carried out in the morning of the following day, September 2.[24] The Magdalo leadership deferred the attack because the previous night had been very dark. And in lieu of Messrs. Crispulo Aguinaldo and Candido Tirona commanding the operations, General Emilio Aguinaldo himself took over, since the two were resting after an all-night vigil waiting for favorable conditions. General Emilio Aguinaldo himself made this clarification thirty-one years afterwards, in a conversation with this writer, during a public function held at the Noveleta municipal building on August 31, 1927.

A few days after the siege of Lian by the Magdiwang forces, the Magdalo army of Captain General Emilio Aguinaldo attacked Talisay, a town in Batangas province. They blockaded the Spanish troops who sought refuge inside the town church and parish house, and for three days they successfully thwarted all enemy attempts to send reinforcements and relief. Weakened from fatigue, sleeplessness, and hunger, the beleaguered enemy surrendered. The Spaniards who were captured pledged allegiance to the cause of freedom for the Philippines and fought on the side of their former adversaries. In this battle, one of those who rendered distinguished service was Colonel Alapaap (lit., Cloud), Marcelino Aure.

The stepped-up activity from the enemy war vessels, which were spewing bigger and bigger bullets than before, forced the Magdiwang and

---

[23]See pages 51-52 of this volume.

[24]See page 64 of this volume.

Magdalo governments to move to safer places. The Magdiwang transferred its seat to the San Francisco de Malabon school house on October 31, 1896, after shrapnel hit its headquarters at Noveleta. Not long afterwards, the Magdalo followed suit by transferring to the friar estate house at Imus.

XXII

An old tradition in Cavite, the provincial capital, was the yearly observance in November of the feast in honor of the Virgin of Solitude. On this occasion, all the other towns in the province offered various forms of entertainment such as brass bands, giant figures, groups of midgets, gaily decorated carts, paper fishes and lions, etc., which were included in the procession for the Virgin. Another feature of the procession was a puppet suspended face down and with arms akimbo. The puppet preceded the figure of the Virgin. Doves were to snatch away the puppet's feet, hands, and head, until nothing remained of it except the heart with a flower bud perched on its top. A dove would then peck at the bud, which would open and reveal the figure of an angel. The finale was when the angel doused perfume on the head of the Virgin.

After winding through the principal streets in town, the procession ended in the church. Then, various spectacles such as contests, fireworks, and a bullfight took over. People from Manila, the nearby provinces, and other Cavite towns would come in droves to attend this fiesta. Some stayed for as long as nine days after the fiesta. From hawkers they bought boiled turnips, apples, and fish paste made in Cavite, to eat and take home as presents. During those nine days, all forms of gambling such as cockfights and card games like *monte* and *panguingue* were allowed.

The Magdiwang Revolutionary Government cooperated in the celebration of the feast of the Virgin of Solitude, not only because it was a revered tradition, but, importantly, because of the voluntary aid and support given them by the parish priest of San Francisco de Malabon, Fr. Manuel Trias.

In that revolutionary year of 1896, the celebration of the fiesta for the Virgin of Solitude was on November 8. For the reasons cited above, all the leaders of the Revolution cooperated and all attended the festivities. Brass bands paraded ceaselessly from early morning, despite enemy cannonade from war vessels along the seashore areas of Binakayan, Kawit, Noveleta and Salinas. Cannon balls reached as far as the scene of the festivities, but the merrymaking did not diminish at all; instead, cannon fire was greeted as the enemy's contribution to the fiesta. Aside from the contests and card games, there were also speeches, fireworks, and rockets. Fr. Manuel Trias officiated at a beautiful mass and was assisted by a choir of lovely voices. The highlight of the celebration in the evening was the spectacular procession.

Despite the festive atmosphere, the hard business of revolution was not forgotten. At about eleven that morning, Captain General Apoy asked Lieutenant General Vibora and Colonel Santos Nocon (he had not yet been promoted to brigadier general) to accompany him to inspect the fortifications that the Spanish war vessels and garrisons were trying hard to destroy. The three left on horseback. When they reached the village of Bakaw (San Isidro), Captain General Apoy was injured when his horse stumbled on an exposed root of a mango tree. He suffered a slight sprain that prevented him from going ahead with the inspection trip. But his two companions did go, and they saw for themselves how the People's troops defended the fortifications with unflinching courage.

The festivities continued into the night, but as darkness fell the cannon fire intensified. Still, the rebel positions remained unperturbed and the merry-making in honor of the Virgin of Solitude was unabated. Also unstoppable were the speeches, which heightened the people's determination to fight for their freedom.

XXIII

The Spaniards launched a determined siege against the rebel fortifications at Binakayan and Dalahikan at six in the morning following the fiesta. Cannon fire came from opposite directions, from their vessels at sea and from hillside positions. At the first burst of gunfire, Captain General Apoy, accompanied by General Mariano Riego de Dios and some soldiers rushed to Battery No. 2, which was then being bombarded by the enemy. Major Pio Baluyot, who succeeded the late Major Aklan, was commander of the post; assisting him were Captains Gregorio Ganak and Hipolito Sakilayan and Major Epifanio Malia. Their principal weapon was a small native cannon for which they had improvised missiles made from two handfuls of scrap iron bits. These were sufficiently destructive up to a distance of about 500 arms-length. A total of twenty-three persons, from the major down to the last soldier, defended the fortifications; and except for one with a Mauser, all the rest were armed with Remingtons. An old woman, named Gloria, joined them and refused to leave. She said she wanted to avenge the death of her husband who had died in the siege against the enemy position at Dalahikan.

As the shelling continued, General Apoy instructed his troops to refrain from returning the gunfire until the enemy was at closer range. Only when they had approached the foot of the demolished bridge did he give the order to fire and duck at the same time. The oncoming front line disintegrated instantly, while the rear line beat a hasty retreat. General Apoy's tactics seemed to be paying off well. He wanted the enemy to come closer so that each one of our bullets would take care of four or five men of the other side.

Then suddenly the woman named Gloria climbed atop the fort and stood there bravely shouting and waving a white piece of cloth. This cloth, they said, was a cover for the chalice used by a priest in saying Mass, and the poor woman waved it as a charm to ward off bullets. But contrary to other hopes, she hurtled and dropped dead to the ground after being hit instantly.

The battles at Dalahikan and Binakayan were fiercely fought. Mortar fire roared incessantly like thunderclaps; bullets exploded and guns flashed everywhere like lightning in a storm. The hail of bullets on all sides—in front, at the sides, above and below—sounded like the fearsome hiss of destruction and death. Fighting became more intense as the sun rose higher; and before noon, the enemy had made four attempts to capture the fort at Dalahikan. But each time they only heaped their maimed and dead in front of the fortifications of the People's troops. Thus repulsed, they retreated farther and farther from their former position, but they began shelling anew with bigger cannon balls. At noon they breached our fort, and a piece of shrapnel pierced the left ankle of Katipunero Gregorio Diaz, while another piece wounded the left ear of a child named Ambrosio. At the time, Captain General Apoy was between the two who were wounded, and he himself barely missed being hit. A bullet grazed the pith helmet he was wearing. The shock felled him, and afterwards he felt a big bump swelling above his left ear. General Mariano Riego de Dios rushed to his side and gently ministered to him; soon he was up and about again.

By two o'clock in the afternoon, the retreating army had left hundreds of their dead and wounded in front of the fortification. They continued to fire from farther and farther away, missing their target, the fort, by greater and greater margin. The relaxed situation made it easier to bring in food, and it was only then, several hours after lunch time, that the People's troops were able to eat. General Mariano Riego de Dios led General Apoy home so that his wound could be dressed. After they left, General Mariano Trias, Lieutenant General Artemio Ricarte, and other officers of the Magdiwang army arrived to take over the command of the Dalahikan fort.

Meanwhile, the rebel forces at the Binakayan front were not doing so well. Their fortification was captured by the Spaniards at two in the afternoon, at about the same time that their comrades at Dalahikan were successfully repulsing the enemy in that sector.

The Battle of Binakayan was clearly a Spanish victory. Aside from taking over the fort, they also killed and wounded many of the People's troops. They burned the village so that they could have an unobstructed view of the surrounding area. But they made a tactical error that was providential for the People's forces at Dalahikan. If they had gone on to Dalahikan after rampaging Binakayan, they would have surprised the defenders of Dalahikan.

Despite his wound, Captain General Apoy returned to the Dalahikan defense position at six that same afternoon. He was greeted by the awful and piteous sight of Tagalog casualties and heaps of the dead and wounded enemy. But no one dared approach the wounded Spaniards to give them first aid, because they would pretend to be dead but would shoot at the first chance they had. And so the wounded enemy were left alone until they were so weakened from hunger, exhaustion, and exposure as to make them practically harmless; even so, they were approached very cautiously.

After the guns and ammunition had been collected, General Apoy ordered three large graves to be dug near the bridge of Dalahikan, at the site where the dead and wounded Spaniards were scattered. They buried the enemy dead in these graves and brought the wounded to the army clinic under the charge of the chief physician of the Revolution, Major Juan Maibay.

The day following these big battles, the Magdalo army staged a valiant offensive to recover the Binakayan fortifications they had lost the previous day. After a brief exchange of fire, the People's troops hurled themselves in man-to-man combat, as breast-to-breast, belly-to-belly, they wielded their daggers, lances, and machetes. As they hacked away furiously, they heard these last laments from the dying Spaniards, "Jesus, Mary and Joseph!," "Mary, most holy!" and "Mother!"

On the other hand, the Sons of the People shouted a ringing "Charge!" as they hacked and stabbed. Guns became useless as the enemy reinforcements dared not fire them since their comrades-in-arms were everywhere, prostrate, hovering between life and death. Finally, those of the enemy who were still on their feet began to flee.

This time it was a victory for the Magdalo army, but a costly one, nevertheless. They recovered the Binakayan fortifications with great loss in lives. Among the many who died was Secretary of War Candido Tirona. His death was mourned deeply because he was one of those responsible for the fine reputation enjoyed by the Magdalo. Dr. Daniel Tirona donned his dead brother's cap. By this symbolic gesture, the Magdalo leadership recognized him as the heir and successor to the office of Secretary of War. This position he occupied until April 1896, when the Spaniards captured San Francisco de Malabon and Tanza. Incidentally, when the enemy occupied Santa Cruz in the town of Tanza, Mr. Tirona introduced Brigadier General Juan Cailles to the Spanish commanding officer as a Magdalo comrade.

XXIV

After the victories of the rebel forces in Cavite, peace was restored to the province. And since for some time the enemy was repulsed in its efforts to enter the province, to the people this was proof enough of the integrity of the revolutionary movement. News of these achievements spread quickly and was received with much enthusiasm and pride. Respect for the Katipunan grew, especially when the people learned about the gallantry of its sons who had shed blood and given up their lives in defense of freedom and of the noble precepts of the Katipunan. For example, an overriding principle that motivated Katipuneros was the unselfish love for humanity shown in their defense of their brethren's life, family, livelihood, and property. They came to pin their hopes on the Katipunan as the only force that could free the people from oppression. Thus, Cavite became the refuge of many people from Manila and the other provinces.

Among the first ones to seek residence in this rebel province was Mr. Teodoro Gonzales. He arrived with his wife and small children, all of them destitute looking. At first he was timorous about meeting President Mainam and General Apoy because he feared that they might not acknowledge his membership in the Katipunan. But when he did meet them and he tearfully recounted the hardships that he and his family had had to undergo, they embraced him warmly and gave him and his family all the assistance they could give. The Gonzales family enjoyed the proffered hospitality until they decided to move in with the Magdalo community.

Another one who sought refuge with the Magdiwang was General Ramon Bernardo, Commander of the Army defeated by the enemy in the Battle of Santa Mesa on August 29-30, 1896. General Bernardo recounted to the Magdiwang leaders the saga of his army's struggle and defeat and his flight to Cavite. He also told them of his vain efforts in the search of Supremo Andres Bonifacio. (This account of historical value is included in the present work). Through General Bernardo, the Magdiwang Council found a courier familiar with the mountainous terrain of Rizal province. They assigned this courier the task of looking for the Supremo and delivering a letter to him.

After the Supremo was located, he corresponded two or three times with President Mainam regarding the latter's invitation to visit Cavite. President Mainam wanted the Supremo to see for himself the conditions of the armed struggle in his province. In reply, the Supremo said that he was happy over the Katipunan victories in Cavite. He praised highly the establishment and growth of the Revolutionary Government that had come to be supported by many municipalities. This feat he recognized as "the cornerstone in the towering fort flying the banner of Freedom."

The Supremo also wrote that, despite their efforts and sacrifices that included the shedding of blood and the giving up of life itself, regretfully they had so far not taken even a single town that they could use for assembly and for defense. They were holed up behind small, dispersed fortifications in the mountains from where they went on forays against the enemy. He added that he was accepting the invitation to visit Cavite so that he could exchange fraternal embraces with brethren and so that he could see for himself the new developments that could further promote the Revolution. He did not intend to stay long in Cavite because it was necessary to harass the enemy from another front so that freedom could be attained sooner. He would not interfere with local Katipunan matters; he would respect and make others respect the leadership and their policies, for in unity there was strength. Moreover, they were all motivated by the noble Katipunan principles of fraternal love and defense of freedom for the Motherland.

The Supremo arrived in Cavite in the late afternoon of December 17, 1896. Stopping at Imus, he stayed in the house of Mr. Juan Castañeda. The following morning, Messrs. Emilio Aguinaldo, Baldomero Aguinaldo,

Daniel Tirona, Vicente Fernandez, and others visited him. Upon seeing Katipunero Vicente Fernandez, the Supremo invoked his authority as Supremo and ordered Fernandez arrested and rigorously interrogated. He accused Fernandez, a lawyer, of negligence that had led to the defeat of the People's troops in an encounter on August 29, 1896. But the Supremo's order was taken as a joke and ignored right there in the center of the revolutionary struggle, so he stopped talking and kept his thoughts to himself.

On the same occasion, Major Esteban San Juan of the Magdiwang army introduced himself; and in the name of the Magdiwang Council, he extended greetings and invited the Highest Chief of the Katipunan to visit them. The Supremo cordially acknowledged the respectful greetings and readily accepted the invitation of the Magdiwang spokesman. He thanked everyone for the warm reception accorded him.

The Supremo left Imus for Noveleta in the company of Messrs. Emilio Aguinaldo, Daniel Tirona, Baldomero Aguinaldo, Esteban San Juan, and others. They did not stop at Kawit, although it was on their way to Noveleta. When they reached Noveleta before two in the afternoon, they were joyfully greeted by the Magdiwang leaders and troops. They were welcomed by a brass band, flags, fireworks and gunfire, and by shouts of "Long live the Supremo!" The Supremo would then answer back, "Long live the Motherland!"

The party was led to a house where they ate and rested for a while. At past three that afternoon, the Supremo and Secretary Emilio Jacinto boarded a luxurious carriage pulled by a well-fed, swift white horse to inspect the defense positions of the Katipunan territories. A cavalry detachment led by Colonel Santos Nocon provided the honor guards in front, on both sides, and at the rear of the carriage. Astride a magnificent horse, Magdalo Secretary of War Daniel Tirona rode abreast on the right side of the Supremo and Secretary Emilio Jacinto. His sword was drawn and he was wearing a cap. Whenever they passed a crowd he would shout, "Long live the Supremo!"

On the left side was Major Esteban San Juan, and at the rear were Magdiwang infantrymen. They were followed by a cavalry detachment and armed troops dressed in red. After inspecting the Katipunan country and its defenses, they proceeded to San Francisco de Malabon. There the Supremo was also welcomed most warmly. There was a brass band, pealing of the church bells, and a *Te Deum* said by Fr. Manuel Trias, a Katipunan member.

Along the streets, some shouted, "Long live the King!" to which the Supremo would answer, "Long live the Motherland!"

At San Francisco de Malabon, the Supremo stayed for some time at the house of Colonel Santos Nocon and later moved to the house of Mrs. Estefania Potente.

XXV

After Christmas of 1896, various rumors smearing the character of the Supremo Andres Bonifacio circulated in the rebel communities. Among these were that the Katipunan members from Manila refused to be identified with the Supremo because he was an agent of the friars and that he was hired to create trouble; that he absconded with Katipunan funds; that he had a beautiful sister who was the paramour of the Spanish curate of Tondo and who was the secret liaison between them. There were others who said that Andres Bonifacio was a bad character, that he flaunted the title "Supremo," but that this should not be accepted because only God could rightly be called Supremo. Aside from these rumors, Mr. Daniel Tirona's act of escorting the Supremo on the latter's arrival in Cavite and shouting, with his saber drawn, "Long live the Katipunan Supremo!" all along the way did not meet with approval from the Magdalo Government. It will be recalled that Mr. Tirona was the Magdalo Secretary of War at the time. However, many suspected that the same Mr. Tirona was responsible for the many poison letters circulating in the rebel towns, especially in San Francisco de Malabon, where the Supremo Bonifacio was greatly admired and respected. The letters vilifying the Supremo stated that as a Mason, he abhorred religion and therefore did not believe in God; that he was a man of little education and was just a lowly hired hand in a German firm dealing in tiles on Nueva Street in Manila, and that this was his only source of livelihood; that he was undoubtedly an agent of the friars. Some of the letters reached the Supremo himself when recipients voluntarily turned them over to him. However, if many came to believe the slander, a still greater number did not; and what was more, the latter erased doubts from those who previously believed the rumors.

Not long after this smear campaign, the Supremo Bonifacio met Secretary of War Daniel Tirona in the home of Colonel Santos Nocon in

San Francisco de Malabon. Tirona was talking to President Mainam when the Supremo arrived. Immediately the Supremo demanded an explanation for the derogatory letters about him. Striking a defiant posture, Tirona airily tried to dismiss the accusation. Provoked, the Supremo aimed his revolver at Tirona. However, President Mainam and some women who were providentially present dissuaded the Supremo from shooting; otherwise Tirona would never have been able to leave as he did, but would have fallen right then and there.

Meanwhile, the Magdiwang Secretary of Justice, Mr. Mariano Trias, began organizing his own private army and commissioning officers outside the jurisdiction of the Magdiwang army. Captain General Apoy thought these actions of the Secretary of Justice unseemly and accordingly informed the Secretary of War, Mr. Ariston Villanueva, about it. The Captain General believed that the times called for better discipline in the revolutionary ranks and concluded that what Mr. Trias was doing was a contravention of the revolutionary effort. Subsequently, two Magdiwang leaders, Secretary of War Ariston Villanueva and Secretary of Justice Diego Mojica, privately confronted Trias to rebuke him.

"In order that the Revolutionary Government be respected, obeyed, and accepted by all," they told Trias, "it is necessary to lay down a correct policy of a united command under the leadership and responsibility of the Captain General. Only this army should be recognized and no splinter ones should be allowed."

Mr. Trias was obviously displeased with the rebuff. He simply ignored it and veered the talk to other matters.

After a few days, when Secretary Trias perhaps understood the full import of the thinking of his peers in the Revolutionary Government, he asked Secretary of War Ariston Villanueva to approve the promotion of Captains Mariano Gabriel and Julian Montalan to the rank of major. The War Secretary objected on the grounds that the commission did not come from the Captain General. Offended, Mr. Trias asked the Council for a meeting where he intended to present his resignation. The Council acceded and a meeting was arranged at the Roman Catholic church of San Francisco de Malabon. In this gathering, Mr. Trias delivered a valedictory speech, which he began by saying that he was happy to have had the pleasure of serving the Magdiwang Government and to have had a chance to see for himself, in his capacity as Justice Secretary, the patriotism of the people and their devotion to the cause of freedom for the Motherland.

After this introduction, he distributed to each one present a gold coin worth four pesos, which was nicely mounted on a pink ribbon. This memento he pinned on the left breast over the revolutionary uniform. Then he resumed his speech, asking that he be relieved of his duties so that he could rest. While his resignation was not accepted, still the upshot of the meeting was that Mr. Trias eventually moved over to the Magdalo Council, where he assumed the position of lieutenant general. He brought over with him the detachments of Captains Mariano L. Gabriel and Julian Montalan.

One afternoon, also in December 1896, the Supremo Bonifacio received Mr. Edilberto Evangelista in the home of Colonel Santos Nocon in San Francisco de Malabon. Mr. Evangelista read to him a constitution which he wanted the Supremo to adopt for the Revolutionary Government. After the reading, however, the Supremo said that a better constitution for the Motherland could be written by educated Filipinos, of whom there was a great number. He said that it would be utterly disgraceful to use such a model since it was very similar to the one written by a Spaniard, (Antonio) Maura, the Minister of Foreign Relations of the Spanish government. Maura's treatise was entitled, "Royal Order concerning the Establishment of the Judiciary in the Philippines by the Spanish Government."

Mr. Edilberto Evangelista studied in Belgium, where he obtained a degree in civil engineering. On his return to the Philippines, he immediately joined the revolutionary forces of General Emilio Aguinaldo. The latter commissioned him Lieutenant General in the Magdalo army in recognition of his patriotism and erudition. Mr. Evangelista was the one responsible for the construction of fortifications in Bacoor, Binakayan, and Kawit. He served his country faithfully and died in action defending the shoreline bordering the Zapote fortifications on February 16, 1897.

XXVI

On the initiative of the Magdalo faction, the Revolutionary Governments of Magdiwang and Magdalo met at the friar estate house in Imus on December 29, 1896. The purpose of the meeting was to settle differences in order to further the revolutionary effort. They explored the possibilities of a merger between the Magdalo and Magdiwang so that there would be a unified leadership. But because of a dispute over which faction should prevail, the proposition came to naught, because each group insisted on a "mine" rather than an "our" point of view. They discussed the framing of a constitution, although the Katipunan already had one that had been adopted by the Revolutionary Councils and chapters. However, they approved a motion creating a Legislative Committee to be headed by the presiding officer, the Supremo Andres Bonifacio. The motion also empowered the Supremo to organize its membership. They also discussed a plot to snatch Dr. Jose Rizal from the firing squad the following day, December 30, 1896, the scheduled date of the execution. For this purpose, General Apoy pledged to send troops armed with bladed weapons to infiltrate Manila that very night and later to mingle with the crowd who would come to witness the execution. At this point, when they were discussing the feasibility of saving Dr. Rizal from the firing squad, Mr. Paciano Rizal arrived at the meeting. He said that his brother, Dr. Rizal, would be agreeable to the plan if only one other life would be at stake. In Dr. Rizal's view, any other life equaled his own in terms of service potential. However, if the plan would jeopardize two other lives he would never agree to it, since the services of two individuals would never equal that of a single one. Because of these considerations, all discussion about the proposal had to be laid aside.

The Supremo Bonifacio asked the secretary of the meeting, Mr. Baldomero Aguinaldo, to record in the minutes the decision regarding the motion to frame a constitution; but Mr. Aguinaldo requested that the task be deferred since at the moment the meeting was in disarray because crowds were milling around Mr. Paciano Rizal. He promised to accomplish the task immediately afterwards, however. The meeting ended then and there, but because of the debates, no minutes were taken of the matters discussed.

Dr. Jose Rizal was shot at Bagong Bayan (now the Luneta) in Manila, the morning of December 30, 1896. At past one o'clock in the afternoon of the same day, Josefina (Josephine Bracken) and Trining (Trinidad Rizal), widow and sister respectively of Dr. Rizal, arrived at San Francisco de Malabon accompanied by Mr. Paciano Rizal. The Supremo received them at the house of Mrs. Estefania Potente. The Rizals had with them two small sheets of folded paper that they found under a burner they had taken from Dr. Rizal's cell when they last visited him. On one was the "Last Farewell," written in very fine script in Spanish. The Supremo asked to keep it for some time so that he could translate the poem into Tagalog. His was the first translation of the farewell poem. The other manuscript, which was in English, was translated by Mr. Lorenzo Fenoy from Batangas.

Dr. Jose Rizal's widow and sister stayed at the friar estate house in Tejeros, San Francisco de Malabon. They realized later that, aside from his words of solace for Josephine, his sisters, brother, and parents, Dr. Rizal had an urgent message for his sister Trining. He instructed her to look for something important, upon his death, inside the shoe on his left foot. However, Trining had not able to do so because a tight security of enemy troops prevented anyone from coming near the corpse. What could be the important thing that was buried with the great Hero of the Race?

XXVII

It should not be forgotten that before the Magdiwang and the Magdalo Councils moved to San Francisco de Malabon from Noveleta and to Imus from Kawit, respectively, the Councils had agreed to solicit contributions from well-to-do citizens in order to help support the Revolution. The Magdiwang Council chose the following to solicit contributions in the corresponding municipalities within the Magdiwang territory: Mr. Ariston Villanueva in Santa Cruz de Malabon (Tanza), Rosario (Salinas) and Naic; Mr. Emiliano Riego de Dios in Maragondon, Ternate, Magallanes, and Bailen; Mr. Mariano C. Trias in Indang and Alfonso; and Mr. Diego Mojica in San Francisco de Malabon and Noveleta.

In Cavite province during the Spanish regime, the friar estates were located in the bigger municipalities of Dasmariñas, Imus, Bacoor, San Francisco de Malabon (General Trias), Rosario (Salinas), Santa Cruz de Malabon (Tanza), and Naic. These estates occupied parts of private lands in different municipalities. The powerful estate owners known as *uldog* were regarded with awe by the tenants. The uldog in return rewarded the sycophants, their own paramours, and the latter's kin with good lands. When the uldog was displeased, his usual form of punishment was ejection from the land. It did not matter to him if an old tenant had been working on the land all his life, nor would he consider the improvements that added to the value of the land. In many instances, tenants were deprived of the land they had been tilling all their lives not out of anger or displeasure by the landlord, but because some favorite, or a paramour or her kin, coveted the land. To dispossess the old tenant, the uldog would raise the rent. The inability to pay the new, higher rent was enough excuse to expel the tenant whose family might have been tending the land with life-long care and devotion for fifty to a hundred years.

The leaders who solicited contributions were rebuffed by the landed gentry on the grounds that because of the unsettled times they could neither save nor sell their crops. In his disgust with those who refused to help, Secretary of War Ariston Villanueva resorted to violent methods. He ordered his troops to arrest and bind with rope outside the fort all the wealthy people who refused to help the Revolution, for he considered them enemies of the Motherland. Mr. Mariano Alvarez, the exalted President of the Magdiwang Government, also resorted to harsh measures against those who refused to cooperate with them. He summoned all those whose land had been grabbed from them by the friar estates. In front of a crucifix placed on top of his table, he made them take an oath and recount the experience they suffered under the land grabbers and to identify the parties to whom their land had been given. He ordered the land restored to their rightful owners after hearing their testimony.

The aggrieved peasants then and there took up arms, returned to their farms to repossess them and to harvest whatever crops remained. These radical measures resulted in benefits for the cause of the Motherland because the rich began to unite with them and support the Revolution. Their motive, of course, was to save their lives and properties. Thus, the Magdiwang Government was able to raise much-needed funds. They allocated funds for the salaries of soldiers and officers below the rank of colonel; those with higher rank and up to the presidency got only clothing and meal allowances. The Magdalo Council also collected contributions from among the wealthy citizens in the area under their jurisdiction without resistance because the latter were fearful that the Magdiwang measures might be applied to them. The Magdalo Council therefore had a comparatively easier time solving the problem of financing the People's troops.

It should be remembered that just before the Magdalo Council moved to Imus, General Crispulo Aguinaldo launched a bitterly-fought, two-day offensive that swept across Muntinglupa, Taguig, and Pateros. Hordes of residents of these towns fled with him when he retreated to Cavite. Among those refugees were Mr. Pedro Dandan, canon of the Manila Cathedral; he died of fever in the countryside on Magallanes, Cavite, at about the time the Peace of Biyak-na-Bato was to be proclaimed.

XXVIII

Much gaiety accompanied the celebration of the feast of St. Francis of Assisi, patron saint of the town of San Francisco de Malabon, on the first Saturday of January 1897. Sanctioned by the Revolutionary Government, it drew the cooperation of all the townspeople. Fr. Esteban del Rosario, parish priest of Ternate, celebrated the High Mass; he was assisted by a choir of beautiful voices with enchanting accompaniment. From the pulpit, he spoke of St. Francis's great love, hope and faith, and of the sacrifices and hardships he bore until his death.

After affirming the eventual triumph of goodness, he said: "My brethren, in our struggle to be free and independent, our hardships and sacrifices and the blood and life we give up for love of the Motherland will not be in vain. The victory which we all devoutly wish for is near at hand because the Lord God, King of the Armies, is with us in our sacred enterprise. We are puny and weak, but the struggle against the enemy has made us strong and alert. Despite our disparate resources—our adversary has much more than we have—still we are victorious in every encounter. We should take care not to jeopardize our holy mission, so blessed it is by the all-powerful God. To avert ruin, we should not allow arrogance and avarice to prevail over our God-given wisdom and strength. We should avoid disintegration by preserving and cherishing our solidarity so that we could reach our divine goal."

In the sermon, there were other exhortations along the same vein, but all were relevant to the conditions of the time.

The following narrative is related to an episode which occurred during that fiesta at San Francisco de Malabon:

Mr. Mariano San Gabriel had been a soldier in the Spanish army in his youth. He had been assigned to join an expedition against the Moros [Muslim Filipinos] in Jolo. At the outbreak of the Revolution, he was sixty years old living in retirement in his hometown, San Francisco de Malabon. He used to regale the townspeople with tales of his exploits and adventures in the Spanish army, like when they were surrounded by the Moros and only a few of them survived unscathed. In one encounter, this was where the *kris* [long knife] hit him; in another, there was where he had it, etc., etc. Luckily, he said, he had a tough skin and so he survived the attacks with little wear and tear. But all around him his comrades were being felled; with single strokes of the kris one was beheaded, another was halved across the waist. Only a few of them survived intact in this encounter. Afterwards, the Moros came to respect and befriend him. They installed him as *datu* [headman], bestowed him with riches, and made him pick twelve lovely women to make up his harem.

Because of these stories about his exploits, the old soldier was believed to be protected by some *anting-anting* or amulet, and his reputation as a man of worth grew in the retellings of his awed admirers. Well, in revolutionary times, men of such reputations were picked and given responsible positions. Thus was Mr. Mariano San Gabriel commissioned captain and assigned to keep watch over Battery No. One at Dalahikan.

On the eve of this fiesta for St. Francis Assisi in San Francisco de Malabon, Captain San Gabriel asked permission to leave his post to attend the festivities in his hometown and be among his children and grandchildren. But he was refused permission because of the critical position of Dalahikan, which was then under threat of enemy attack from the warships in Manila Bay. In his disappointment, the captain sought solace in drink. On the day of the fiesta, he asked for a big bottle of gin. He kept drinking all morning and by one o'clock in the afternoon, when all the gin was gone, he abandoned his post, taking along with him all his troops to San Francisco de Malabon. He rushed drunkenly, as if he was late for the fireworks, brass bands, and the various games and contests that were part of the fiesta fare. As he was nearing his destination, he met the Secretary of War, accompanied by two soldiers. When asked to explain why he had abandoned his post, he ordered his troops to disarm the aides of the Secretary of War. After this incident, he continued on his way with a mocking smile on his face and every now and then threatened to shoot the soldiers accompanying him.

The Secretary of War reported the matter to the Captain General, who forthwith mounted a swift horse to discipline the erring officer. The newly-promoted Brigadier General Santos Nocon rode after him. The pursuers saw the man they were pursuing at a store in the site known as Pasong Tarika. On seeing his superiors, Captain San Gabriel aimed his gun at them and warned them with a wave of his hand not to approach him.

"Do you know who I am?" Captain General Apoy asked, not heeding the warning.

"No!"

At this impudence, General Santos Nocon suddenly confronted the defiant captain and disarmed him. However, when he had subdued the officer and was to take him in custody, he could not find any of his troops. They had fled in fear and had gotten lost among the merry-makers during the encounter. The captain took advantage of the general's discomfiture to escape and return to his post at Dalahikan.

The Captain General quickly signed an order to all troops in the army to capture Captain San Gabriel, dead or alive, and to bring the prisoner immediately to his presence. However, on the intercession of Revolutionary Delegate Aquilino Monton and Lieutenant General Vibora, he consented to countermanding the order, but insisted that San Gabriel be stripped of his rank of captain.

The festivities continued into the night. After the procession, people gathered in front of the house where the Supremo Bonifacio and President Mainam were staying and where a gaily decorated platform had been erected. The Supremo and the leaders of the Magdiwang Council spoke on the platform. Among the speakers, aside from the Supremo Bonifacio, were President Mariano Alvarez, Secretary of War Ariston Villanueva, Secretary of Treasury Diego Mojica, Lieutenant General Vibora, Colonel Nicolas Portilla, and Mr. Santiago Rillo. The last named was the elected representative of Batangas province to the Magdiwang Government; on his request he was allowed to use a seal with the motto, "*DEUS OMNIPO-TENS.*"

XXIX

Despite the constant bombardment of rebel towns in the province of Cavite by cannon from Spanish warships, the people went about their affairs unintimidated. All who were able wholeheartedly contributed to the war effort. They celebrated their town fiestas, like the one at San Francisco de Malabon, with undiminished gaiety. When their turn came to celebrate their own fiestas, the people of Naic and Ternate also organized rallies where the speeches were revolutionary and agitational in character. The only exception was that of Secretary of War Ariston Villanueva, whose speech in Ternate was spiced with banter.

Judging by the lightheartedness with which the people conducted themselves in the face of grievous danger, no one would suspect that a widening rift among their leaders threatened to jeopardize all of them. Andres Bonifacio and Emilio Aguinaldo tried to conceal their growing differences, but the unfolding events tended to exacerbate them instead. Loose talk tended to smear each other's reputation until things came to a head one evening in

January 1897. It was nearing full moon when General Emilio Aguinaldo and Secretary Mariano Trias, on one hand, and the Supremo Bonifacio and his brother Procopio, on the other, departed that night from the house of Mrs. Estefania Potente in San Francisco de Malabon. Mrs. Potente's house was then being used as headquarters of the Magdiwang Government. The four men going down the stairs were each armed with a gun. They walked to an alley inside the town and positioned themselves two feet apart from the other pair, under the foliage of a tree. At first the parties exchanged some heated words and then aimed their guns at each other. At this point General Apoy suddenly appeared and stood between the adversaries and said sternly, "Shoot me first before you proceed with what you intend to do!"

General Apoy, who had been secretly watching the goings-on from the house where the four men had come from, rushed out in time to stop a mishap that should never be allowed to happen. Shortly afterwards, General Vibora arrived on the scene and helped to mediate. The antagonists were persuaded to talk things over at the home of Secretary of the Treasury Diego Mojica. Then they fetched the parish priest, Fr. Manuel Trias, uncle of Secretary Mariano Trias. The priest tried his best to restore amicable relations; he had them embrace each other and afterwards thanked God and prayed for peace and love among them. Finally, he kissed each one on the cheek and blessed them in the name of God and the Trinity.

Not long after this event, a detachment of troops from Manila and Bulacan came to San Francisco de Malabon. They elected Messrs. Arsenio Mauricio and Pedro Giron to be their leaders. Their troops were assigned as additional guards in the Dalahikan fort of Noveleta.

The Magdiwang Revolutionary Government, which had jurisdiction over the territory from Noveleta and San Francisco de Malabon in Cavite to the province of Batangas, effected various changes such as promotions in rank for some brave and meritorious Sons of the People, the transfer of Council headquarters to San Francisco de Malabon, and the assignment of additional qualified leaders. The following was the new roster of Magdiwang officers:

Venerable Over-All President:	Mariano Alvarez
Vice President for Batangas:	Lorenzo Fenoy
Over-All Minister of Interior:	Pascual Alvarez
Over-All Minister of War:	Ariston Villanueva
Vice Minister of War for Batangas:	Ananias Diokno

Over-All Minister of Welfare and Justice:	Mariano Trias
Over-All Minister of Economic Development:	Emiliano Riego de Dios
Over-All Minister of Finance:	Diego Mojica
Over-All Captain General:	Santiago V. Alvarez
Assistant Over-All Captain General:	Artemio Ricarte
Assistant Captain General for Batangas:	Miguel Malvar
General, Cavite Division:	Mariano Riego de Dios
General, Batangas Division:	Paciano Rizal
Brigadier Generals for Cavite & Batangas:	Nicolas Portilla
	Santos Nocon
	Eleuterio Marasigan
	Luciano San Miguel
	Pablo Mojica
	Arcadio Arrieta
Colonels for Cavite & Batangas:	Juan Cailles
	Jose del Rosario
	Severino Caoibis

The Magdalo Government, whose jurisdiction extended from Kawit, Cavite, to the province of Rizal had the following officers:

Venerable Over-All President:	Baldomero Aguinaldo
Over-All Minister of War:	Candido Tirona
Over-All Minister of Finance:	Cayetano Topacio
Over-All Captain General:	Emilio Aguinaldo
Assistant Over-All Captain General:	Edilberto Evangelista
Brigadier Generals:	Crispulo Aguinaldo
	Vito Belarmino
	Tomas Mascardo
	Mariano Noriel
Colonels*:	Pantaleon Garcia
	Pio del Pilar
	Agapito Bonzon
	Marcelino Aure

* A few of them were quickly promoted to generals because of their bravery and gallantry.

As has been related before, Secretary of Justice Mariano C. Trias of the Magdiwang Council, together with Captains Mariano San Gabriel and Julian Montalan, defected to the Magdalo on February 8, 1897. Trias accepted the position of Lieutenant General in the latter Council, but he tried to maintain cordial relations with his former comrades by saying that his transfer was in response to a Magdalo need for reinforcements.

XXX

A Filipino officer in the Spanish army revealed to General Apoy the spying activities of a Filipino woman agent of the Spanish government. His name was Tomas Pastor, a native of Pampanga and a first lieutenant in the 73rd Infantry of the Spanish army. He said that on February 10, 1897, a woman courier of a certain Captain Ado came to Palanyag (Parañaque, Rizal) to inform the Spanish authorities, who had established headquarters in that town, of a little known path to Silang in Cavite. Unguarded by the Katipunan, they could use this path to penetrate the town of Silang. The name of this woman informer was Cesarea Belarmino, herself a native of Silang. According to Lieutenant Pastor, the woman appeared before the Spanish Major Enrique Sotto to give the information. Major Sotto, of the Fourth Infantry Battalion of the Spanish Army, asked Captain Villalon of the same battalion to bring the woman to Governor and Captain General Camilo Polavieja, who was then at the parish house of Palanyag directing operations against the Cavite rebels.

Very early in the morning of February 16, 1897, Spanish troops under General Polavieja started their assault of Bakood (Bacoor) and Silang. This was a determined and fierce attack on the fortifications defended jointly by the Magdalo and Magdiwang forces. Leading the Magdalo were General Emilio Aguinaldo himself, with Lieutenant General Edilberto Evangelista, General Tomas Mascardo, Colonels Pio del Pilar, Mariano Noriel, Agapito Bonzon, and Major Lucas Camerino. The Magdiwang contingent was led by General Luciano San Miguel of the Supremo's staff, and Captains Mariano San Gabriel and Mariano Ramirez.

Despite three days of heated offensive using superior arms from land and sea positions, the Spanish troops failed to take even a bit of Katipunan territory. Finally, they had to retreat, but not without exacting their toll in casualties from the People's Army. Among the corpses were those of

Lieutenant General Edilberto Evangelista, Captains Mariano San Gabriel and Mariano Ramirez, and among the serious wounded were Generals Tomas Mascardo and Luciano San Miguel.

The People's troops who defended Silang were under the command of General Vito Belarmino of the Magdalo army; aiding him were Colonels Ambrosio Mojica, Marcelina Aure and Captain Hipolito Sakilayan, all of the Magdiwang. They put up a determined and pitched defense against the Spanish forces headed by General Jose de Lacambre. The shooting mowed down whole detachments on each side, resulting in a great number being wounded and killed. After three days of fighting, the surviving Sons of the People were forced to retreat because they had run out of ammunition. On February 19, 1897,[25] the enemy entered the town and burned everything except the town church and parish house, which they occupied.

Meanwhile, at the Noveleta front, the enemy did not send group troops, but instead bombarded the town from warships along the seashore. Simultaneously bombarded with Silang and Bacoor, Noveleta was defended by the Magdiwang army led by Captain General Apoy, Lieutenant General Vibora, Generals Mariano Riego de Dios, Santos Nocon, Nicolas Portilla, and Major Pio Baluyot. For three days, there was no respite from countless cannon balls that, when fired in unison, sounded like the loudest thunderclap, while gunfire as sharp as lightning thrusts slivered the streets in halves. The whole town was in chaos as people fell on their bellies, while corpses and fallen trees lay strewn around the fortifications. Nobody and nothing was spared—people, animals, houses, and trees. The People's troops kept within their defense positions; their canons, guns, machetes, spears, daggers, arrows, and arquebuses were ready, but they kept from returning the fire in order to conserve their ammunition for the distant enemy. They had anticipated ground troops to pursue the offensive, but this did not materialize; instead, the enemy retreated without landing a single foot soldier.

When the Spaniards left the Noveleta shoreline in their warships, the Supremo Bonifacio decided to go to Silang for a determined effort to get back that town from the Spaniards. Joining him in this expedition were Generals Mariano C. Trias, Pascual Alvarez, M. Riego de Dios, Nicolas Portilla, Lieutenant General Vibora, Colonel Crisostomo Riel, and Major

---

[25]The typescript had the date as October 19, 1896, an obvious mistake. Cf. *Aguinaldo and the Revolution of 1986*, 222.

Cristobal Bustamante. They entered into an agreement with the Magdalo to make a joint offensive to capture Silang. They agreed to surround the area, with the Magdalo under General Emilio Aguinaldo moving in from the north and the Magdiwang from the west and south. Assigned to lead the Magdiwang positions were Secretary of Development Emiliano Riego de Dios, General Mariano Riego de Dios, Colonel Crisostomo Riel, and Major Cristobal Bustamante.

The organization and preparations over, the joint armies attacked early the following day, but they failed to rout the Spanish troops who outnumbered and overwhelmed them. Both sides suffered heavily in the bloody encounter, with many killed and wounded. Finally, General Aguinaldo had to withdraw his troops and retreat to Imus. The Magdiwang were not aware of the Magdalo withdrawal until later. They followed suit after leaving a detachment under Captain Julian Montalan to guard and waylay the enemy at the site known as Putik.

On hearing about the debacle, Captain General Apoy led a cavalry detachment to reinforce the beleaguered forces in Silang. He started out the day following the withdrawal; with him were Colonel Arcadio Arrieta, Major Damaso, Captain Romualdo, two lieutenants, and twelve cavalry troops. It was nearing noon when they reached the place called Paso near the waterfalls on the big river in Silang. They took refuge from the noonday heat of the sun at the house of Mr. Blas Medina.

To the tired, hungry and thirsty General Apoy, a big watermelon he saw on the vine in an open field looked very tempting indeed. The owner obliged when he asked for it. Due to his great thirst, General Apoy was tempted to eat the watermelon despite the warning that it was not good to eat it right then because it was still hot from exposure under the blazing sun. After eating four slices, he lay down on a narrow bench near the window while waiting for lunch. But he soon got up and quickly ran down the stairs to relieve himself in a corner in the yard. Colonel Arrieta went out to look for him when he failed to return after a while. He saw General Apoy clutching his belly, vomiting and defecating at the same time. Quickly running to his general's rescue, Colonel Arrieta brought him up to the house. They boiled a concoction of leaves and made him drink it. The stomach ache was relieved a little but the vomiting and loose bowls were not abated. When his companions had eaten, they helped him to his horse and took him back to the Magdiwang headquarters since there was little medication to be had in the place where he fell ill.

Meanwhile, the Supremo Andres Bonifacio went to the Magdalo headquarters in Imus to confer with General Emilio Aguinaldo about plans to retake Silang from the enemy. He was accompanied by Generals Mariano Trias, Pascual Alvarez, Nicolas Portilla, and Artemio Ricarte. After discussing their plans about Silang, the Supremo asked if it were true that Mr. Daniel Tirona was secretly giving Magdalo commissions to Generals Pascual Alvarez and Artemio Ricarte. The two gentlemen dismissed the matter as a joke, but glanced meaningfully at Secretary Tirona.

XXXI

On February 27, 1897, the Spanish troops at Silang attempted to take the neighboring town of Perez-Dasmariñas. However, they were repulsed by the People's troops who fought valiantly despite their lack of ammunition.

When the Magdiwang and the Magdalo leaders learned of the aborted attempt, they coordinated plans for the defense of Dasmariñas. They packed two big stone houses in town with many troops armed with machetes, daggers, and spears. On February 28, just as the Katipuneros had finished sharpening their weapons, a great number of enemy troops arrived, the day after they had been driven back. This time the enemy succeeded in penetrating the town despite the efforts of the People's Army to repulse them again. It was as if the enemy knew of the Katipunan secret plan, because they ringed the town and burned all houses except the church and parish house, which they always respected.

The fire forced out the armed defenders, who were mowed down by bullets from all sides. Only a very few were lucky enough to survive. The combined Magdiwang and Magdalo forces under the Supremo Andres Bonifacio and General Emilio Aguinaldo, respectively, made some attempts to strike back, but these were unfortunate. Among those who lost their lives were Magdiwang stalwarts Mariano Yenko, Pio Rodas, Esteban Montoya, and Alipio Dragon.

Soon after the Spaniards had taken Perez-Dasmariñas, they next tried to take Imus, but they were steadfastly repulsed even from the outskirts of the town. They retreated to the friar estate house at Salitran, a village between Imus and Perez-Dasmariñas. From the headquarters that they had established at Salitran, they sent out missions day and night against the People's Army in order to take Imus. In one offensive, when they tried to penetrate Katipunan forces under General Crispulo Aguinaldo, the Spaniards failed again and lost many lives, including that of their commanding officer, General Antonio Zabala. As a consequence of this blow to the enemy forces, some rebel officers were promoted in rank: General Crispulo Aguinaldo was promoted to lieutenant general, Major Lucas Camerino to lieutenant colonel, and Captain Antero Riel to major.

The Revolution was facing a grave crisis. The Katipunan forces in Cavite were suffering defeat after defeat with great loss of life. Magdalo territories had passed to Spanish hands after the battles of Salitran, Zapote and Dalahikan. Imus, the rebel capital, was in a state of imminent collapse. To strengthen defenses so that they could stop the Spanish advance into the rest of the province that was still held by the Magdiwang, and to forestall the loss of more lives, the Supremo Bonifacio, with the approval of other revolutionary leaders, called a meeting of the leadership of the Magdalo and the Magdiwang. This meeting, scheduled for March 24, 1897, was postponed for the next day because of the death of Lieutenant General Crispulo Aguinaldo, General Emilio Aguinaldo's brother, on that day in the battle of Salitran.

The Magdiwang leaders were waiting for their Magdalo counterparts at the Tejeros friar estate house, the designated place, long after lunch on that day. They had to start in the afternoon to allow the usual enemy raids, which came in the morning, to subside before they ventured out to Tejeros, a village in the municipality of San Francisco de Malabon. When the Magdalo group finally came at about five in the afternoon, they brought with them the sad news of the death of General Magdalo's own brother. Heading a small group, General Magdalo recounted the circumstances of the heroic death of his patriot brother. Then he begged to be excused to attend to arrangements for his beloved brother's funeral. Thus the meeting was put off for the next day at the same place.

But before dispersing, Secretary Treasurer Diego Mojica proposed a resolution of condolence and prayers for patriots who had died heroically like Lieutenant General Crispulo Aguinaldo. The Supremo Bonifacio thought this was superfluous and objected to such a resolution. "True love of country," The Supremo argued, "and service to the cause of freedom for the Motherland are the most noble attributes that would ensure one's place in heaven. Lieutenant General Crispulo Aguinaldo and their comrades who died before him are all truly blessed and are now in their respective places in the heavenly kingdom. Moreover, they will always occupy an honored place in the history of our country."

XXXII

The assembly at Tejeros was finally convened on March 24, 1897. The invitations to the meeting were signed by Secretary Jacinto Lumbreras of the Magdiwang Council, and he presided over the assembly. Seated with Lumbreras at the long presidential table were the Supremo Andres Bonifacio, Messrs. Mariano M. Alvarez, Pascual Alvarez, Ariston Villanueva, Mariano C. Trias, Diego Mojica, Emiliano Riego de Dios, Santiago V. Alvarez, Artemio Ricarte, Santos Nocon, Luciano San Miguel, Pablo Mojica, Severino de las Alas and Santiago Rillo, all of them of the Magdiwang. Among the Magdalo seated at the head table were Messrs. Baldomero Aguinaldo, Daniel Tirona, and Cayetano Topacio.

It must be mentioned that, before the assembly was convened, Secretary of War Ariston Villanueva of the Magdiwang Council received the confidential information that Mr. Daniel Tirona of the Magdalo faction was set to undermine the proceedings of the assembly and that he had already succeeded in enjoining many among the Magdiwang leaders to ally with him. Secretary Villanueva kept silent, but nevertheless alerted Captain General Apoy, who had troops in readiness for any sudden eventuality.

The leaders were seated at the presidential table, as previously described, and all the others were standing in groups on both sides of those seated. After Chairman Jacinto Lumbreras had declared the assembly open, he announced the main topic of discussion, which was how to bolster the defenses in the areas still under Magdiwang control. Presently Mr. Severino de las Alas rose to speak, and when he was recognized he said, "Before we discuss minor details, let us first tackle the major issue such as what kind of government we should have and how we should go about establishing it. Once we make a decision about these questions, the problem of organization and strengthening of defenses will be resolved."

"As initiator of the Revolution," Chairman Lumbreras replied, "the Katipunan now holds authority over the Islands. It has a government of law and a definite program. It is obeyed and respected by all, because it stands for freedom, brotherly love, and a well-organized and well-run government. The purpose of this meeting is to discuss the best measures to take to strengthen the Magdiwang Government vis-à-vis the enemy. We should avoid surrendering the headquarters of the Katipunan army should the Magdalo eventually lose out."

The chair next recognized the Supremo. He concurred with what Chairman Lumbreras had just said and explained that the "K" in the middle of the Sun in the Katipunan flag used in the Revolution stood for *Kalayaan*, Freedom.

Mr. Severino de las Alas spoke again. He countered that the letter "K" and the Sun on the flag did not indicate whether the Revolutionary Government was democratic or not.

The Supremo replied that from the rank and file to the highest levels, the Katipunan was united in its respect for universal brotherhood and equality of men. It was risking bloodshed and life itself in its struggle against the King, in order to establish a sovereign and free government. In short, it stood for people's sovereignty, not a government led by only one or two.

Mr. Antonio Montenegro spoke in defense of Mr. Severino de las Alas's stand. He argued that if they would not agree on the kind of Revolutionary Government they were to have and that if they were to let the status quo prevail, then they who were in the Revolution would be no better than a pack of bandits or of wild, mindless animals.

General Apoy was hurt by these words of Mr. Montenegro. He quickly stood up and looked angrily at the previous speaker.

"We of the Katipunan," he began, "are under the jurisdiction of our respected Highest Council of the Sons of the People. This Council is the defender of, and has authority over, the Magdiwang and Magdalo Governments of Cavite. We are true revolutionaries fighting for freedom of the native land. We are not bandits who rob others of their property and wealth. Nor should we be likened to beasts, for we know how to protect and defend others, especially the political refugees who seek asylum with us. We are rational and we do not expose those who talk big but do not accomplish anything. If you want to establish a different kind of government that is to your liking, you must do as we have done: Go back to your localities and snatch them from Spanish control! Then you can do what pleases you; but don't you dare seek refuge among cowards who might call you bandits and beasts. And for everybody's satisfaction, I am now ordering your arrest!"

Captain General Apoy stopped speaking and looked intently at the person he was alluding to and ordered a detachment under Major Dalmasio Fojas to keep him under guard. After a short while, Dr. Jose Rizal's sister, Trining, and his widow, Josephine, pleaded with General Apoy not to arrest Mr. Montenegro, but to let him stay at the estate house where they themselves were staying. They volunteered to be held personally responsible for Mr. Montenegro while in their custody. Captain General Apoy easily acceded to the request.

The strong and excited denunciation by Captain General Apoy of Mr. Montenegro alerted the Magdiwang troops. The leaders eyed everyone suspiciously and were only awaiting a signal from General Apoy for them to begin shooting. Disorder ensued and disrupted the assembly.

When order was restored, some wanted the convention adjourned, but the Supremo Bonifacio prevailed upon the others to continue. However, the presiding officer, Mr. Lumbreras, refused to resume his role of chairman. He wanted to yield the chair to the Supremo whom he thought to be the rightful chairman.

"The Katipunan, as you know," Mr. Lumbreras explained, "was responsible from the beginning for the spread of the revolutionary movement throughout the Philippines. But because of the disaffection of some, this assembly was called to establish a new overall Revolutionary Council. If we are to pursue this ambitious and important undertaking, only the Supremo has the right to preside at this assembly, for he is the Father of the Katipunan and the Revolution."

Mr. Lumbreras's speech was well received and his proposal was unanimously accepted. The Supremo Bonifacio assumed the chairmanship accordingly and said, "Your aim is to establish a new over-all government of the Katipunan of the Sons of the People. This would repudiate the decisions made at the meeting held at the friar estate house in Imus. In my capacity as President-Supremo of the Most Venerable Katipunan of the Sons of the People, I agree and sympathize with your aspirations. But I wish to remind you that we should respect all decisions properly discussed and approved in all our meetings. We should respect and abide by the wishes of the majority."

Because of a repeated clamor for the approval of the establishment of a Government of the Philippine Republic, the chair proceeded to prepare for an election to the following positions: President, Vice President, Minister of Finance, Minister of Welfare, Minister of Justice, and Captain General.

The Supremo spoke again before the election began. He said that the candidate who would get the most number of votes for each position should be the winner, no matter what his station in life or his educational attainment. What should matter was that the candidate had never been a traitor to the cause of the Motherland. Everyone agreed and there were shouts of approval such as "That is how it should be—equality for everyone! Nobody should be higher nor lower than the other. May love of country prevail!"

The Supremo Bonifacio appointed General Artemio Ricarte as Secretary. Then, with the help of Mr. Daniel Tirona, he distributed pieces of paper to serves as ballots. When the ballots had been collected and the votes were ready to be canvassed, Mr. Diego Mojica, the Magdiwang Secretary of Treasury, warned the Supremo that many ballots distributed were already filled out and that the voters had not done this themselves. The Supremo ignored this remark. He proceeded with the business at hand as if nothing unusual had happened.

When the votes for President were counted, Mr. Emilio Aguinaldo won over Mr. Andres Bonifacio, the Supremo. The winner was acclaimed by applause and shouts of "Mabuhay! [Long live!]."

Mr. Severino de las Alas spoke again to say that since the Supremo Bonifacio had received the second highest number of votes for the presidency, he should be proclaimed Vice President of the Government of the Philippine Republic. When nobody signified approval or disapproval of the proposal, the presiding officer, the Supremo Bonifacio, ruled that the election be continued. For Vice President, Mr. Mariano Trias won over Mr. Mariano Alvarez and the Supremo Bonifacio. General Vibora was elected Captain over General Apoy. General Vibora demurred, saying that he had neither the ability nor the right to assume the new position. But General Apoy cut short his objections by saying that he personally vouched for General Vibora's competence and right to occupy the position to which he was elected. General Apoy's endorsement was greeted with shouts of "Long live the newly elected Captain General!"

Mr. Baldomero Aguinaldo wanted the elections to be completed before it got too dark. To facilitate the counting of votes, he suggested that for all other positions to be voted upon, voters should stand on one side of the hall if in favor and on the other side if against. The suggestion was adopted for the rest of the election. For the position of Secretary of War, Mr. Emiliano Riego de Dios was elected overwhelmingly over Messrs. Santiago V. Alvarez, Ariston Villanueva, and Daniel Tirona. After the voters had given the proper honors to the new Secretary of War, they proceeded to elect the Secretary of Interior. Mr. Andres Bonifacio, the Supremo, won over Mr. Mariano Alvarez. The crowd broke into shouts of "Mabuhay!" Mr. Daniel Tirona requested for a restoration of order and then spoke aloud:

"My brethren, the office of Secretary of Interior is of so great a scope and of such sensitivity that we should not entrust it to one who is not a lawyer. One among us here is a lawyer. He is Mr. Jose del Rosario. Let us reconsider the choice for the last position, for he has no credentials to show attesting to any educational attainment."

Then in as loud a voice as he could muster, Tirona shouted, "Let us elect Mr. Jose del Rosario, the lawyer!"

Greatly embarrassed, the Supremo Bonifacio quickly stood up and said, "We agreed to abide by the majority vote and accept its choice no matter what the station in life of the person elected. And because of this, I demand of you, Mr. Daniel Tirona, an apology. You must restore to the voters and the one they elected the honor you have only now besmirched."

Then he pulled out his revolver and took aim.

Instead of replying, Mr. Tirona ignored the Supremo's remarks and, perhaps because of fear, he slid away and got lost in the crowd. Disorder ensued as the convention Secretary tried to disarm the Supremo, who was intent on shooting Mr. Tirona. The people began to disperse and the Supremo adjourned the meeting with these words:

"In my capacity as chairman of this convention and as President-Supremo of the Most Venerable Katipunan of the Sons of the People which association is known and acknowledged by all, I hereby declare null and void all matters approved in this meeting."

Then he left quickly and was followed by his aides and some others present.

Mr. Baldomero Aguinaldo, the Magdalo President, did not leave San Francisco de Malabon that night, in order to convince the Magdiwang leaders to reconvene the disrupted meeting the following day. They agreed to his proposal. That same night, rumor had it that Messrs. Mariano Trias, Daniel Tirona, Emiliano Riego de Dios, Santiago Rillo, and others were in the parish house of the Catholic church at Tanza (Santa Cruz de Malabon), and that they were conferring with the priest, Fr. Cenon Villafranca. Many attested to seeing them, but no one knew what they talked about.

On the request of Magdalo President Baldomero Aguinaldo, a meeting was called at the same friar estate house in Tejeros. Called on the day after the tumultuous convention, its purpose was to continue and revalidate the proceedings of the election meeting, to revive their former alliances, and to restore cordiality and fraternal love in their relations. Aside from the Supremo Andres Bonifacio, among the Magdiwang leaders who attended were Messrs. Mariano Alvarez, Diego Mojica, Ariston Villanueva, Pascual Alvarez, Jacinto Lumbreras, Santiago Alvarez, Artemio Ricarte, Nicolas Portilla, Santos Nocon, and Fr. Manuel Trias, the parish priest of San Francisco de Malabon. They waited until five that afternoon, but none of the Magdalo members came, not even their President who had initiated what would have been a reconciliation meeting.

That same night it was rumored that the Magdalo leaders were holding their own meeting at the parish house in Tanza. Though it had reason to be apprehensive because the Magdalo were meeting in territory under its jurisdiction, the Magdiwang leadership looked the other way because the Magdalo were hard pressed for meeting places since its territories had all been taken by the Spanish enemy.

The next morning, March 27, 1897, eyewitnesses who had spied on the proceedings revealed that, indeed, a meeting had taken place at the Tanza parish house, and that the Supremo's decisions regarding the election at the friar estate house were not respected. These revelations surfaced despite denials from many sectors.

At the gathering in the Tanza parish house, those elected at the Tejeros convention knelt before a crucifix and in the name of the Holy Father, the highest pontiff of the Roman Catholic Church, invoked the martyred saints and solemnly took their office. Father Cenon Villafranca officiated. With Messrs. Severino de las Alas and Daniel Tirona as witnesses, the following took their oaths of office: Messrs. Emilio Aguinaldo, Mariano C. Trias, and Artemio Ricarte. Conspicuously absent was the Supremo Andres Bonifacio, who was not invited although he was one of those elected to office. It will be recalled that as chairman of the Tejeros convention, he declared null and void all matters approved by the assembly because of a grave violation of a principle agreed upon before the election.

It should be noted here that, unknown to the Magdiwang Council, the Magdalo posted troops to guard the Tanza parish house for their oath-taking ceremonies. The troops were under strict orders not to admit any of the unwanted Magdiwang partisans. If the news about the secret ceremony had leaked out earlier, and the underdogs in the power struggle had attempted to break into it, they would have been annihilated then and there.

XXXIII

The Spaniards captured and occupied the town of Imus in the afternoon of March 25, 1897. They left Imus three days afterwards and marched into the San Francisco Malabon territory up to the village of Bakaw. When they reached Bakaw, they were intercepted by Magdiwang troops led by the Supremo Bonifacio and General Apoy. A pitched battle ensued. But the Magdiwang initiative was foiled by the arrival of a great number of enemy reinforcements at the height of the encounter. In the face of such an unfavorable situation, the Supremo decided on a tactical retreat to their fortifications. General Apoy on his part ordered Major Baluyot to rally all other armed units of the Magdiwang army and assign them to the Tarike fortifications in San Francisco de Malabon.

After the battle, the Spaniards encamped and rested in Bakaw, but throughout the night they were harassed with potshots from small Katipunan bands.

Anticipating that the enemy encamped at Bakaw would try to penetrate the strong Dalahikan fortifications in Noveleta from the rear, General Apoy ordered General San Miguel to pull out all troops from Dalahikan and transfer them to some other fort.

On April 3, the Supremo made a bid to recapture Noveleta. General Vibora and General Santos Nocon accompanied him in the offensive, which lasted the whole day. But despite a fierce determination on their part and heavy enemy losses, they were unable to dislodge the Spaniards.

A few days after the Supremo's unsuccessful attempt to retake Noveleta, fresh Spanish reinforcements began arriving in great numbers in the open fields to the west of Bakaw and along the seashores in Noveleta and Salinas. At nine that morning, artillery fire from mountain cannons began battering the San Francisco de Malabon fortifications, extending from Tejeros to Tarike. Two hours of shelling was followed by ground attack by cavalry and infantry troops.

After preliminary skirmishes, man-to-man combat broke out at the Tarike fort. It became a fierce battleground as the rebels made a valiant defense. Every head that emerged from either side was quickly bashed in or severed at the neck. All that could be heard was the rattle of gleaming blades, the burst of gunfire, and the thud of bodies as they fell against the earth. Wielding a variety of arms such as spears, machetes, daggers, revolvers, and rifles, the combatants locked in struggle and fell together. In one instance, the tip of a bayonet piercing somebody's middle came out straight through the back of another who himself had a pointed machete sticking in his chest. In another instance, one who was mortally wounded by a sharp dagger inflicted by the other was in a death embrace with his assailant who was himself killed by the other's gun. Another pair who fell together each had bayonet thrusts, one through the navel and the other above the chest. Some had severed heads, others severed hands or feet.

General Apoy and the Supremo Bonifacio lost many gallant troops in this bloody and miserable battle. Among those who died were the valiant Major Pio Baluyot, head soldiers Francisco Arnaldo, Juan Brosas, Lucio Poblete and Nicomedes Esguerra. The enemy rode roughshod over their bodies as they rushed into town to raise their flag of victory and to burn houses.

Very early that morning before the battle, Captain General Apoy had visited the Tarike fort to boost the morale of the Magdiwang and the Balara troops. Then at past seven o'clock, they saw the Spaniards massing a great number of their troops. The commanders of the Magdiwang and the Balara contingents thought it was the better part of discretion if the Captain General was not with them inside the fort when the expected attack took place. Thus Major Baluyot and Captain Olaes escorted him across the river to the west of the town of San Francisco de Malabon.

General Pio del Pilar and his troops, along with a small detachment from Imus, came to help in the defense of San Francisco de Malabon, but for some unknown reason he withdrew even before the enemy could attack. He made his withdrawal without notifying those inside the fort.

Coming from Imus and Kawit, the enemy took Noveleta without resistance. They captured the fortifications and collected Katipunan arms and ammunition. Coming in and spreading out into the open fields around Imus, Kawit, Noveleta, and San Francisco de Malabon, they overwhelmed the People's troops with their sheer number. After capturing Noveleta, General de Lacambre, the head of the expeditionary force, issued a decree granting amnesty to all those who would surrender and accept Spanish authority. Notice to this effect was circulated before they attacked the fortifications of San Francisco de Malabon.

Guiding the Spanish expeditionary force was one Francisco Valencia of Tanza. He sent word to his fellow townsmen not to panic, but to prepare for the entry of the Spanish forces by flying white flags on their houses. The Tanza townsfolk cooperated. They greeted the Spaniards with the ringing of church bells and shouts of "Long live Spain!" All over town they flew white flags alternating with the Spanish banner. They readily accepted amnesty and turned hostile to those who were in the armed struggle—they refused to have anything to do with the rebels, much less to shelter and feed them.

With the approval of Secretary of Justice Mariano Trias, well-known gentry of the town led by the Ferrer family rushed to seek amnesty. Some rebel dignitaries also presented themselves to the Spanish authorities to surrender. Among them were Mr. Daniel Tirona (the Magdalo Secretary of War), Brigadier General Juan Cailles, and Colonel Jose del Rosario[26] of the staff of Captain General Apoy. Colonel del Rosario was a secret ally of Mr. Daniel Tirona, while General Cailles organized mercenary troops for Mr. Francisco Valencia.

Because of the fall of Imus and San Francisco de Malabon, the Magdalo and Magdiwang Governments were constrained to move out their headquarters from these towns. The Magdiwang, together with the Supremo Andres Bonifacio and the Highest Council of the Katipunan, transferred their seat of government from San Francisco de Malabon to the friar estate house in Naic. The Magdalo could not find any suitable place since most of their territory had been taken by the Spaniards. However, the lack of a government center did not deter the Magdalo leaders from holding meetings and making decisions, which they coordinated with the Magdiwang and the Supremo Bonifacio's Highest Council of the Katipunan.

XXXIV

With the fall of Imus and San Francisco de Malabon, other disconcerting developments reached the ears of the Supremo. One was the voluntary surrender and offer of cooperation with the enemy by Messrs. Tirona, Cailles, and del Rosario. Another was the Magdalo Government's decision to set free Spanish prisoners of war and to turn them over to the Spanish authorities who had captured San Francisco de Malabon. Still another was the news that Francisco Valencia had been installed as municipal executive of this town. Angered by these events, the Supremo ordered the troops under General Pio del Pilar, Colonel Mariano Noriel, and

---

[26]The lawyer proposed by Daniel Tirona, speaking at the Tejeros Assembly, for the position of Secretary of Interior instead of Andres Bonifacio.

Pedro Giron to arrest and bring before him at Tanza the Spanish prisoners who were freed, as well as their protectors and escorts. He gave this order at two o'clock in the afternoon of April 7, 1897.

General Apoy learned of these developments when, at past three that same afternoon, General Luciano San Miguel arrived breathlessly at his temporary residence in the house of Magdiwang Treasurer Blas Arenas. General Apoy decided to see the Supremo immediately. He left the house in the company of General San Miguel, Magdalo Minister of Finance Cayetano Topacio, and other leaders. In the middle of the street, they encountered a large group of infantry soldiers surrounding three Spanish prisoners, an elderly woman, and two men. He learned from the head soldiers that the prisoners were to be brought before the Supremo. General Apoy escorted them to the Supremo's office at the Naic friar estate house.

News of this event soon reached the other revolutionary leaders. When the Supremo reached the Supremo's headquarters at dusk, and as he was coming near the stairway, he heard the sound of guns being cocked and soldiers barking, "Stay out!"

He bounded up the stairs and discovered that sentinels from the Balara detachment were barring the entry of General Emilio Aguinaldo and Magdalo President Baldomero Aguinaldo. At once, he ordered the guards to lay down their arms and, putting both hands on the shoulders of the Aguinaldos, he escorted them up to the Supremo's office.

"The Balara troops are fearless," General Magdalo remarked.

"Please excuse them, for probably they did not recognize you," General Apoy apologized.

When they stood face to face with the Supremo, the latter declared, "Everyone in the Katipunan is bound by a solemn and patriotic vow to defend the country even at the risk of death, and this vow he sealed with a signature in his own blood. The surrender to Spanish authority by prominent leaders of the Revolution like Messrs. Tirona and Cailles of the Magdalo Government is clearly a supreme treachery against the Motherland to whom we owe life and livelihood. We should take care that their example should not be emulated, for such a despicable deed brings dishonor to the Revolution. We should warn and punish any son of the Philippines who secretly or openly collaborates with the Spanish enemy."

General Aguinaldo also deplored as shameful and dishonorable the surrender to the enemy by two ranking leaders involved in the defense of the Motherland. All those present were elated by these remarks. Fraternal feelings were rekindled among comrades united in a common cause, and the two leaders embraced.

"Victory for the Motherland!" General Apoy exclaimed.

"Long live!" chorused everyone.

About a week of close comradely cooperation between the Magdiwang and Magdalo troops followed this detente between the Magdiwang Supremo and General Magdalo. The Supremo agreed to a plan of lending guns to the Magdalo troops who volunteered to do the fighting while the Magdiwang men took a brief respite. All the Magdiwang leaders wholeheartedly concurred with him on the decision for the sake of fraternal unity in a common cause; moreover, the arrangements made possible a maximum utilization of scarce firearms. Without any misgivings whatsoever, the Magdiwang loaned some two out of three of their firearms to their Magdalo comrades who were without guns. The Balara contingent of the Supremo Bonifacio likewise loaned their guns for the sake of good fraternal relations. Nobody had any inkling or foreboding of the utter injustice that would result from the sincere gesture of friendship they offered. With Magdiwang guns, the Magdalo troops entrenched themselves in all defense positions. After less than a week of such accommodation, something which nobody expected surfaced. All troops, from the lowest to the highest ranks, received commissions authorized and signed by the Magdalo leadership.

XXXV

General Emilio Aguinaldo was able to effect a reconciliation with many revolutionary leaders through the intercession of his followers present at the Tejeros assembly. Having consolidated his forces, he called a meeting at the friar estate house in Naic after Holy Week of 1897. Captain General Apoy and other Magdiwang ministers and colonels did not attend this meeting because, in their opinion, the main task was the struggle against the enemy. Other matters should be attended to only after victory was achieved, or at least after a reassuring turning point had been reached where their position was stronger than the enemy's. These considerations were ignored by the organizers of the meeting. They pursued their plans and established a Government of the Philippine Republic without an election of any kind. Magdalo President Baldomero Aguinaldo read to those present a proclamation and a list of officers of the Republic, which follows:

President:	Mr. Emilio Aguinaldo
Vice President:	Mr. Mariano Trias
Director of Interior:	Mr. Pascual Alvarez
Director of State:	Mr. Jacinto Lumbreras
Director of Finance:	Mr. Baldomero Aguinaldo
Director of Welfare:	Mr. Mariano Alvarez
Director of Justice:	Mr. Severino de las Alas
Director of War:	Mr. Emiliano Riego de Dios
Captain General:	Mr. Artemio Ricarte

Before the meeting adjourned, the new Council gave approval to change the emblems for the Army officers.

It should be noted that, except for a few minor changes, the composition of the above Council was substantially the same as that resulting from the election at Tejeros. As will be recalled, this election was declared null and void by the presiding officer because of the disorder that ensued, and that despite this declaration, those elected nevertheless took their oath of office at the parish house in Tanza.

With the establishment of a new Government of the Philippine Republic with offices at the friar estate house in Naic, the Supremo's position and influence were virtually abolished and negated. People who came for some litigation or else sought the advice of the Council, never were able to see Andres Bonifacio again; those wanting to see him were directed to the new offices of the national government, for as was claimed, authority was vested in them alone. Greatly grieved by this turn of events, which he saw as an insult to his person and a repudiation of his authority, Bonifacio decided to leave the province of Cavite.

In the encounters with the enemy who wanted to capture Naic, the Magdalo troops were gradually losing stamina, thus requiring a search for replacements for the weary soldiers. The Magdiwang troops offered to replace them, only to be rebuffed and repaid with grievous injustice. The Magdiwang loaned their guns to the Magdalo for the sake of comradeship, but the latter not only did not return the guns but also gave them to others. The Magdalo troops claimed that they were so instructed by their commanding officer. Besides this, the Magdalo required the Magdiwang to produce commissions from the Magdalo Government before they were allowed to possess firearms. The Magdiwang insisted that they were the true owners of the guns and that it was from them that they were borrowed, but their arguments were ignored.

Colonel Antonio Virata reported these developments to General Apoy. The latter, in turn, lost no time in relaying the news to Major Cristobal Bustamante, who was then at a site between the villages of Redepispo and Timalan. Major Bustamante collected guns from twenty-one persons and gave them to the troops of Colonel Virata.

Because of the fear that the enemy would eventually take the few remaining towns still in the hands of the revolutionary forces, General Apoy began looking for a new defense site. He surveyed the areas and investigated the conditions in such places as Kaytitingga in the municipality of Alfonso, Cavite, and Pitong Gubat and Luok in Batangas province.

At Luok he stopped and rested for four days in the big estate house of Mr. Pedro F. Roxas. His investigation of the place showed that trails to the east led to Pitong Gubat and that a road westward led to the sea. The village was composed of some one hundred bamboo and *nipa* huts clustered around a house of medium size. Set quite apart from the village was the estate house, which had a water tank near it and which was raised some three arms' length from the ground. East of the estate house was a building which served as the village church.

General Apoy arrived at the estate house on a Saturday. That evening he was welcomed at a dance attended by young men and women of the village, who participated in such dances as the *balitaw*, the *pandanggo*, the *lolay*, and the *banahaw*. Swirling and keeping time in the fashion very agreeable to our young people during these times, they danced animatedly to the sweet Tagalog melodies, made more appealing because of the castanet accompaniment. The instruments used to provide dance music were a bamboo flute and a guitar made from the wood of the *langka* [jackfruit] tree.

General Apoy heard Mass in the chapel near the estate house very early the following day, which was a Sunday. He noted that the instruments used to accompany the choir were a guitar and a flute, as in the dance the night before, and that the choir sang the *Salve Maria* very well.

He left Luok for Naic escorted by a few cavalry troops. Because of the unsuitability of the places he visited, General Apoy did not see fit to recommend to the Council any one of them as sites for retreat and defense.

XXXVI

From the very beginning, we (in the Magdiwang) adhered to and respected such Katipunan principles as equality and freedom. Thus, in our actions, we refrained from being arrogant, for we believed that all men were equal. And to attain freedom for our Motherland, we risked property, bloodshed, and life itself. In line with these tenets, the Magdiwang Government and the Katipunan Highest Council, headed by the Supremo Andres Bonifacio, wholeheartedly loaned guns to their Magdalo comrades at a time when the latter sorely needed aid because of the serious threat on their defense positions by the enemy. On their part, the Magdalo justified the loan of guns to them on the grounds that the arrangement would also benefit the Magdiwang. They said that it would give those of them who had sufficiently rested a chance to relieve the Magdiwang troops, thus giving the latter a chance to rest and recuperate. At the same time, they said, it would give them an opportunity to help defend the Magdiwang fortifications. However, the guns were never returned, but were kept by the head soldiers commissioned by the Magdalo Government. This happened before the appointment of the entire cabinet of the newly established Philippine Republic, described in the previous pages.

Despite the cooperation by the Highest Council of the Katipunan with the new Government of the Philippine Republic, the Magdiwang was stripped of all authority, and this became patent especially after their guns were not returned to them. This development added to the disenchantment of the Supremo Bonifacio, who then decided to transfer his headquarters, on April 4, 1897, from the friar estate house in Naic to the village of Limbon in Indang. From Limbon, he planned to prepare to leave Cavite, finally, and head for the hills of Silangan in San Mateo, Rizal.

In his peregrination to Limbon, the Supremo was accompanied not only by his troops, but also by followers, men and women, old and young alike. In this new site, they built fortifications and established a head government and its army. But everyone in the community wanted to go back to their homes.

Food was scarce in the village, and their appeal for food donation was largely unheeded. To solve the problem of rations, the Supremo ordered that all those not in active duty should fend for themselves and look for their own sustenance. He had hoped to procure food for the troops from the townspeople, but he was sorely disappointed when the men he sent for the purpose to the Indang municipal government office were turned away. Mr. Severino de las Alas refused to extend any help to the Supremo for whom he had a low regard. He threatened the Supremo's men with harm should they ask for aid again.

When the Supremo heard this report, he was so furious that he could hardly speak or breathe. He sighed heavily several times before he finally found words so bitter they were like thorns being plucked from his breast: "Treacherous brethren! They won't recognize nor aid us! And here we are ready to offer our blood and life itself for the cause of freedom, and what do we get in return? Threats! Tell me, what do we do in the face of such behavior?

"Burn the town! Spare no one! Begin with the parish house and church, so that they would know what is the rational dessert of those who deny sympathy and succor to the needs of the Motherland!"

This was the Supremo's answer to his own questions and it was overheard by many passersby. It was not surprising that, on that very day, news spread in town that the Supremo Andres Bonifacio was ordering the burning of all houses in Indang, including the parish house and the church.

The following day, General Apoy visited the fort east of the church. He was still weak, having just recovered from a fever, but he managed to make the visit with Colonel Pablo Mojica aiding him. He came from the village of Tambog in Indang, where he had temporarily established himself in the house of Benito, the headman of the village. Also visiting the fort was General Vibora, who had with him a copy of a Spanish newspaper, *El Comercio*, an issue in that month of April that was then a few days old. The two of them sat on top of the fort to read the paper when they saw the following news printed in bold type:

TWO TOP REVOLUTIONARIES IN CAVITE, GENERALS S.V. ALVAREZ AND E. AGUINALDO FALL IN SPANISH HANDS. TIGHTLY BOUND, THEY ARE ACCOMPANIED BY SPANISH TROOPS ON A WARSHIP ON THE WAY TO MANILA. WITH THEIR CAPTURE, THE REVOLUTION IN CAVITE IS FINISHED. EVEN THE SO-CALLED SUPREMO IS AFRAID AND DOES NOT KNOW WHERE TO HIDE.

That was the translation of the news in Spanish. All those present burst out in laughter at the utterly false piece of reporting. Then some soldiers called their attention to a rumor that the Supremo had ordered the burning of all houses in Indang. General Apoy assured them that it was not true and that they should not believe such senseless talk.

XXXVII

General Apoy's wife, Paz, gave birth to a baby girl, who was baptized soon after at the Catholic church of Indang, on the morning of April 21, 1897. Given the name of Maria Paz, she had, for baptismal sponsor, Maria, the wife of Colonel Jose Koronel. Among those present at the ceremony were the revolutionary leaders Generals Artemio Ricarte, Santiago V. Alvarez (the baby's father and author of the memoirs), Luciano San Miguel, Colonels Pablo Mojica and Jose Koronel, and many other friends.

During the baptismal ceremony, rapid gunfire from the enemy suddenly jolted the pleasant sounds of the singer's sweet voice, the pealing of the church bells, the music of the brass band, and the gunshots of the People's Army. Firing from the outskirts, the enemy prepared to enter the town. The people panicked, and the officiating priest wanted to flee and leave his unfinished business, but General Apoy prevailed upon him to stay. He convinced the priest to stay, telling him about the strength of the fortifications and the great number of troops defending it. He said that no matter how hard they tried, the Spaniards would never be able to capture the fortifications in four hours. With his assurance, the ceremony was resumed. However, it ended amidst a rain of bullets from a large enemy contingent, on one hand, and from the Sons of the People on the other. The enemy were looking for a way into town and were firing hard into a thick grove which they suspected was a Katipunan lair.

The story of this baby girl baptized by the Revolution should not be forgotten in a collection of anecdotes of the period. Combining to make an unusual event were the hissing of bullets, the ringing of church bells, the music of a brass band, the gunfire from both camps, the townspeople's apprehension, and the officiating priest's terror.

Nicknamed Pacita, the baby was cradled in a hammock made from a sheet, which was slung around the neck of Lieutenant Abiyog. Hugging the baby close to him while fleeing the enemy, he scaled the steep mountain-sides of Tagaytay, Sungay, and Paliparan, and descended the precipitous cliffs that served as places of refuge during heavy rain, in the dark night, or after treading slippery paths. The baby was believed to be a miraculous savior by the many comrades and the multitudes who joined them in the flight from the pursuing Spaniards. The refugees hurried to abandon a site, no matter how adverse the weather, every time the baby had a crying fit; they always took it as a warning for them to leave.

It often happened that the enemy would come soon after they had abandoned a place, and thus was reinforced the belief that the baby's cries were some sort of a divine warning system. A large following clustered around carrying the baby, to make sure they would not miss a cue to run for their lives. The group broke up and dispersed only when they reached the safety of Paliparan.

XXXVIII

Because of the rumor that he ordered the burning of all the houses, the church, and the parish house in Indang, the townspeople began to turn against the Supremo Andres Bonifacio. The day after the baptism of baby Pacita, the President of the Philippine Republic, Mr. Emilio Aguinaldo, received the following information: that Andres Bonifacio was a paid *agent provocateur* of the friars; that Andres Bonifacio ordered his men to burn the houses, church and parish house of Indang as soon as the Spaniards had entered the town; that Andres Bonifacio ordered his troops to catch carabaos and other farm animals in order to slaughter these for food; that Andres Bonifacio was organizing a great number of men to destroy the new Government of the Philippine Republic, which he did not want to acknowledge and respect.

After reading the letter of denunciation that was signed, among others, by Messrs. S. de las Alas and J. Koronel, General Aguinaldo mulled things over for some time and kept the information he received from people he suspected to be followers of the Supremo Bonifacio. The Supremo's followers were unaware of the rift that was destroying the unity of the Katipunan, and they were stunned by the sudden and violent emergence of a split between them.

The open break came when President Emilio Aguinaldo issued on April 27, 1897, a stern order for the arrest of the Supremo Andres Bonifacio and his men. He assigned the task to head soldiers Colonel Agapito Bonzon (alias *Intong*), Felipe Topacio, and Jose Pawa (alias *Insik Pawa*), and instructed them to bring the prisoners dead or alive before him at the headquarters of the Philippine Republic.

The arresting officers with some soldiers left Naic for Indang in the afternoon of the same day. From Indang, they went to Limbon where the Supremo was then staying. On their arrival, they were greeted cordially by the Supremo.

"Where are you going, my brethren?" the Supremo inquired. "Do you want to see me?"

"No, we are only looking for trails the enemy might use," one of the party answered. Then they proceeded to walk up to the village of Banay-banay, in the municipality of Amadeo, but later returned stealthily to Indang. The fact that they did not arrest the Supremo at once indicated that they wanted first to survey the premises and the armed strength of the Supremo's forces, without appearing belligerent and giving away their intention. Should they find out that they were not equal to the task, then they could make the necessary preparations before they attacked.

Very early in the morning of the next day, April 28, the Supremo's troops assigned to guard the fort of Limbon were surprised by the sudden assault of the detachment under Colonel Bonzon and Insik Pawa. Caught unprepared, the guards fell into disarray. As a consequence, Ciriaco Bonifacio, elder brother of the Supremo, was killed at once, and the troops with him were captured and their arms confiscated. When he heard the gunshots, the Supremo quickly came down from his temporary residence inside the fort to investigate; with him were Katipuneros Francisco Carreon, Alejandro Santiago, and others. He was about to approach the daring Colonel Bonzon and Pawa when Bonzon rushed headlong and shot him with a revolver. Seriously wounded on the left arm, the Supremo was easy prey for Insik Pawa, who then stabbed him on the right side of the neck with a dagger. Blood spurted and made the Supremo dizzy. When Pawa made another move to attack the piteous Father of the Revolution, Mr. Alejandro Santiago rushed forward and pleaded that they take his life but not that of Andres Bonifacio.

(What great cowardice! It would be such a shame if the people would know about this episode. It should not have been written at all into our history. Why did the followers and comrades of the Supremo Andres Bonifacio fail to give up blood and life in defense of the true hero? Why was it that all they could do was say, "Kill me, but not him?")

The captors subdued the weakened Supremo and laid him on a hammock. They bound Ciriaco, the Supremo's brother, and rounded up the others and brought all of them to Indang. From Indang they proceeded to

Naic, where they locked the Bonifacio brothers in a narrow, dark room under the stairs of the friar estate house. The thick wooden doors were barricaded with stones and strictly guarded by loyal troops. The two prisoners were not allowed any visitors and were prohibited from talking to anyone. In the three days that they were detained, they were fed only twice with food that had better not be mentioned at all. After a while, President Aguinaldo organized a military tribunal and appointed Colonel Pantaleon Garcia as Judge in the trial of the Bonifacio brothers and their companions.

Let us skip over the delicate matter of the trial for the present and go back to a sad episode in the life of the Supremo Andres Bonifacio. This was when the Philippine Republic had not yet been established and the Highest Council of the Katipunan along with the Magdiwang Government had their headquarters at the friar estate house in Naic. It will be recalled that the pharmacist Feliciano Jocson, a Katipunan member, solicited a great sum of money from the Magdiwang and Magdalo Governments, and from the Highest Council of the Katipunan, for the purpose of buying guns in Japan. Jocson got the money on his promise to deliver the guns about the middle of April 1897. He was to arrive on the same boat carrying the cargo of guns. To unload the arms, the boat would drop anchor at night near a mountain on the coast. The site would be identified by means of big bonfires in tripod formation that the men on board could easily spot with a telescope. The ship could only stop briefly, owing to the danger involved, and so it was necessary to have many boats and men to unload the guns quickly.

The Supremo Bonifacio, Secretary Pascual Alvarez, Mr. Emiliano Riego de Dios, and others, made a reconnaissance journey on horseback to the Maragondon mountain range to look for a high peak close to the sea. In such a site they planned to establish a base for unloading guns according to the above plan. As they were following a trail up the mountainside near the place they had chosen as a likely site, they saw looming before them a branch of a tree across their path. Of an ordinary size, the branch would have reached up to Secretary Alvarez's chest if he had not ducked past it on his horse. He was the tallest among the group and his was the highest horse. Those riding ahead did not find the branch too bothersome as they playfully bowed their heads to avoid it. But when the Supremo's turn came he rode smack across it and fell on his back on the ground. This was surprising since he was shorter than those riding ahead and his mount was the smallest of all. His companions who came to his rescue were perplexed no end; they could not understand why he had failed to negotiate the obstacle safely.

The Supremo immediately rose to his feet and after some reflection said, "An old belief is that an event such as this is an omen of defeat. If by an unfortunate chance we are defeated and we are pursued by the enemy up here, this is where I shall die and be buried."

His companions broke into laughter. They then all mounted their horses again and proceeded on their way. (Today this site is pointed to by supposed witnesses as the same one where the Bonifacio brothers were killed and buried.)

On the evening of April 29, 1897, some Magdiwang leaders met at the invitation of Secretary of War Ariston Villanueva and Secretary of Finance Diego Mojica in a house in the village of Malainin in Naic. The purpose of the meeting was to discuss a plan to rescue the Supremo Bonifacio and his brother, who were then held prisoners by the Magdalo. The organizers purposely did not invite General-in-Chief Mariano M. Alvarez and his son General Apoy, because the former was then with the Magdalo-sponsored Philippine Republic, as Director of Welfare, while the latter was patently opposed to any move that would lead to a civil war. Those present resolutely approved of a plan to organize a bolo regiment that was to pretend to reinforce the infantry contingent guarding the Naic estate house. At a given signal, it was to make a sudden and simultaneous attack and then capture the guns and the fortifications. That was how they envisioned they would liberate the Supremo and his brother. The plan never materialized, however, because of an unexpected attack by the Spaniards, which led to the capture of Naic and Indang.

The next day General Luciano San Miguel visited General Apoy at Indang to report to him what had transpired at the meeting. The latter advised against such a plan as was approved because he thought it would lead the country to perdition.

"What will happen if a small number of comrades split and engage each other in armed struggle?" General Apoy asked. "Should that happen, the enemy horde will ride triumphantly over us and we will not be able to effectively defend ourselves against them. This will come about because of our arrogance, and avarice will prod us to betray our own brothers despite our commitment to the common goal of freedom for the Motherland."

In the course of his briefing, General San Miguel told of the news circulating among the top military echelon of the Philippine Republic, to the effect that many among the chiefs of government and of the army of the Philippine Republic objected to the arrest of Andres Bonifacio and his followers and instead favored a grace period for them.

"I am thankful that the plan did not materialize," General Apoy reiterated. "However, we should be reminded that in order for us to achieve our goal of Freedom, to which we dedicate our blood and our lives, we should first be united. I wholeheartedly acknowledge the existence of the Philippine Republic, although on principle I was against its establishment. I am hoping that from the new Government of the Philippine Republic will come the deliverance of our country, which is at present still in the clutches of the Spanish enemy.

"I hail the well-deserved promotion of General Artemio Ricarte to Captain General. Likewise, Magdiwang President Mariano M. Alvarez welcomes his appointment as Minister of Welfare in the Philippine Republic. This office he is serving well, and the only reason he cannot go to his office is because of his inability to walk because of arthritis. As you can see, I continue to serve even if I am not the Captain General of the Philippine Republic; it is General Vibora who holds that office. I am with the Magdiwang army, and up to now I cannot say that we should dissociate our army from theirs, for I am an advocate of unity and against self-defense.

"The enemy is now overwhelming us; we are weak and without defenses we can be proud of. We shall be forced to form small bands roving mountain and plains, each one looking out for itself. If we are not united, there cannot be a single government from which will emanate our common decisions. The resulting chaos will make for disparate policies and responsibilities. If this happens, what nation will take us seriously, if we are to carry on the Revolution but our laws are for the benefit of selfish interests, and not of the people? We cannot have Freedom under those conditions."

The listener (General Luciano San Miguel) found these statements very convincing.

XXXIX

The trial of the prisoners, the Supremo Andres Bonifacio and his companions, was held on April 29 and 30, 1897, in Naic, Cavite, before a court martial headed by Colonel Pantaleon Garcia.

The following is a deposition of General Mariano Noriel which was presented before the court:

Colonel Agapito Bonzon reported to General Mariano Noriel that he had arrested the Supremo Bonifacio and his companions in the village of Limbon. He said that he had tried his persuasive best to convince the Supremo Bonifacio to go with him to comply with summons from the Government of the Philippine Republic, but that the Supremo not only had refused him, but also had shown a belligerent attitude and had ordered his troops to shoot. Colonel Bonzon's troops had been forced to shoot back in self-defense. Thus the unexpected shedding of blood and taking of lives had occurred. These could have been avoided if only Colonel Bonzon's pleas had been heeded. Two soldiers of the Philippine Republic and a brother of the Supremo had been killed. Because of the seriousness of the Supremo's wound in the throat, they had left him at Indang. Twenty of his men, including another of his brothers, had been captured with the Supremo; all of them had firearms.

The above is the report of Colonel Bonzon which I am submitting to you.

(Sgd.) Mariano Noriel
Brigadier General

To the Honorable President of the Philippine Republic Mr. Emilio Aguinaldo:

This letter should be acknowledged by the War Council which should appoint a Colonel as Judge to try the case.

(Sgd.) Emilio Aguinaldo

The President's memo was sent to Colonel Pantaleon Garcia, who was then appointed Judge Advocate in the trial. As soon as Colonel Garcia received his appointment, he immediately set up a court in Naic and appointed Colonel Lazaro Makapagal as Secretary.

The trial started on April 27, 1897, before the officers of the court martial, Colonels Garcia and Lazaro Makapagal. The accused answered the questions asked of them truthfully and in a straightforward manner. The following are samples of their testimonies on the first day of the trial.

Testimony of Benito Torres

He was one of the head-soldiers of the Supremo Bonifacio, with Pedro Giron as Colonel, Roxas as Captain, and Juan Liwanag as Lieutenant. He did not know where their guns came from, but even when they were still at Balara, the Supremo Bonifacio already had many guns. He was not aware of a government with higher powers than the Highest Council of the Katipunan of the Sons of the People. He knew that they were getting ready to leave Cavite province and were only waiting for the Supremo's order to that effect. He had no knowledge of the trouble at the municipal hall in Indang; all that he knew was that the troops sent by the Supremo Bonifacio were not only refused aid, but also scolded.

Testimony of Procopio Bonifacio

He was not aware, because he had not heard any news about it, of the existence of a new government vested with superior power that had been established in Cavite. He did not know how many guns they had, but all of them were already in their possession when they came to Cavite from Balara. He did not know if the Government of the Philippine Republic had one or two guns mixed with the ones from Balara. In the event that this had happened, Pedro Giron should know, for he was the only one authorized by the Army to come in and go out of camp freely.

They had prepared to retreat to the hills of Rizal province, where they had planned to regroup and establish a new front in order to disperse the enemy forces. They had envisioned this to be of benefit to Cavite province because the concentration of enemy forces in the area would be broken. But since they were not yet ready to retreat, they had encamped at Limbon to defend it and keep the enemy from entering Indang. They did not know of the existence of a government with power over them and from whom it was necessary to ask permission for the army of the Highest Council of the Katipunan of the Sons of the People to stay at Limbon. He had not written to any head soldier nor to any soldier (in the Magdalo camp) to encourage, entice, or bribe them to join their group. No one can attest, whether secretly or openly, that he had prodded anyone to defect to their army; his brothers Andres and Ciriaco could attest to this.

No meeting whatsoever was held at Limbon. If the Katipunan Supremo had occasionally received one or two visitors, their talk was about things that already had happened and not about decisions and future plans.

Aside from his natural disposition and force of habit, it was also his duty as Supremo to cultivate fraternal love and sympathy not only among men of sympathy and good will, but even among those considered to be dangerous to society. He could make them embrace in brotherly love for the sake of freedom for the native land. And now it was he who was considered dangerous!

There was never any meeting or private conversation in Limbon that was against the Government they said had been established, or against President Aguinaldo. And there was no plan whatsoever to overthrow the said Government of whose existence we were not even aware.

On the second day of the trial, the following depositions were made:

Testimony of Rafael Non

He did not know that there was established a new government vested with superior authority. He knew about the Magdalo Government at Imus when the town was not yet captured by the Spaniards. He did not know whether Andres Bonifacio was vested with authority and had the right to have an army. However, he knew that Mr. Andres Bonifacio was the Supremo who established and headed the Katipunan and the Revolution. He did not know how many troops and how many guns they had because he did not pay attention to these matters. He did not know whether the Supremo Bonifacio had permission or not to stay and mass troops at Limbon. He did not know of any meeting held in Limbon, and he did not see people go there in order to hold a meeting.

He did not know of any head soldier whom the Supremo tried to lure or bribe, secretly or openly, to defect to his army. He did not know or had not heard of any case where the Supremo wrote to a head soldier, so he could not comment on that matter. He knew that from the beginning, the Supremo had been organizing many men for the purpose of defending the Freedom of the Motherland and not to attack and overthrow a national Government and its President. No one among his comrades could say that he had any such plan or threat.

He was not in the fort when fighting started between the troops who arrived and those whom they found in Limbon.

He was free to look after his own needs.

Testimony of the Supremo Andres Bonifacio

His position was that of Supremo of the Katipunan and President of the Revolution. He did not know of any other government that should be respected and established by the revolutionary nation. He knew that there was an army in the province of Cavite and that its leaders were Generals Santiago V. Alvarez, Emilio Aguinaldo, Artemio Ricarte and Pio del Pilar. He could not say whether he was vested with authority or not (by the new government) because he was not even aware of the establishment of this so-called government. As organizer of the Katipunan, authority emanated from him and he did not ask permission from anyone. He followed the same procedures because he was not aware of the existence of a newly-established superior government.

He had fifty guns which he brought to Cavite to help defend the province. However, he had only seventeen Remington guns left after Magdalo troops borrowed the others; those seventeen guns he brought to Limbon. He was not sure whether there were some which were marked "Magdalo" among the guns they had, but that should not be the case since none of the guns borrowed from them were ever returned.

He knew Messrs. Benito Torres, Pedro Giron, Modesto Ritual, and Pio del Pilar. He had never written to any of the above gentlemen for the purpose of enticing them and the troops under them to defect to his army.

He did not call a meeting at Limbon, and while there he had talked only with his own men. He never even once met with Pedro Giron who claimed to have been ordered by him to kill the President of the new government. Giron's claim was a lie and was motivated by avarice. Messrs. Silvestre Mojica and Diego Mojica had passed by Limbon on their way to Buena Vista, but they stopped very briefly. They barely had time to exchange greetings because the Mojicas were in a hurry.

He had given no orders whatsoever to his brothers and his men that would violate the peace and freedom of the troops who attacked them. When they saw these troops, they had already surrounded his residence; this was witnessed by everybody, including the villagers.

One colonel had asked permission to talk to him. He said that they had to do something about the news they had heard at Indang to the effect that the Balara detachment was planning to ambush his troops at Paso. After seeing for themselves that everything was peaceful and that the news was false, he had to apologize.

He [the Supremo] would not let the colonel go until they had shared a meal. The colonel said that they were to make a reconnaissance trip, and when they left, he [the Supremo] had presented them with several packs of cigarettes and some matches.

After a while, one of his [the Supremo's] soldiers had come in to report that their outside battery had been captured by those to whom they had just given presents, and that these [men] had given stern orders not to let anyone go out or come into the fort. They also had seized the guns of troops guarding the fort, raided all houses and ordered the detainment of his [the Supremo's] troops.

In order to find out if the report was true, he [the Supremo] had sent some men outside to investigate. When these did not return at once, he had asked Captain Martin[27] and General Santos Nocon, and later Dorong Puti, to do the same. However, these emissaries could report nothing except that the head of the assaulting party refused to make any explanations.

Very early the next morning, the troops of Colonel Intong (Colonel Agapito Bonzon) had started attacking their position again by firing five consecutive shots from their Mausers. But, strangely enough, they had continued their assault even as they kept shouting, "Brother! Brother!"

He [the Supremo] had ordered Major Benito Torres to tell his troops to desist from shooting back in retaliation. After a while, someone had shouted, "Come out, you shameless Supremo! You who ran away with our money!"

He had came out and faced his accusers. He told them, "My brethren, I am not doing anything shameless. I did not run away with money, nor do I have any intention of doing so."

In reply, the major on the opposite camp had ordered his men to fire. A single bullet had plowed through his shoulder and rested in the chest of a soldier behind him. He [the Supremo] had said bitterly, "My brethren, see what you have done! You have killed a fellow brother!"

They had ignored this remark and instead had fired simultaneously. Then one of them had rushed forward and stabbed him in the neck. He had fallen prostrate and unconscious. To satisfy the desire to annihilate them

---

[27]Agoncillo identified Captain Martin as "Captain Martin of Silang," implying that this individual was at one time administrative head of that town in Cavite Province (Teodoro A. Agoncillo, *The Revolt of the Masses: The Story ofonifacio and the Katipunan* [Quezon City: University of the Philippines, 1956], 251).

completely, the attackers had confiscated the few clothes and some money they had with them.

Colonel Intong had made a move to take his [the Supremo's] wife to an unoccupied house, but thanks to the intercession of some of his [Colonel Intong's] own head-soldiers, he had been thwarted in his beastly intention. The same Colonel Intong had made a second attempt to abuse his wife while they were at Indang. She had been dressing his [the Supremo's] wounds when suddenly there barged in a head soldier who claimed to be a major. This interloper had insisted on taking his [the Supremo's] wife away, but she was luckily spared again by the propitious arrival of General Tomas Mascardo.

His [the Supremo's] weapons had been a dagger and a revolver which remained fully loaded. In the confusion, he had not noticed what weapons his two brothers had. He had not shot, neither had he unsheathed his dagger to fight his attackers and captors, because he did not believe in fighting his own brethren; instead, he had wanted to talk things over and to settle their differences amicably. Because of this non-belligerent frame of mind, the attackers had been able to get near them. Before they knew it, their arms had been seized from them and they had been shot at without defense. Thus, he could not tell what weapons were carried by whom among his men. He did not know that two men were shot dead outside the fort. However, he had seen two dead bodies inside the battery; the bodies had later been taken to the clinic.

He recalled having been present at the meeting at Tejeros for the purpose of electing the President of the Islands. Disorder had broken out because of a serious violation of a principle that had been approved by the people. Before the election started, this principle had been approved through persuasion and by authority of the chairman of the meeting. But everyone saw that what had been agreed upon was violated. Besides, a manifesto signed by more than forty councils of different provinces strongly objected to the violation of the principle and supported the stand of the presiding officer.

For the same reason, General Artemio Ricarte who had been elected Captain General declined the position. He explained his stand in a speech and in a manifesto he circulated during the meeting. Under these circumstances, the affiant President Supremo of the Katipunan of the Sons of the People and presiding officer at the meeting held at Tejeros could not say whether Mr. Emilio Aguinaldo was elected President of what was purportedly established as Government of the Republic of the Philippines.

If his election as President was acknowledged and respected, still these questions had to be answered: Why was he not so proclaimed? And why were policies and guidelines not disseminated? Instead, hasty decrees were imposed on people who were not aware of them. For instance, people had been grilled on whether or not they accepted the existence of a Government of the Philippine Republic, or if they had permission to stay in a given place, or to assemble people and weapons. These interrogations had been untenable since no decrees or orders to that effect had been promulgated. Moreover, these were revolutionary times, and it was the duty of all who were able to be ready to defend the freedom of the Motherland.

Why did Mr. Emilio Aguinaldo insist on his claim to the presidency despite the decision of the presiding officer of the meeting held at Tejeros and the speeches and manifestos circulated by many leaders during the election? Why did he take his oath of office in secret with a Catholic priest, Fr. Cenon Villafranca, officiating when he knew that the latter was under the jurisdiction of the Roman pontiff? In all the history of the nation, no one had read or heard about a national president taking his oath of office in secret before a representative of the Pope in Rome. This was unthinkable considering that the Philippine Revolution was the result of outbursts of nationalist feelings of Dr. Rizal, Burgos, Zamora, and other defenders of freedom. (Fathers Jose Burgos, Mariano Gomez, and Jacinto Zamora were executed by the Spanish authorities in 1872 for alleged complicity in a mutiny in a Cavite arsenal in that year. Dr. Jose Rizal had dedicated his second novel, *El Filibusterismo*, first published in 1890, to the memory of the martyred Filipino priests. The Philippine nationalist movement is reckoned to have begun with the repercussions of that execution).

For reasons already stated, he was not aware that Mr. Emilio Aguinaldo was President of the Philippine Republic.

Made in the name of God and the Motherland, the valuable statements above composed the deposition of the Supremo Andres Bonifacio.

Testimony of Mrs. Gregoria de Jesus [Wife of Andres Bonifacio]

She did not know who had fired the first shots because she had run to the woods as soon as she saw the great number of men attacking the place where they were staying.

She had seen the five men who were captured and punished by Ciriaco Bonifacio. These men had admitted that they were spies for the Spaniards and were assigned to report on the position and number of guards in the revolutionary forces. They had been promised to be well rewarded if they could give a good report. After they had confessed, they had begged for mercy and asked that their lives be spared. They had promised to serve in the People's Army and not ever leave its ranks. Their lives had been spared, but Ciriaco had had their heads, eyebrows, and eyelashes shaved to keep them from escaping. To avoid condemnation from others, word had been spread around that the prisoners were being punished for theft.

Not a single meeting had been held at their residence in Limbon. She did not know that the Philippine Islands had a President. She did not know of any instructions the Supremo Andres Bonifacio issued to the effect that his men were to halt all troops passing by the Limbon fort. (The supposed order to halt was to be given three times; and if after the third time any passing troops did not take heed, then they were to be fired at with a machine gun.)

XL

The trial of the Supremo Andres Bonifacio and his wife, Mrs. Gregoria de Jesus, was held in Maragondon, Cavite on May 4, 1897.

In its search for truth, the court interrogated many persons at Naic and Maragondon, and almost all of the witnesses, except for one or two, proved that the Supremo Andres Bonifacio was innocent of the charges against him.

Among those interrogated by the court martial were Messrs. Andres and Procopio Bonifacio, Alejandro Santiago, Benito Torres, Nicolas de Guzman, Francisco Carreon, Rafael Non, Julian Aguila, Narciso Tiolo, Bibiano Rojas, Pedro Giron, Cayetano Lopez, Domingo San Juan, and Mrs. Gregoria de Jesus of A. Bonifacio.[28]

---

[28]In the typescript copy, the name of this witness appears as "Juan Aguina," but a comparison of the same documents as they appear in other sources shows that the name as it appears in the typescript was either incorrectly recorded in the original manuscript or miscopied. Cf., Teodoro A. Agoncillo, *The Writings and Trial of Andres Bonifacio* (Manila: Bonifacio Centennial Commission, 1963), 35, and Taylor, "Court Martial of Andres and Procopio Bonifacio and Others," 312.

One of those who testified against the Supremo Bonifacio was Pedro Giron. In the presence of the colonel of the court martial in Naic on April 30, 1897, Pedro Giron stated that:

> He knew of the existence of the superior Government and Army of the Philippine Republic. He did not know of any right or authority given to the Supremo Bonifacio to organize an army. He did not know how many men and guns Bonifacio had, for he was but a humble soldier, not an officer. He did not want to join Bonifacio because he had been aware of his bad intentions from the time of the election for President at the friar estate house in Tejeros. One day (the exact date he could not remember) the Supremo had told him that they should leave Cavite because the leaders (of the Revolution) in this province were not in good terms with each other. He had wanted them to recognize his leadership over them because he had founded the Katipunan and started the Revolution.
>
> When the People's troops had been in Naic after the capture of Tanza by the Spaniards, the Supremo had called for him and told him that the situation was getting worse for them, and that if Mr. Emilio Aguinaldo would not subordinate himself to his [the Supremo's] authority, he would have Mr. Aguinaldo killed. The Supremo had given him ten pesos and repeated his statement that should Mr. Aguinaldo refuse to recognize his authority, he would have him killed. The Supremo also had assured him of his patronage and protection no matter what happened.
>
> After this interview, he finally had left the Supremo's forces. He knew that the Supremo was massing a great number of troops. He quoted the Supremo as saying, "Should the enemy be able to take Naic and Indang, we will be forced to go. Otherwise we shall not leave."

Following the first name of Narciso Tiolo the typescript has a question mark, indicating that the surname was unknown to the author. The missing surname appears in both sources cited above.

The name Bibiano Rojas is Basilio Roxas in the typescript. It is corrected here to conform to the name as it appears in the sources above.

The rendering of Bonifacio's wife's name, Mrs. Gregoria de Jesus of A. Bonifacio, was an influence from the Spanish practice. It was adopted by upper- class Filipinos in the urban areas and persisted until the American occupation.

In their desire to avoid trouble, many officers had tried to convince the Supremo to move out. But the latter had refused, for fear that the officers who had repudiated him would accuse him of cowardice and weakness. His two brothers had nothing to do with this matter.

Meetings had often been held in the Supremo's residence at Limbon. He had not recognized the people who came to see the Supremo since he was not from Cavite province. He did not know what they talked about because he had had no occasion to be near them.

The one who had opened fire [in the engagement that led to the capture of the Bonifacio brothers] was Ciriaco Bonifacio, the Supremo's older brother. He [Pedro Giron] had tried to avert the killing of Ciriaco by standing in front of his friend who was aiming his gun at Ciriaco. However, this friend had shot Ciriaco just the same. In the exchange of fire, two soldiers of Colonel Intong had been killed.

At the continuation of the court martial proceedings in Naic, Mr. Domingo San Juan[29] testified as follows:

He was not aware of the existence of a Revolutionary Government and its authorized army. He was not aware of any authority vested in Mr. Andres Bonifacio and his two brothers, nor of any recognition of their authority by the vested Government of the Philippine Republic. He was also not aware of any permission given by the said recognized government for the Supremo A. Bonifacio to reside at Limbon and there organize an armed force. He did not know if meetings had been held at the Supremo's residence because he did not stay there. And he did not know where the Supremo A. Bonifacio's guns came from. He had not been at the battery when the shooting had started so he did not know who fired the first shot.

---

[29]Corrected to conform to the record of the trial. *Cf.* Taylor, *The Philippine Revolution*, 304, and *The Writings and Trial of Andres Bonifacio*, 43. In the typescript of these memoirs, the name appears as Domingo S. Juan.

The present writer reiterates that in this account, only a few of the many witnesses in the trial have been mentioned. Moreover, it was only Mr. Pedro Giron who testified that the Supremo Bonifacio plotted to destroy the Government of the Philippine Republic and to assassinate President Emilio Aguinaldo. All the other witnesses testified that they did not know of the alleged plots and had not even heard about them.

XLI

In his refusal to recognize the said Government of the Philippine Republic, the Supremo Andres Bonifacio was motivated not by treachery, but by his adherence to what was rational. The Revolution, representing reason, was ranged against forces representing avarice and violation of a principle agreed upon in the meeting held at the friar estate house in Tejeros, San Francisco de Malabon.

Colonel Pantaleon Garcia submitted all the documents pertaining to the trial to President Emilio Aguinaldo. On May 4, 1897, in the town of Maragondon, President Aguinaldo appointed General Mariano Noriel Judge advocate of the court martial, and, as such, he was to study the case and render judgment.

General Noriel convened the court martial on the following day, May 5, 1897, in the place called Pluhan in the municipality of Maragondon. President (aside from the accused Katipunan Supremo and his companions) were the defense attorneys Teodoro Gonzales and Placido Martinez, the prosecutor Mr. Jose Elises, and other advocates of the court.

Judge Noriel ordered the brothers Andres and Procopio to appear before the court; and when they were arraigned, the secretary read aloud the charges against them and their companions. These charges resulted from the investigations made by the Judge Advocate, Colonel Pantaleon Garcia. After the reading, the prosecutor, Mr. Jose Elises, asked the Judge for permission to speak.

"According to the documents that have just been read," the prosecutor said, "which were the results of the interrogation of the Bonifacio brothers, it is clear that the accused are really plotting to destroy the Government of the Philippine Republic and kill the Highest President. They also induced Mr. Pedro Giron to join them in the plot. They told Giron to get ready for an attack not against the Spanish enemy, but against other enemies of the People's Army. This was indeed what happened, and it resulted in the death of two soldiers of the Philippine Republic and of a brother of the accused Bonifacio. Procopio is a co-plotter with his brother Andres and is equally guilty of scheming to overthrow the government and assassinate the highest President of the Philippine Republic. In view of the seriousness of their crime, I ask this court martial that the accused be executed in the open, ten paces away from the firing squad."

After asking the Judge's permission, the Supremo Andres Bonifacio's defense attorney, Mr. Placido Martinez, stood up to speak.

"It is impossible," Mr. Martinez said, "to defend Andres Bonifacio of his grievous crime. He deserves a heavier penalty than the death sentence, if indeed that were possible, for he plotted to take over the government and assassinate the Highest President. By so doing, he did not realize that he was jeopardizing the interests of his own brethren, kin, and people. In spite of all these, however, this honorable court is reminded that since man is a creature of sin, we have to give allowance in making judgments. And where the individual is being led to do wrong, it is our duty to provide straightforward advice.

"This was the experience of Mr. Andres Bonifacio when he was captured at Indang: he was wounded, stripped of his clothes, divested of his belongings, placed under guard, locked up in the dark, held incommunicado, and deprived of proper food. And up to now he is still under heavy guard. Because of the distress and hardships he has already suffered, I beg of you to forgive him of the crime he is accused of, or if this is not possible, to mitigate his sentence. You know that we are guided by the basic tenets of the Katipunan that clearly state that we are all brothers who should love and cherish one another and that we should love our brethren like we love our own selves. Besides, our Lord Jesus Christ whose example we follow did not only forgive those who tortured and killed him, but also asked God the Father to forgive them, too. He begged forgiveness for them because He believed that they were inflamed by their passion against which they were unable to struggle, and for this reason they committed the transgressions innocently. And in consonance with our daily prayer, 'Our Father, forgive us our sins as we forgive those who sin against us,' I wholeheartedly beg your forgiveness of the crimes attributed to Mr. Andres Bonifacio. May he be set free as a true comrade and brother in the defense of freedom for the Motherland.

"But before I end my piece, I implore this honorable court to put to trial Colonel Bonzon, who attempted to dishonor the wife of the Supremo

Bonifacio, Mrs. Gregoria de Jesus of Bonifacio. I know that she is extremely pained about the incident and that it compounds her distress over the fate of the Supremo."

Mr. Teodoro Gonzales, defense attorney for Procopio Bonifacio, stood up to speak after obtaining the court's permission.

"According to my clear understanding of all the depositions signed by the accused, likewise of all the statements made by Mr. Procopio Bonifacio, it appears that he is innocent and that he had nothing to do with the matter the Supremo Andres Bonifacio is being accused of. And nobody ever testified, even from hearsay, that the said gentleman was ever involved in whatever capacity, either openly or secretly, in the matters that his brother the Supremo is being charged with. Since in this world justice and reason prevail, and all peoples from the smallest tribes to the biggest races never punish except those who are guilty, it becomes superfluous to defend anyone. And now, in my capacity as defense attorney for Mr. Procopio Bonifacio, I hereby ask for complete freedom for my innocent client."

The Supremo Andres Bonifacio asked the court to be permitted to speak, but was denied the privilege on the objections of the counselors of the court. He repeated his request to be allowed to speak, but was again rejected. The defense lawyer said nothing further. The counselors agreed to adjourn the trial and to promulgate the sentence within twenty-four hours.

The following composed the court martial: Judge, Mr. Mariano Noriel; Counselors, Colonel Mariano Riego de Dios, Messrs. Crisostomo Riel, Esteban Infante, Tomas Mascardo, Sulpicio Antony and Placido Martinez.

The court martial convened again on May 6, 1897, to approve the sentence to be meted out to the Supremo Andres Bonifacio and his companions. The following were the matters they established and agreed upon in the meeting:

Andres Bonifacio knew of the establishment of the Superior Revolutionary Government. He had no permission to reside at Limbon and to organize troops and collect arms. He ordered his men to fire if the government troops of the Philippine Republic were to approach their garrison. Finally, he and his men were captured and brought here (at Naic) to the government headquarters. He bribed many officers, along with their soldiers, to defect to his army. He massed many troops at Limbon in order to overthrow the Government of the Philippine Republic and to kill the Highest President.

Because of their serious crimes, Andres and Procopio Bonifacio deserved the death penalty. And because they were accomplices, his officers and soldiers were to be detained by the government army in order to serve as orderlies in the war effort. Andres Bonifacio was to pay life pensions to the widows and orphans of the two soldiers killed by his troops.

That was the decision approved by the Council of War (i.e., the court martial). It was signed by all council members except Mr. Mariano Riego de Dios, who absented himself. The Judge Advocate, General Mariano Noriel, sent the decision to President Emilio Aguinaldo who, in turn, forwarded it on May 7, to the auditor, Mr. Baldomero Aguinaldo, for his study and approval. The latter concluded that:

"Mr. Andres Bonifacio stayed at Limbon for the purpose of collecting troops and weapons with the help of his brothers Ciriaco and Procopio. He often called meetings with the connivance of Messrs. Diego Mojica, Silvestre Domingo, Santos Nocon, and others. These men were also present at these meetings.

"The matters discussed were the overthrow of the Government of the Philippine Republic and the assassination of the Supreme President. When the latter learned of the plot against him, he sent troops with firearms to Limbon. The Bonifacio brothers ordered their men to shoot and to close the door of their fort when they saw the government troops approaching.

"When their men did not obey the orders, Ciriaco started shooting and thus killed two of the approaching soldiers. Finally, Ciriaco himself was also killed. Andres and Procopio resisted inside the fort, but when the former fell, the latter surrendered.

"These events clearly attest to the fact that the Bonifacio brothers organized armed troops at Limbon and that they held secret meetings in order to overthrow the Government of the Philippine Republic and kill its President. These were the circumstances reported and proved to us by our comrades, Messrs. Pedro Giron, Bibiano Rojas, Benito Torres, and many others who, because of their great number, need not be mentioned here.

"From his relationship with Messrs. Diego Mojica and Ariston Villanueva, it is evident that Mr. Andres Bonifacio was the mastermind behind the evil plot. Besides, he also distributed money to officers and their men to bribe them into defecting to their side. On this matter it is necessary to investigate and put to trial the accomplices and those secretly helping the Supremo Bonifacio in the evil designs against the Government and the

Highest President of the Philippine Republic. Among these are Messrs. Diego Mojica, Ariston Villanueva, Santos Nocon, and others.

"The court martial's death sentence to Andres Bonifacio and his brother is just and must be carried out. Still, the disposition of the case rests with the Highest President of the Philippine Republic. We await his final decision."

Addenda:

"The proceedings of the trial should be transcribed so that these can be used in the investigation of the accomplices, Messrs. Diego Mojica, Ariston Villanueva, Santos Nocon and others. All materials seized from the army of the Supremo Andres Bonifacio—firearms and bladed weapons, documents, seal, and equipment of the troops—should be part of the property of the Government of the Philippine Republic."

Thus was the communication sent on May 7, 1897, by the auditor, Mr. Baldomero Aguinaldo, to the Highest President of the Philippine Republic, General Emilio Aguinaldo.

XLII

After studying the court martial's decision of a death sentence on the Supremo Andres Bonifacio and his brother Procopio, and after reviewing the opinion of the auditor, Mr. Baldomero Aguinaldo, the President-General Emilio Aguinaldo made the following deposition:

That the trial court verified the charges imputed against the Supremo Andres Bonifacio and his companions and that these crimes were voluntarily and deliberately committed:

1) not recognizing and not respecting the Supreme Government of the Philippine Republic;
2) organizing many men and collecting firearms for the purpose of overthrowing the Supreme Government; and
3) plotting to kill the national President.

That it was proven that the funds used in enlisting officers and men and in carrying out their evil intentions came from the contributions collected by Messrs. Diego Mojica and Ariston Villanueva.

That after a careful and proper trial, the court had no doubt whatsoever about the guilt of the Supremo Bonifacio and his companions, and, therefore, it immediately imposed the death sentence on the Bonifacio brothers and detention and garrison servitude to the others.

That the crime of disrespect and rejection of the Government of the Philippine Republic was committed when the Supremo Bonifacio ordered his men to halt the approach of government troops and to fire at them. Properly obeying superior orders, the government troops went to invite the Supremo Bonifacio to confer with the national government officials in the latter's desire to clarify issues. But they were fired upon, and this resulted in the killing of two of the government troops and of Ciriaco Bonifacio, elder brother of the Supremo. Because of this provocation, the national government troops counter-attacked those whom they then considered their enemy and captured the wounded Supremo and his brother Procopio and their officers and men with firearms.

It is necessary that we all acknowledge the authority of the court and its right to impose the death sentence on anyone who intends or carries out the crimes mentioned above. But for the sake of brotherly love and patriotism, the President, in his exercise of his rights as the highest official of the national government and his privilege to revise the final decisions of the military and civil courts, deposes and says:

That he (General Emilio Aguinaldo) was commuting the death sentence to the Bonifacio brothers, and in its stead, he was decreeing their banishment to the mountains where they were to be held incommunicado and would not be allowed to see anyone except those with express permission from the Superior Government. This decree, which carried his signature along with that of Auditor Baldomero Aguinaldo, he sent to the trial judges for their affirmation and signature. The decree should also be sent to the following for the same purpose: the prosecutor, the counselors of the court, the defense attorneys, and the condemned men.

Afterwards, the document was to be returned to the custody of the Secretary of the Supreme Government.

(Sgd.) Emilio Aguinaldo
Baldomero Aguinaldo

Colonel Lazaro Makapagal was assigned to obtain the signatures needed to finalize the decision in the case against the Bonifacio brothers. He secured the signatures of all except that of the Supremo, who could not sign his name because his wounded arm was swollen. Makapagal deposited the document for safekeeping with the Secretary-General's office.

The news spread that the Supremo Andres Bonifacio and his brother Procopio were spared their lives and were to be banished in the mountains. Their fears assuaged, many started speculations that sooner or later the feuding officials would patch up their differences and resume their amicable relations; this was only rational since they represented the beginning, the present, and the logical ending of the Revolution.

XLIII

At a time when people were speculating about the eventual fate of the Bonifacio Brothers, two Alvarez cousins, General Apoy and General Bagong Buhay [lit., "New Life," *nom de guerre* of Pascual Alvarez], were hoping for a pardon and commutation of the death sentence. With deep feeling, the latter related his reminiscences of the trial to the former.

"I was with General Emilio Aguinaldo, Mr. Baldomero Aguinaldo, Mr. Pedro Lipana and others, hiding in a small room of the *nipa* house in Maragondon where the Judge, General Mariano Noriel, was hearing the case against the Supremo Bonifacio and his brother Procopio. We did not make our presence known to the persons present at the trial, including the Bonifacio brothers who, we were absolutely certain, would get a death sentence. The prisoners presented a most piteous sight. There they were, wordless, but as if their inner selves were rebelling against the injustice brought upon them. Anybody seeing them could not help but shed tears over their plight.

"General Emilio Aguinaldo was torn about the possible death sentence; perhaps his merciful nature made him wish that it were a mere banishment to the mountains. Moreover, there was the nagging realization that the Supremo was a true hero and patriot whose life must be spared not only for its worth, but also for the sake of brotherly love. He mulled over these thoughts even as he well knew that the decision had been made by General Mariano Noriel and was ready to be promulgated.

"I don't know," General Pascual Alvarez continued, "whether they talked about other things when I left the house for a personal necessity. They had already started the trial when I returned. After a biased trial that gave little credence to reasonable defense, the death sentence was imposed on the Brothers Andres and Procopio Bonifacio.

"I knew that General Emilio Aguinaldo's commutation of the sentence would not be carried out anyway, because I saw that the scale of justice was weighted in favor of the necessity of eliminating the Supremo Andres Bonifacio and his followers. And so I became resigned to the idea that the saga of the Supremo would be like that of Christ—like Him, he would rise and be with God the Father. When his end came he would certainly follow in the footsteps of Christ. May he rest in peace!"

The might of the Revolutionary Government prevailed over that of the Supremo Andres Bonifacio and his brother and comrade-in-arms Procopio. It prevailed over a patriotic Father who never wearied of his love for freedom. The justification was so that thousands of brethren might be united to rally in defense of the Motherland.

Just before the Supremo met his doom, it was as if a thick and heavy cloud concealed the straight path he was taking. Then suddenly it was light again, and out of the blue there appeared a former loyal aide who greeted him most affectionately. After an initial exchange of warm felicitations, the visitor's behavior turned treacherous. To the stunned Supremo, again it was as if a sharp lightning bolt and a deafening clap of thunder hit him and literally rendered him unconscious.

When he came to, he was already in jail and guarded heavily by armed troops. Tightly bound, he was conducted to and from the court martial that condemned him to death. Despite a commutation of the sentence by the President of the Philippine Republic, the Supremo was nevertheless executed.

Why was there no investigation whatsoever to find out who violated the decree commuting the death sentence on the Bonifacio brothers?

The following is an account of events as confided to the present writer by Lazaro Makapagal. Colonel Makapagal was the officer commissioned to carry out the execution order:

"With some troops, I was ordered to escort the Bonifacio brothers to Mt. Buntis. I was instructed to stop before reaching the summit of the mountain at a concealed yet spacious place; there I was to put the prisoners under heavy guard. Then I was to open the sealed letter to be given to me by General Mariano Noriel and to read it to the Bonifacio brothers.

"I followed the instructions carefully. I chose a suitable place at the foot hills to open the letter of instructions so that I would know where to bring the Bonifacios. First I read the letter by myself. When I had understood its contents, my lips trembled and I was speechless for some time. Oh, what compassion I felt!

"The instructions said I was to obey strictly the order to shoot the brothers. Should I fail to do so, it would be I who would be shot on my return to headquarters or wherever pursuing troops might overtake me, should I attempt to flee.

"After I had read the order to the prisoners, Procopio wept, embraced Andres, and asked, '*Kuya* [Elder Brother], what are we to do?'

"Andres did not say a word. He bowed his head and sobbed while bitter tears welled in his eyes and rolled down his cheeks. Not able to bear it, I turned my back; and when I faced them again, the deed was done. My men had fired the shots and the poor Bonifacio brothers were prostrate and dead. Then I paid proper respect to their remains."

The news about the execution spread quickly. The widow of the Supremo, Mrs. Gregoria de Jesus, was immediately escorted to San Pedro Tunasan by Colonel Antonio Guevara. There she was put in safe hands, away from the evil intentions of those who would dishonor a respectable woman. After a few weeks rest in San Pedro Tunasan, she went to Pasig, where she met and later married Julio Nakpil. Mr. Nakpil was at that time working for the Katipunan in the village of Palatiw in Pasig as deputy of the Supremo Andres Bonifacio.

After the death of the Supremo Bonifacio, many patriots formerly serving the Revolution in the province of Cavite, Manila, Rizal, and Laguna lost heart and withdrew from the struggle. They no longer joined or got involved in any undertaking having to do with the Revolution. Keeping a distance, they contented themselves in adopting a wait-and-see attitude. This alienation on the part of many revolutionaries led to a further deterioration of the movement. Many were distressed at this turn of events, but some Cavite folk found it not unpleasant when hordes of people who earlier flocked to the province returned to their own hometowns. All in all, the revolutionary forces disintegrated as each one resorted to individual efforts to save himself by retreating to open fields and hill country.

XLIV

Titingga was the name of the village in the western part of the municipality of Alfonso, Cavite. Located on one of the highest elevations in the area known as Tangway, it was adjacent to the expanse called Pitong Gubat [Seven Woods] that was part of Batangas province. A wide and deep river separated Cavite and Batangas provinces, and a trail along the riverside served as the link between the Batangas area and Titingga. A considerable length of this trail was so narrow that if one were on horseback or were leading a horse, he had to call out loudly to alert other parties coming from the opposite direction; if one were to cross unhindered, the other had to give way. Thus, if one were traveling astride a beast or were leading a herd and failed to give a signal on approaching the narrow pass, he ran the risk of an argument over who should pass and who should back out. And often arguments were reduced to a show of bladed weapons, and the better part of valor for those who preferred peace was flight. The aggressive party then slaughtered the abandoned beast and led his own livestock over the carcass.

Towards the interior, Titingga had a valley ringed with mountains that descended in steep cliffs to the west. To the east of the village was the revolutionary town of Alfonso.

The Magdiwang Revolutionary Army and Government changed the name of Titingga to "Mainam," *nom-de-guerre* of the Father of the Revolution in Cavite province, the Honorable Mariano M. Alvarez. He was the first general in the army, Highest President of the Revolutionary Government of Magdiwang, and Minister of Welfare when the Government of the Philippine Republic was established. The village became the lively town of Mainam when many people settled there. It became a trading center for produce coming from Manila, Rizal, Batangas, Laguna, and other places. It was also here where the Magdiwang Government, under the leadership of General Apoy, established its headquarters and built new defense fortifications. Simultaneously, the Government of the Philippine Republic was being organized in the town of Maragondon.

At a time when many people were reflecting on the sad fate that befell the Bonifacio brothers, Mr. Feliciano Jocson arrived at the Maragondon headquarters of the Government of the Philippine Republic. It will be recalled that this gentleman solicited a great sum from the Magdiwang and Magdalo Governments and from the Katipunan Council, with the understanding that he would use the money for buying arms and ammunition. But no guns nor ammunition materialized, and neither was there an accounting of the money collected for the purpose. Yet this man had the temerity to barge into town shouting at the top of his lungs, "Long live the Philippines!" He tantalized the revolutionary troops by saying that if only they would fight a little longer, the guns and ammunition he brought from Hongkong would arrive and ensure certain victory.

After Mr. Jocson conferred with the President, General Emilio Aguinaldo, at the parish house, the latter agreed to establish a government in Central Luzon which was to be known as "Departmental Government." It was to include the provinces of Manila, Rizal, Laguna, Tayabas [now Quezon Province], Bulacan, Nueva Ecija, and Bataan. This government was to be organized along the same lines as that of the Philippine Republic.

Elected President of this government was Fr. Pedro Dandan.[30] [30] Anastasio Francisco was chosen Vice President; Feliciano Jocson, Minister of the Interior; Teodoro Gonzales, Cipriano Pacheco, and Antonio Montenegro, Governors of Manila; Paciano Rizal, Governor of Laguna.[31]

The staff officers of the army of the "Departmental Government" were: Severino Taeniyo, Brigadier General, whose assistant was a woman, Mrs. Agueda Kahabagan, popularly known as "General Agueda"; Mamerto Natividad, Major General for Central Luzon, and under him were the following officers—Mariano Llanera, Colonel; Isidoro Torres, Lieutenant

---

[30]Fr. Dandan's name has been supplied by the translator; the typscript contains the list of officers beginning with the Vice President. One of the priests involved in the struggle against the Spanish friars over the question of the Pilipinization of the parishes and implicated in the Cavite Revolt of 1872, Fr. Dandan was exiled to the Marianas. He left his parish in Quiapo, Manila, to join the rebels at the outbreak of the Revolution in 1896. He died in January 1897, in the Magallanes mountains in Cavite where his Katipunan detachment led by General Crispulo Aguinaldo retreated after a two-day siege of Spanish positions in Taguig, Pateros and Muntinglupa.

[31]Teodoro M. Kalaw lists the departments to which the men were elected in a manner which differs from the Alvarez version. Kalaw's listing is as follows: Fr. Pedro Dandan, president; Dr. Anastasio Francisco, vice president; Paciano Rizal, secretary of finance; Cipriano Pacheco, secretary of war; Teodoro Gonzales, secretary of interior; and Feliciano Jocson, secretary of welfare (Teodoro M. Kalaw, *The Philippine Revolution* [Manila: Manila Book Company, 1925], 58).

General; Gregorio del Pilar, Colonel; Manuel Tinio, Francisco Makabulos, Simeon Tekson, and (Tomas) Kabling,[32] Brigadier Generals.

However, this staff of the "Departmental Government" was not yet fully constituted when, six months later, it was suddenly dissolved with the adoption of a constitution framed by Mr. Isabelo Artacho at Biyak-na-Bato. When Mr. Jacinto Lumbreras died, Mr. Antonio Montenegro succeeded him as Secretary of State, while Mr. Isabelo Artacho assumed the office of Secretary of Interior, Vice President Mr. Pascual Alvarez, who became Intendant General of the army of the Philippine Republic.

The lone objector to the dissolution of the "Departmental Government" was Mr. Feliciano Jocson, who did not resign his position in that government. But when he realized that no one acknowledged nor respected that office, he changed his tune. He then claimed that he would defend the cause and carry on the struggle began by the Supremo Andres Bonifacio, the Father of the Katipunan, who had been betrayed by avaricious elements. The Katipunan saw through his machinations, however, and shied away from him; they had not forgotten his failure to deliver the guns whose purchase had been entrusted to him. General Apoy received two letters from Mr. Jocson requesting an interview; but because of pressure of work and his disaffection for the man, he did not make any reply.

Towards the end of May 1897, the Spanish enemy attacked Maragondon. The fighting was so fierce that the dead and wounded littered the streets from the trenches up to the center of the town in front of the church and parish house. In this battle, the army of General Mariano Riego de Dios displayed an uncommon valor and gallantry. But despite their resoluteness, strength and courage, the defenders lost; because they were not only outnumbered but, more significantly, because they were sadly wanting in arms and ammunition. Maragondon was captured by the enemy, and the Government of the Philippine Republic was moved to Mt. Buntis, located between Maragondon and the site called Luok in Batangas province. And it was while the exile government was in hibernation in this wilderness that the Bonifacio brothers were executed in that vicinity. As was narrated earlier, they were killed despite the commutation of their sentence.

----

[32]Kabing, without a first name, in the typescript; Cabiling, also without a first name, in the *Ricarte Memoirs*, 51; Tomas Kabling, *The Philippine Revolution*, 59.

It should also be revealed that the ones who instigated the assassination of the brothers Andres and Procopio Bonifacio were officials who wanted to ingratiate themselves to General Emilio Aguinaldo.

XLV

Something that should not be overlooked in the chronicles of the time is the fact that the Supremo Andres Bonifacio had been a prisoner for two days at the friar estate house in Naic, then the seat of government of the Philippine Republic, when the rumor spread that all those suspected of being Bonifacio partisans would be arrested and investigated. Also, they would be accused of plotting to overthrow that government and to kill its Highest President, General Emilio Aguinaldo. According to reliable sources, all Magdiwang leaders would be investigated, among them General Apoy; the only one exception was General Mariano M. Alvarez, Minister of Welfare in that government. Subsequent events proved that the rumor was indeed based on facts.

General Apoy firmly believed that only two or three individuals were responsible for the terrible state of affairs that was wrecking their unity. And these same persons were hiding behind an armed force that they all had helped to build. Reflecting on this situation, General Apoy concluded that it was not necessary for many to give up their lives in this internal struggle; it was enough that one leader should give way to the other, but no blood need be spilt, for all available life was needed in the defense of freedom for the Motherland.

After these ruminations, General Apoy had to do something to ease the tension brought on by the disturbing rumors. At one o'clock on the same day that the news reached him, instead of taking an afternoon rest, he dressed and strapped a leather belt around his waist, tucked in a revolver and a dagger, and asked an aide to have a horse ready for him. Unlike his usual wont, he did not ask any of his mounted aides, of whom he normally had six, to escort him. Before leaving, he admonished Major Jose Mojica never to forget their commitment to the freedom of the Motherland no matter what rumors might reach them. He reminded them to be faithful guides, defenders, and benefactors of the parents, wives, and children of those brethren who would fall in the dark.

In the village between Naic and Indang, a nipa house stood along a roadside; two bamboo posts supported the end of the shed which covered the bamboo ladder leading up to the house. Around the yard was a bamboo fence with a gate opening out to the road on the east. Encircling this house were gun-carrying troops, the majority of whom were on guard at the backyard.

Inside the house upstairs, was a matron from Medicion, Imus (Cavite) known by the name of Tinang. She was related to both General Magdalo and General Apoy. When the latter stopped his horse at this house and was about to go up the stairs, the guards stopped him, their eyes flashing belligerently. Preparing himself for any eventuality, General Apoy tried to behave as prudently as he could; but he could not help taking a chance when he handed over to the guards the care of his horse while he quickly bounded up the stairs. He was met at the door by the matron who thereupon broke into wails which shook her frame. General Apoy gave her a comforting pat on the shoulder and then proceeded to join Generals Emilio Aguinaldo, Tomas Mascardo, Baldomero Aguinaldo, Mariano Trias, and other officers who were secluded in a small room in the house. He recalled that he saw Mr. Teodoro Gonzales and General Mariano Noriel, among others, rushing into the room as he came in.

The group received General Apoy most cordially. They said nothing that could have dampened the warmth of their old relationship or caused any dissension among them. They complimented General Apoy for his fine revolver and dagger; and forthwith, the latter offered, without hesitation, to give the weapons to whomever fancied them. He unsheathed the arms to show that he was earnest, but there were no takers. The visit ended with their customary light-hearted banter, and General Emilio Aguinaldo's parting words had a touch of humility:

"We are hoping that you will not part ways with us."

"No," General Apoy answered, "never shall I part with you in the defense of our Motherland."

Meanwhile, the matron Tinang had not left her place at the door where she had greeted General Apoy. She was still sobbing and weeping when he saw her again. He asked her why she was crying. She did not answer him directly, but when he was leaving she put a hand on his breast and whispered, "Be careful, my son. May God protect you!"

For a while, General Apoy was taken aback, but he quickly regained his composure. As he bowed in farewell with a smile, he was measuring in his mind's eye the height of the window from the ground below and was watching covertly the movements of the gun-toting guards. Thus he girded himself for any happenstance.... When he reached the foot of the stairs, a soldier brought him his horse. He quickly mounted it and sped away.

XLVI

The days passed with both factions—the Aguinaldo and the Bonifacio—feeling their way and gauging each other. Secluding themselves in the new town of Mainam, the Bonifacio group watched and waited, adopting a hands-off policy towards any decisions the other group was implementing.

With the advent of June 1897, the Spaniards easily took the remaining municipalities under the jurisdiction of the Magdiwang Government. These were Mendez Nuñez, Amadeo, Alfonso, Bailen, and Magallanes. They fell to enemy hands with only minimum resistance because of a dearth of ammunition among the People's troops and a decline in zeal among many resulting from the execution of the Bonifacio brothers.

Meanwhile, General Emilio Aguinaldo, accompanied by many refugees, left Mount Buntis to escape the hunger and disease that had begun to decimate them. The refugee group led by General Aguinaldo was composed of men and women, old and young. They tarried at Tagaytay and at the site called Amuling, then moved on to Talisay. At Talisay he told them:

"I commiserate with you in your suffering. I know that hunger and disease will eventually kill us if we do not do something now. I would be very happy if I could help and protect all of you; but as you can see, I am helpless now, and even the soldiers, whose lives are at stake at every moment, are complaining about the lack of food. But above all else, on behalf of the Government of the Philippine Republic that I represent, I wish to acknowledge your unforgettable and unstinting patriotism, and I pray that your love for the Motherland will endure. But because of our present predicament, the most sensible thing to do, it seems to me, is for you to return to your homes and seek the amnesty offered by the Spaniards to all those who surrender to them. This you should do in order to be able to rest and recuperate and to recover your means to livelihood, so that when sufficiently strong again, you can go back to the service of the Motherland."

After that little speech, General Emilio Aguinaldo joined his troops in a long trek to the hilly areas of Rizal province, to look for a better site for a defense position. All through the dark night, while the rain was light and heavy by turns, the General led the multitude of old and young, men and women. With the armed troops ahead of them, they trekked over the dangerous and slippery ridge on the mountains of Singay and Tagaytay. On both sides of the ridge were sheer cliffs, at the bottom of which were huge boulders. Shivering with cold and hunger, the people either quickened their pace or slowed down, depending on whether they were ascending or descending the precipitous slopes. And looming above all these physical hardships was the fear that the enemy was spying on them from some hidden lair. Those in the vanguard held up bamboo torches, but when the flame flared taller than the tips between the thumb and the little finger of an open hand [a *dangkal*], the flame was extinguished by hitting it against the ground, until only the embers were left along the path to guide the others following them. But because of the length of the line, many in the rear lost their way because the embers had burnt out by the time they caught up with them.

Most of these people came from Talisay and Atimonan (Mendez Nuñez) and had been deprived of basic needs for some time. All they had to eat in place of rice were root crops and vegetables such as squash, gourds, bananas, and wild fruits. Sometimes they had meat of wild boar or deer, but they had no salt. And since they were so many and food was so scarce, hunger was still the order of the day. Besides, they found little to shelter them except the foliage of trees; the alternating heat and cold of the earth on which they slept increased the incidence of fevers and chills.

On their way to Paliparan, the army of General Emilio Aguinaldo stopped at Mt. Kabangaan. They had only very little food left. The following day, General Apoy, accompanied by his family and some soldiers, also arrived at the same place; they, too had run out of food. General Apoy thought that he could borrow some from those who had came earlier, so for this purpose he went up the shack where Generals Emilio Aguinaldo, Pio del Pilar, Mr. Baldomero Aguinaldo and their companions were resting. When the latter group brought out all their remaining stock for all to see, they had only less than a *ganta* [measure equivalent to four kilos] of rice left, and this they were keeping for General Emilio Aguinaldo. This sad revelation was a source of mirthless laughter for everyone. General Aguinaldo had some troops go look for food to augment their very meager store in the hope that there would be enough to go around.

General Apoy got half of the little remaining stock of rice; but of course, he needed much more for his men; so he ordered those who still had some strength to rummage around for more. After procuring additional provisions, they quickly prepared a meal, which they ate at about five o'clock that afternoon. That meal was their only one that day—it was their breakfast, lunch, and supper all rolled into one.

What a painful experience it is to recall the suffering and hardship one had to endure for the sake of the Motherland.

Generals Apoy and Pio del Pilar inspected the fastnesses of Mt. Kabangaan. Deep cliffs protected the eastern side as well as the upper and lower areas, and on the western approaches were ages-old thick stone doors wrought by nature. In terms of security it was a good site; but because of its small size, it would not be able to hold a great number of troops. Moreover, it lacked basic necessities such as water; and if the enemy should blockade it, the defenders would not be able to hold out for more than two or three days.

General Emilio Aguinaldo and his companions left Mt. Kabangaan and proceeded to Malapad-na-Bato in Guadalupe, where they rested for some time. Then they crossed the Pasig River to make their way to Biyak-na-Bato.

XLVIII

While General Aguinaldo's forces headed for Biyak-na-Bato, General Apoy and his group proceeded to the community of San Vicente, in the municipality of San Pedro Tunasan, which at the time was headed by Colonel Antonino Guevara. Even before coming to San Pedro Tunasan, where he settled for some time, he had assumed the name of Salvador Alvaro. During his stay in that place, he saw how patriotic its citizens were. With all their hearts they helped and protected the Sons of the People, although ostensibly they appeared loyal to Spain (since the Spanish Government there had not yet been overthrown). More than a thousand rebels and refugees were welcomed and billeted in the best homes, where they were fed, clothed and cared for unstintingly. Needless to say, the people of San Pedro Tunasan wholeheartedly supported the Katipunan; they had a council with jurisdiction over local Katipunan councils in the towns of Muntinglupa and Biñan. Everyone belonged to the brotherhood, but no one thought of giving preferential treatment to any brethren because of their affiliation to either the Bonifacio or Aguinaldo factions. They considered all who sought sanctuary with them as Sons of the People and Katipunan brethren. Besides, they provided food and other necessities to troops in the field, such as the contingent headed by Colonel Lucas Camerino and other armed groups. The storehouse in the rice mill of "old Man Pirion" in San Vicente was the repository and source of provisions, and a special guard on duty everyday was in charge of all incoming and outgoing material for distribution to the people and the armies in the field. It also served as local post office for those involved in the struggle.

On the other hand, the municipal hall was the headquarters of the Spanish enemy. The Katipunan council kept a secret watch over the movements of this enemy camp. Thus all the actuations of the Spaniards in Muntinglupa and Biñan, which were saturated with their troops, were quickly reported to the Katipunan headquarters. And so it was that when the enemy finally reached San Pedro Tunasan, everyone had already been alerted and everything seemed peaceful, orderly, and gay; and the municipal captain or president and other local officials were at their posts at the municipal hall ready to do the Spaniards' bidding.

Mention of the tested patriotism of Katipunan members from Muntinglupa, San Pedro Tunasan, and Biñan, should not be overlooked in all the important historical accounts of the country, for they, too, risked life and blood in encounters with the enemy. They defended the Motherland; and while they fought, they gave a chance for other freedom fighters to rest and regain their strength. In San Pedro Tunasan, the leading figure responsible for rallying the people for the resistance up to 1897 was Colonel Antonio Guevara. He was aided by his brother, Pepe Guevara, and all the leading citizens of the town.

Very early one morning about the end of June 1897, when General Apoy was still staying at San Pedro Tunasan, the Katipunan council of the town received an urgent message from the Biñan chapter that one Julian Lopez (alias *Pokiap*) was being fielded by the Spaniards to spy on the Alvarezes—the father, Mariano M. Alvarez (General Mainam) and his son, General Apoy. The Spaniards received information that the Alvarezes were the leaders of many rebels who were hiding and resting in that town. The horse the spy was going to ride belonged to a Katipunan member. The latter resorted to all manner of ruses to delay the departure; for instance, he pretended to give the horse a bath before the trip. The Spaniards planned that their agent would leave at about ten o'clock that morning, and should he take more than one and a half hours to get back to Biñan, they would send reinforcements to aid him. This information was speedily relayed to General Apoy.

As soon as he learned of the plot, General Apoy went to the sugar mill which served as rebel field headquarters in the village of San Vicente. From there he immediately summoned Colonel Lucas Camerino and the two detachments with firearms under Captain Honorio Camerino and Captain Andres. With Major Jose also present, there were fifty-one men altogether. Afterwards he went to town to organize many bolo-bearing troops to reinforce the detachment with firearms.

Julian Lopez, the spy, was a native of Naic, Cavite. Before the Revolution, he had been one of the better-educated gentry. A former *directorcillo*[33] in his hometown, he spoke Spanish fluently. He had become a captain in the People's Army when the Revolution broke out, but he defected to the Spaniards when they captured Naic.

Julian Lopez arrived at San Pedro Tunasan during a critical moment for the revolutionary forces. They needed to strengthen both their gun and bolo detachments, but some troops were still aimlessly wandering the streets. Lopez came on horseback, as did his companion, a boy some thirteen years old. They met an advance guard whom Lopez had known when he was still with the rebel forces.

"Antonio! Why are you here?" Julian greeted the guard.

"I enlisted here, sir."

"Who of our former comrades are here?" Julian asked again.

"I can recognize only a few among those who enlisted."

"Have you seen General Apoy and his father?"

"No, sir, but we heard recently that he went to the municipal hall to pick the troops who would escort him to Pasig."

"Do you live here?" Julian changed his line of questioning.

"Not very far from here, sir. I live in the village of San Vicente. Come with me, sir, so you can rest."

"Yes, indeed. I'd like to talk to you some more before I leave. But if we talk here, I run the risk of being arrested by the Spaniards."

"Let's go, sir."

Julian followed Antonio, little suspecting that he was walking into a trap laid for him by troops of the People's Army.

---

[33] An extra-legal officer who acted as advisor to the *gobernadorcillo*, or municipal executive. The directorcillo exerted enormous influence in municipal affairs (Nicholas Cushner, *Spain in the Philippines, from Conquest to Revolution,* IPC Monographs no. 1, [Quezon City: Ateneo de Manila University, 1971], 264).

XLIX

As they talked, Antonio was leading Julian Lopez towards a contingent that was lying in wait. Suddenly, Colonel Lucas and Captain Andres appeared as if from nowhere and ordered them to halt. The others came out of their concealment and all aimed their guns at Julian. At first, Julian remonstrated, claiming that he was a captain of the People's Army. He produced his commission, but this was ignored. He and his companion were ordered to dismount and to put their hands up. After they were searched, Julian was relieved of his revolver, but no arms were found on the boy with him. Then Captain Andres asked for Julian's commission, and after reading it he asked, pointing to the signature,

"Who signed this?"

"My General Apoy," Julian answered.

On hearing this the captain ordered the soldiers to bind Julian tightly.

"If you acknowledge General Apoy as your General and you accord him befitting respect, why are you looking for him so that you can deliver him to the enemy for a price? Why did you not go back to your masters in Biñan instead of telling them what you did—to send soldiers after you if you did not return to them within an hour."

Julian Lopez trembled and reddened when he heard those words. Speechlessly he fell in a heap on the group. Two soldiers were ordered to beat him up, after which another two dragged him by both feet until they reached the rebel headquarters at the sugar mill. His companion was also taken, but he was not tortured, for they knew that he was a mere boy and orderly.

As soon as they reached the headquarters, Julian was brought before General Apoy. On seeing the General, Julian feel on his knees and shed copious tears. Finally he confessed that he had turned spy for the Spaniards because he needed money. He also disclosed that the Spaniards were offering one thousand pesos and a high-salaried job in their government to anyone who could identify and be instrumental in the capture of Generals Apoy, Mainam, and Magdalo. Julian said that the Spaniards considered these three to be the leaders of the great disorder in Cavite that was causing much loss of life and blood. He added that the rumored execution of Andres Bonifacio pleased the Spaniards no end.

After this confession, Julian promised that he would never again do anything treacherous against his country and people. Then in all humility, he begged to be forgiven and be spared from death. Everyone present—officers, soldiers, and townspeople chorused, "Kill that man, otherwise he will have you killed! If you allow him to escape, all of us from San Pedro Tunasan will be shot without mercy. Have him killed, or give us the authority to do so!"

When Julian heard this clamor, he collapsed and lost consciousness for a long time. Finally, General Apoy ordered that Julian and his servant be brought to headquarters and guarded closely. He himself would go there afterwards to resolve the case.

General Apoy arrived at headquarters at noon of the following day. With other officers away visiting their families, the only one left to act as officer-in-charge was Captain Honorio Camerino. The General approached Julian. He saw that the prisoner could hardly move from the many wounds and bruises he had all over the body. All night long he had been beaten up by the soldiers guarding him, but his servant who slept apart from him had received only two blows. He had lost his voice from crying; and when he cried, tears would not well any more, for the well itself had dried up. He had not been given any food nor even a drop of water to drink. Swollen, bruised, and wounded in the body and head from lashings of the *hampas tigbalang* [thorny vine], all he could do was to roll from side to side. Wordlessly, he used his eyes, which he opened and closed, to implore for mercy.

General Apoy could not stand such a look. Involuntarily, he turned his back, his heart beating fast. Overwhelmed by feelings for a fellow human being, the flaming anger inside him was smothered by the cool water of pity. After calling for Captain Honorio to tell him to feed the prisoner, he left immediately.

In the evening of the same day, Colonel Lucas Camerino came to San Pedro Tunasan to see General Apoy. He wanted to know the General's decision about the prisoners. He was of the opinion that individuals like Julian Lopez should quickly be done away with, for they had no jails to keep them in. Neither was there room for them in their barracks, which were so cramped that if the enemy should suddenly attack, the troops could easily be dispersed. But the most important consideration was that if the spy would be able to escape, he could inflict a greater harm especially to the peaceful and cooperative haven for insurgents that was San Pedro Tunasan. This was why this dangerous prisoner was beaten up. It was to weaken him so that he would not be able to escape and do more damage.

General Apoy said that up to that moment he had not yet decided on what punishment to impose on one who would sell a comrade's life and blood, but he cautioned against taking undue advantage of a defenseless person since this would be a violation of human feelings. Then he gave instructions to Colonel Lucas (Camerino) for the prisoner to be guarded closely, but at the same time to be treated well and fed properly. He added that within two days he would be back to render a decision about what to do with the prisoners.

It should be recalled that at noon of the same day that Julian Lopez and his companion were captured, over a hundred soldiers entered the town of San Pedro Tunasan from Biñan. They mixed among the people, but thanks to the discreet behavior of the townsfolk, the Spaniards did not detect the presence of rebels among them. Thus an outbreak of open hostilities was averted because of the people's loyalty to the cause of the Motherland.

Two days later, General Apoy visited the outpost at Paliparan to see the prisoners again. Colonel Camerino took him to the prisoners, and he saw that his instructions had been dutifully followed. They were strictly guarded—they could not leave the shack where they were detained without permission and without a guard—but still they were well-treated and were given the same rations as the troops. In the presence of General Apoy, Julian, the traitor against the Motherland, became as gentle as a lamb. He stood erect with arms folded; his tear-stained eyes had a sad look that matched the rest of his visage, and his voice was soft and hoarse.

With mixed feelings of indignation and pity, General Apoy interrogated Julian Lopez.

"Do you realize that you are a Filipino," General Apoy began, "a son of the Philippines, our Motherland?"

"Yes, sir."

"Do you realize that in the past, you risked spilling blood and losing life itself in defense of the freedom of our Motherland?"

"Yes, sir."

"Do you realize that one who betrays one of his race, or a kinsman, a brother or a comrade, is at traitor to the honor of the native land?"

"Yes, sir."

"If you do, then why are you betraying a brother and comrade to the enemy?"

"On my knees I already begged your forgiveness. I confessed to you that I was led to this dastardly act because of pecuniary interest; I needed the money that was promised as my reward. But when I realized my error, I regretted what I did; and even now, in your honorable presence, I promise never again to commit the same mistake. I implore you to forgive me, and I promise to continue serving the Motherland, and never again to stray from my comrades-in-arms."

General Apoy was lost in thought for some time. Then he turned to the prisoner, and in the presence of Colonel Lucas Camerino and other officers, he said "Since the circumstances did not permit that your evil intentions be carried out, and considering that the Motherland needs all of us who could serve her cause, I hereby forgive you and your companion. For the sake of love for one's fellowman, I absolve you from the terrible punishment that you deserve, but I also forbid you to leave this outpost. You must serve Colonel Lucas Camerino and help with the secretarial work of the Revolution while your young companion must serve here as an orderly. Both of you will be treated well, but if any of the troops catches you in a treacherous act or in an attempt to escape, you will be shot to death without mercy."

With his attendant following suit, Julian Lopez raised his right hand and said, "In the name of the Motherland, I promise to respect, obey and acknowledge your honorable decision."

That marked the beginning of Julian Lopez's rather long service with the revolutionary forces, which culminated in his being private secretary to Colonel Lucas Camerino. But as soon as he had ingratiated himself to his superior, and after he had taken care to provide for his personal needs, he suddenly disappeared together with his servant. They were not heard from again.

L

Before we resume chronicling the events of the Revolution, let us evaluate the relationship between General Magdalo and General Apoy. Were they brethren and comrades, or were they enemies? Readers of this account are well aware of the beginning as well as the end of the alliance between the two leaders. It will be recalled that General Apoy had to force General Magdalo to share the little remaining rice the latter had just before they parted ways at Mt. Kabangaan. Then, partisans of General Magdalo who were not pleased with the nationalistic stand of the group of the Supremo Andres Bonifacio began to poison his mind against the latter faction.

Among the leaders of the Supremo's partisans in Cavite were General Mariano M. Alvarez and his son, General Apoy.

General Magdalo was pleased by the attention of sycophants, but he did not show that their flattery turned his head. He retained his kindly nature and did not threaten or persecute those who were identified with the Supremo. There was talk that the Bonifacio followers would be investigated, but this was not carried out, as in the experience of General Apoy. However, General Magdalo maintained a distance from them, and at times he pretended that he did not know his old comrades-in-arms. While he ignored General Apoy, he never stripped him of his rank, perhaps in recognition of his untiring service to the cause of freedom for the Motherland. He also showed the same attitude to Chief General Mariano M. Alvarez, who was elected Minister of National Welfare of the Philippine Republic. He took no steps at all, whether individually or collectively, against the said generals. He simply ignored them, and the Alvarezes, in turn, did the same.

This state of affairs continued until just before the death of General Mariano M. Alvarez, the Father of the Revolution in Cavite. Before he died on April 25, 1924, the elder Alvarez reminisced about the Revolution and bequeathed a fond embrace and good wishes to all his comrades-in-arms. To General Emilio Aguinaldo, he extended thanks for his goodness and wished him security and success for the sake of the Motherland.

The people paid due homage to General Mariano M. Alvarez for his services during the Revolution. As the recognized Katipunan leader in Cavite, he was elected President of the Magdiwang Council and later was chosen Minister of National Welfare in the government headed by General Emilio Aguinaldo. For days and nights the people kept vigil over his remains, with the Veterans of the Revolution and the Knights of '96 of the Most Venerable Lodge of Isagani standing as honor guards. Among those who attended the funeral on August 31, 1924, were senators and representatives of the Philippine legislature and members of the provincial board of Cavite. Messages of condolence were received from the Governor General, the admiral's deputy, officers of the navy, the American veterans, the veterans of the Revolution from San Juan, Noveleta, Kawit, and Cavite (the provincial capital), and from Generals Tomas Mascardo, (Jose) Alejandrino and (Mariano) Riego de Dios.[34] Messages were also received

---

[34]First names of Generals Alejandrino and Riego de Dios, missing in the typescript, have been supplied by the translator. For Alejandrino, see *Aguinaldo and the Revolution*, 531; for Riego de Dios, see *Ricarte Memoirs*, 13.

from members of "United Filipinos," headed by Representative Pedro Espiritu, and from prominent citizens of Cavite, Rizal and Manila, and hundreds of others from other provinces.

General Emilio Aguinaldo arrived late at the interment because his automobile had broken down on the way. Before leaving, he talked briefly with some American veterans and the President of the Pacific Commercial Company.[35]

The Philippine constabulary band that was expected to play at the funeral failed to arrive. The captain of the band apologized to General Apoy in a letter he wrote afterwards. He explained that they were all set to leave when something unforeseen prevented them from doing so. He added that General Rafael Crame would explain everything.

A few days after the funeral, General Apoy visited General Rafael Crame of the Philippine constabulary. The latter asked enigmatically,

"Have you read the 'Song of Florante'? If you have, then you should always keep in mind its warning about a person who pretends to be your friend and to be happy to be with you...." Then he added, "Now I see that even the dead are not spared from the machinations of the living.... A ranking officer of the Veterans of the Revolution stopped the constabulary band from leaving just when they were all set to go to the funeral."

Thus ended the Story of one of the Supremo Andres Bonifacio's loyal partisans and Katipunan brethren, General Mariano M. Alvarez (May he rest in peace!), the Father of the Revolution in Cavite.

LI

Let us now turn our attention to the march of the army of the President of the Philippine Republic, General Emilio Aguinaldo, over the mountains of Rizal and Bulacan. After they left Mt. Kabangaan, they crossed the Pasig River at the site called Malapad-na-Bato and proceeded to Montalban. At the invitation of General Licerio Geronimo, they encamped at Mt. Puray. There they rested several days to allow General Aguinaldo to recover from an illness he had contracted during the march.

They were attacked by the Spaniards as soon as their whereabouts were discovered. The People's troops fearlessly fought against the enemy and

---

[35]The largest distributor of American products in the Philippines at the time.

resolutely defended the Motherland even at the cost of their own lives. After about five hours of fierce shooting, stabbing, and shouting, the Spaniards were forced to retreat, scampering over the many dead bodies of their fallen men. This battle was a signal victory for General Licerio Geronimo, Brigadier General in the army of the Supremo Andres Bonifacio. General Geronimo was then and there promoted to Lieutenant General in the army of the Philippine Republic by President Emilio Aguinaldo.

The leadership of the Republic deemed it prudent that they should continue to look for a more formidable location for its government headquarters. Led by General Licerio Geronimo, the party left Mt. Puray. After stopping at several Katipunan defense positions, they crossed Mt. Minuyan in Norzagaray to Baras-Bakal in Angat. The trek ended at Biyak-na-Bato in San Miguel de Mayumo in Bulacan, where they established the Government of the Philippine Republic. General Isidoro Torres opposed the move and refused to recognize the authority of General Emilio Aguinaldo, causing the latter to feel resentful.

Not all officials of the Philippine Republic went with General Emilio Aguinaldo to Biyak-na-Bato. Among those who were left behind in Cavite were Mariano C. Trias, Vice President; Emiliano Riego de Dios, Minister of War; Jacinto Lumbreras, Minister of State; and Pascual Alvarez, Minister of Interior. These officials established their seat of government in Mainam, the town they founded and named in honor of the President of the Magdiwang Council and who was also the first general of its army. This government had jurisdiction over the mountainous regions of Cavite and of Manila until August 1987, when Jacinto Lumbreras died of malaria and starvation. He was buried in a mountain ridge.

At the suggestion of General Miguel Malvar, the Revolutionary Government at Mainam was later transferred to Mt. Makiling, in the provinces of Laguna and Batangas. Only the Minister of War, Mr. Ariston Villanueva, and his small staff and the Minister of Finance, Mr. Diego Mojica, were left at Mainam. Charged with the defense of this town was a contingent headed by Colonel Arcadio Arrieta[36] and composed of Major Damaso Fojas, Captains Hipolito Rin, Sagas, and Arar; Lieutenants Francisco Castro, Felipe Villanueva, Military Governor Andres Villanueva, and others. Their services and sacrifices for the Motherland were ignored if

---

[36]Anarayata in the typescript and Arayata in the *Ricarte Memoirs*, 52.

not belittled by those who were at the helm of Government of the glorious Philippine Republic.

From Mt. Makiling, the Government of the Philippine Republic, headed by Vice President Mariano C. Trias, prepared to attack the Spanish enemy in the town of San Pablo, Laguna. Led by Trias himself and General Miguel Malvar, the People's Army began the siege of San Pablo in about the middle of December 1897. For three days they effectively encircled the Spaniards, but their ranks were breached when heavy enemy reinforcements came from Nagcarlan, thwarting their attempt to liberate San Pablo from the Spaniards.

In this battle, a woman revolutionary who came to be called Generala Agueda, emerged as a heroine whose daring became an inspiration for many among the People's Army. Astride a horse, she held a revolver in her right hand and the reins and a dagger in the left. Fearlessly and with head high, she charged against the enemy. She rallied the others to do the same, and many did give up their lives valiantly.

LII

Before we chronicle the actions of the Government of the Philippine Republic at Biyak-na-Bato, let us first attend to some important events that happened elsewhere. Let us review the experiences of those patriots who gallantly risked bloodshed and offered their very lives for the sake of freedom.

The patient reader, who has been closely following this account, will recall that an earlier chapter recounted the pitched battle between the Katipuneros and the Spaniards on August 30, 1896, at Mandaluyong, San Juan del Monte, Pandacan, and Santa Mesa. The Supremo Andres Bonifacio and General Ramon Bernardo each led his own Katipunan army in these encounters. And since we already know of the tragic end which befell the unforgettable Supremo Andres Bonifacio (May he rest in peace!), let us now turn our attention to another who, likewise, should not be forgotten. He is General Ramon Bernardo whose Katipunan *nom-de-guerre* was Salogo.

After the battle of Santa Mesa in which they were routed by the Spaniards, only a few of his troops survived. They dispersed and were not heard from again until Salogo went to the Magdiwang Council in Cavite. After the Revolution, Salogo wrote an account of his experience. He entrusted his memoirs to General Apoy, who is still keeping them, along with other valuable Katipunan documents, at the time of this writing in 1927. The following is General Bernardo's account:

We were defeated in the heated battle at Santa Mesa. I had a thousand troops, more or less, who were armed with either bolos or guns. We were overwhelmed by the superior number and arms of our enemy. Many of my men died or were wounded; most of those seriously wounded were captured by the Spaniards. Seeing our state of disarray, I shouted as loud as I could: "Run for your lives, everyone! Save yourselves!"

Afterwards, I also fled along with a few who were armed only with bolos. We walked all the way through Santol, Barongpipa, Kailokohan, and Matalahib. We stopped for a while at Matalahib and then proceeded towards San Francisco del Monte. After negotiating a bend in a trail leading to our destination, we saw Spanish cavalry troops armed with guns. They were riding towards us!

We tried to creep into the woods, but the enemy rained bullets on us from all sides. We were finally encircled. The enemy troops were so numerous that they were able to block effectively all passages for our escape.

It was a gloomy day. The intermittent rain soaked our clothes and we shivered from the cold and hunger. We snatched at fruits and leaves to fill our empty bellies. The sky darkened and the wind and the rain grew stronger towards midday. The heavy hail of bullets whizzing in our direction was not unlike the howling wind and rain. To save ourselves, we each went our own way except for one soldier who stuck to my side. This soldier's name was Florentino Policarpio. Fortunately for the two of us, the darkness and the stormy weather served as screen for our movements. We crawled down the canal along the bamboo thickets and woods to our escape. We did not know what happened to the rest, for we did not see them again.

We walked towards Masambong; on the way, Florentino, my companion, became sick with fever. He was so weak and tired that he wanted to lie down on the road. Finally, however, we reached Masambong. After leaving him in the care of Katipunan brethren, I went on my way to look for the Supremo and his men.

I reached Balintawak past noon, and there I met the headman of the village of Baisa. He invited me to his house; and after giving me lunch, he showed me the trail to Caloocan. I left Baisa at once, and I arrived at Caloocan at about four in the afternoon. I went to the house of Mr. Nicolas de Jesus, father-in-law of the Supremo Bonifacio, to inquire about the latter's whereabouts, but nobody could tell where he was.

It was not safe for me to tarry in the house of Mr. de Jesus, especially since only the day before the enemy had threatened to arrest him along with his daughter, Gregoria, the Supremo's wife, and his sons, Arcadio and Ariston. Moreover, the Spaniards were likely to raid houses and arrest people at that time because of the heated battle at San Juan del Monte in the morning of the same day. Instead of putting me up at his place, he asked the caretaker of a fishpond located west of the Calocan parish church to shelter me. This caretaker, whose name was Valentin, was himself a Katipunero with the *nom-de-guerre* of Bigaa.

I thought that I had a chance to rest in Valentin's hut, so I prepared to retire after supper. But hardly had I laid down my tired frame when a group of men arrived and began to pound on the frail bamboo door of the hut. "Open the door!" they demanded. "We are the law. Anyone who tries to escape will die!"

When I heard this, I quickly stood up—all my drowsiness having left me—and jumped out of the little window in the back of the shack. Meanwhile, Valentin managed to divert the men's attention by pretending the door was stuck so that he could not open it at once. I dashed into the fishpond and walked on my knees across its muddy bottom, meanwhile keeping my nose barely above the water. When I reached the sandy edge of the Manila Bay known as Dagat-dagatan, I crossed a dike and plunged into the water again, walking with my nose and eyes above the water. I went ashore at Maypajo and hid behind a *pagatpat* tree to take off my wet clothes. I squeezed out the water and put on my clothes again. Soon afterwards, I heard the bells ring out the hour of twelve midnight.

It rained hard throughout the rest of the night, and the swaying leaves did not shelter me from the rain. I got drenched again and so I had to take off my clothes once more to squeeze out the water. At about four in the morning, I could no longer stand the chill from my wet clothing so I decided to immerse myself in the water. The warm water relaxed me a bit, and in my fatigue I must have dozed off a while. I panicked when I realized that my head was under water. I got out, gasping for breath, as fast as I could. When I recovered full consciousness, I saw the reddening sky in the east. It was daybreak, August 30, 1896.

I squeezed out the water from my clothes once more and tidied myself a bit. Then I walked towards a nearby village and knocked at the first house I reached. An old woman came to the door and quickly bade me to come in. I followed her to the house and seated myself close to a window. In that position I was concealed from passersby. I asked the old lady where the hut of Valentin was. She pointed to a fishpond dike that she said I could take; and if I went right on, the first hut I could see was Valentin's.

Then the old lady made like she had a coughing spell and put her head out of the window to expectorate. Suddenly she shrugged, pulled back, and told me that in the village there was not a single male individual left because all had gone into hiding.

"Here they come again," she said, "the many civil guards and Spanish soldiers. They will raid the house in search of someone."

When I heard these words, I jumped out of the house without saying goodbye. I ran as fast as I could towards the dike leading to Valentin's hut. I had not gone far when I discerned a figure on the dike walking towards me. Because of the distance between us and the semi-darkness of dawn, I could not make out who he was, but I had no forebodings about him being an enemy. I thought he could be a fisherman or another fugitive like myself. When I came closer I saw that he was Valentin, the person I was looking for.

It turned out that Valentin himself had spent a sleepless night looking for me in the fishponds and in the foreshore area. He took me to his hut, where he fed me and made me rest and sleep the whole day. He put together some provisions for me, and after supper he put me on a little boat and rowed me to Bigaa, Bulacan. We traveled all night and reached Bigaa at about nine the following morning. He took me to the hut of another fisherman, an uncle of his, and put me under his care and protection.

I was well received in that home, not only by the owner himself, but also by all his friends and neighbors. While resting there, I thought of all the things I should do—how to organize men and collect arms, where to build defenses, and which town should first be attacked. I had spent four days thinking about and planning a strategy when I received word at dusk that that evening Spanish civil guards and soldiers were coming to raid the house in search of strangers to the place.

My host gave me a quick supper and then brought me to a ricefield bordered by thick bamboo groves. He brought along a blanket and a mat that I spread over a concealed place in the thickets. This was my bed. Early the next morning before daybreak, my host brought me farther out along the bay among the mangrove stands. In my new hiding place he brought me food and other provisions.

At five o'clock in the afternoon of September 7, 1896, Katipunan Valentin came to see me. He was riding on the same boat he had used to bring me to this place among the mangroves. He said that Katipunan brethren from Malabon, Tinajeros, and Caloocan had asked him to take me elsewhere.

We were back in Valentin's hut by the fishponds by noon of the following day. Soon a group of Katipunan leaders came to talk with me. They wanted to organize a large contingent armed with machetes and daggers for an attack on the Spanish position in the Walled City of Manila. They planned a staggered and undercover entry at the different gates and, once they had penetrated the city, they were to make a concerted attack against the Spanish garrison.

I objected on the ground that we were not ready for such an undertaking. I said we needed time for preparation; and moreover, we needed men with the resoluteness of the Japanese ,who faced all odds fearlessly in the defense of the Motherland. Because of their belief that those who died defending their Motherland had an assured place in heaven, the Japanese were psychologically prepared to die without hesitation in that manner.

"Let us get prepared," I said, "and the moment we are ready, let me know and I shall lead the attack."

In that conversation I learned that the Supremo was in Maypajo, although I could not tell in whose house he was staying, for he always kept on the move and his movements were closely guarded secrets. After our talks, Valentin accompanied me to Maypajo and took me to the house where Katipunero Policarpio Martinez (Mandaluyong) was staying. We passed through fishponds, open fields, and sparsely settled areas. We stopped at a house which happened to be the hide-out of Katipunero Manuel Martinez (Iloy), and by chance luckily stumbled upon the Supremo Andres Bonifacio. The Supremo was with Secretary Emilio Jacinto, council member Aguedo del Rosario, and Procopio Bonifacio. After we had exchanged news and views, the Supremo said that we should disperse, for it would be too risky for us all to be holed up in one house. He then advised me to look for another lodging place. Valentin and I proceeded to where Katipunero Mandaluyong was staying. I spent the night in this house while Valentin went home to his house in Caloocan. We left at past eight that night.

Very early the following morning—it was September 8, 1896—while we were eating breakfast, a Katipunero suddenly appeared at our doorstep and shouted, "The heat is on!"

Then he dashed out and fled.

We all left the table, and from a window we saw a great number of enemy civil guards and infantry approaching. We jumped out and ran for cover. Mandaluyong and I crept into the middle of a sugarcane field and stayed there until after midday when the enemy had left. When all was clear, we went back to the house to finish the meal we had started to eat that morning.

The Supremo Bonifacio and I had agreed to meet somewhere in the open field that day; but since Valentin was not disposed to leave the area, he looked for others who could escort me to where I was to meet the Supremo. He found two Katipuneros who were planning to go in the same direction I was going. They were Cenon (Sargento) and Lorenzo (Lupa). We agreed to leave at seven that evening.

The three of us started out at past seven, after we had eaten our supper. But when we had walked for about twenty-five minutes, Sargento Cenon suddenly realized that he had forgotten to bring with him something very important. Because he had to go back for it, he suggested that we resume our trip the next morning. I agreed, and we walked back slowly, carefully avoiding mudholes and swamps. The darkness and the drizzle that fell throughout the night did not help us any. We were nearing the house of Mandaluyong—that was the name by which all the folk in the area knew Policarpio Martinez—when the church bells rang out the hour of ten. We parted ways with the understanding that my two companions would pick me up at Mandaluyong's house the next day. I walked alone towards the house, but suddenly I had misgivings about spending the night at that house. The lights were already out and the people inside were surely asleep. If I went ahead, the many ferocious dogs they were keeping would raise a howl and create an uproar, so I decided to retire to a brokendown rice mill and barn behind the house. I tried to sleep on top of a big flat stone, but over-sized mosquitoes swarmed about me and kept me awake the whole night. It was only towards morning that I finally fell asleep.

Luckily, Mandaluyong passed by this place at about nine in the morning. He woke me up and took me to the house and gave me provisions. But we were soon to be jolted by shouts. Aling Isiang [Aunt

Isiang], the owner of the house, was shouting excitedly that soldiers were coming.

When we looked out, we saw a large number of troops descending on the place, and so I fled once more and hid in a sugarcane field. When the troops were gone, Mandaluyong came to bring me back the house. There I waited for the two escorts who were to take me to my rendezvous with the Supremo. When noontime came and still they had not arrived, I asked Mandaluyong to give me another guide. He chose Katipunero Ambo, but this one also failed to come.

When it was past four in the afternoon and Ambo still had not come to fetch me, I went down the house and walked to the rundown mill where I had spent the previous night. I had to do something to mitigate my anxiety and irritation. I decided to go back to the house to find out if any of my guides had come. When I turned to go, I saw that a horde of enemy civil guards and infantry troops were surrounding the house. I walked away as quickly as I could, not knowing where I was going. Soon I came upon a main road that was beginning to fill with men who were coming out of a cock-fighting gallery. I walked into the crowd, and whom did I see coming out of the gallery but my guide, Ambo! Then I knew why he failed to pick me up.

It was past six in the evening when Ambo took me to the house of Katipunero Victor, Barrio Lieutenant [administrative village head] of Balintawak. In turn, Victor escorted me to Pasong Tamo and brought me to the house of Juan, whose Katipunan name was Baging. The latter was, like Victor, also a Barrio Lieutenant. We arrived at his house at five o'clock in the morning of the following day, September 11, 1896. Since I had not eaten anything since noon of the previous day, I considered supper the meal I ate at Katipunero Baging's that early morning.

After I had rested a bit, Baging asked his brother-in-law, "Old Man Amboy," to take me to their pasture land in the site called Bilog. We were soon followed to the place by Baging and his son Roberto, also a Barrio Lieutenant. Looking around for a suitable tree where I could hide in the meanwhile, they located a big, tall one with its trunk covered all with balete, and the *lima-lima* vine. The combined foliage of the tree and its creepers was so thick that looking up from its base one would see nothing inside the crown.

They made a bed of bamboo that they hauled up and nestled inside the crown of the tree. This became my place of concealment during the day. At night they put me up in a hut in the middle of a thick strand of trees away from the footpaths. In these retreats, I never lacked provisions and visits from solicitous Katipunan brethren.

On September 13, 1896, some of my callers informed me that Lucino de la Cruz, (Ipo-Ipo) and Luis Malinis were in Balara and were organizing troops. I asked Old Man Amboy, who had been assigned as my look-out, to bring Lucino de la Cruz to see me. Lucino came at about nine in the morning the following day, when I was about to go to my retreat in the tree. Without any warning, he fired a shot and then aimed his revolver at me.

"What is the matter with you?" he reproached me. Close to tears, he was full of bitterness as he continued, "Why do you hide after inciting us to take up arms? Where is that Supremo Bonifacio now?"

"Never," I answered, "never did we hide from you. As a matter of fact, I've been looking for you so that we can talk things over. From the time we were defeated in the battles of Santa Mesa, San Juan del Monte, and Escombre, I have not yet seen any of our troops. I saw the Supremo Bonifacio and last talked to him at the house of Brother Iloy (Manual Martinez) in Maypajo, Caloocan, on September 8; but since we had to cut short our meeting, we agreed to meet again at this place so that we could talk about important matters. I cannot say whether I was too early or too late for this rendezvous, but I was delayed at Maypajo where thrice I nearly fell into the hands of the enemy. I am thankful that I have been spared from untold dangers."

I tried to pacify Lucino by speaking to him in the most placating manner I could. Apparently he was satisfied with my explanation, for afterwards he put his revolver back in its holster. We embraced fraternally. Then he took his leave, saying that he had an appointment with Captain Mariano Llanera of Cabiao, Nueva Ecija. They were to meet in the village of Kamias, and from there they would fetch me so that we could all be together at Balara.

While waiting for Lucino at Bilog, I continued to hide from the enemy by retreating to my shack at night and inside the thick crown of the tall tree during the day. My faith in the eventual victory of the Sons of the People never wavered, and for this end I often said the *Te Deum*. (The reader should know that General Ramon Bernardo (alias *Salogo*) was one of the Filipinos of the time who knew Latin. He was more facile in this tongue than in Castilian, although he studied both assiduously. As an organist in the

Catholic church at Pandacan, he gave lessons and played the organ especially when the more elaborate Masses were offered. A native of Pandacan, he was municipal head of this town at the outbreak of the Revolution. As the town executive, he was known as *Capitan* Ramon by everyone.)

Time flew quickly while I was waiting for Katipunero Lucino de la Cruz at my retreat in Bilog. Finally he arrived at about eight in the morning on Thursday, September 17, 1896. By that time, he had come to be known as General Lucino. He took me to Balara, which was not too distant from where I was staying; and after walking a while, we reached the place where we were to meet some other leaders of the Revolution. There we met Captain Mariano Llanera and his sons Eduardo, Licerio Geronimo, and Luis Malinis. All were accompanied by some troops.

There were also Pitong and Polonio, two Katipuneros from Marikina, who came to convince those bivouacked at Balara to join them at Pantayanin, their native village, which was part of the municipality of Marikina in Rizal province. Aside from its strategic location, other favorable conditions they cited were an abundance of food in the surrounding areas, ease of access to these sources, and availability of many recruits for the army.

However, the Balara forces were not disposed to leave the place; still, they did not dare turn down the invitation of Pitong and Polonio for fear of offending them. While they turned to me for advice, I knew they had no intention of leaving Balara. Lucino and Luis talked to me privately, to ask me to mediate in such a way that the Marikina leaders would not feel hurt about our rejection of their invitation to join them at Pantayanin. Thus I told Pitong and Polonio that, while we appreciated their offer, we could not possibly accept it for the present without hurting the feelings of other comrades and thus jeopardizing the Revolution. I told them that we were awaiting a contingent to join us at Balara and that if we left before they arrived, there would be nobody to attend to their needs. They would go hungry and if they tried to locate us, they might lose their way and eventually disperse; then it would be difficult to assemble them again. We could not afford to take such a risk at a time when we needed all available men and resources for our cause. I promised to go with them to inspect the site, and when I was convinced of its advantages over Balara, then we could move our camp to Pantayanin. But first I should have the troops we were waiting for be fetched so that none of our comrades would get lost.

After agreeing on this plan, the three of us—Pitong, Polonio, and myself—went to Pantayanin. But I had some mental reservations about the transfer. Should the place prove to be a disappointment, I would have the troops in Pantayanin moved to Balara instead.

We reached Pantayanin in the afternoon of the same day. There I found many people, and I saw that it was indeed a suitable base for Katipunan forces. It had an ample supply of food and other necessities, aside from being strategically located.

I chose the top of a hill, called Masuyod, as the site for building our defenses. There we encamped and built a long, barn-like structure for housing the troops. Around it, I ordered the construction of huts for the civilian population. I decreed that all who went up the hill—be they men or women, old or young—should carry with them boulders from below. Thus in a short while, we had collected a big pile of stones that we intended to hurl down upon the Spanish enemy should they persist in attacking us.

When our fort was finished, many people from various localities came in a steady stream to see it and visit us. They brought us rice, cigarettes, cigars, matches, fish, meat, vegetables, clothes, hats, sandals, shoes and other things needed by the troops in the hilly retreat. It was usual for the fort to have more than three hundred visitors during the day and to entertain the crowds; there were card games, cockfighting, and other diversions. Because of a lack of housing, the visitors began to thin out towards evening to go back to their homes in the lowlands.

This idyllic state of affairs posed a problem for me. Should I ask Balara troops to transfer to Mt. Masuyod, or should I let things be and let them stay where they were? If they were to move to this mountainous retreat, we would be overcrowded; moreover, it would still be advantageous to maintain a separate defense position at Balara. I was mulling over the problem when Katipunero Pitong approached me and surprised me with these words:

"From the time you started building this fort, we have been closely watching your every move. We became suspicious of you when we received a letter signed by one Sergeant Lucino Lozada and addressed to "Old Man Mangatlang" of Marikina. It said that you (Salogo) and Laureano Gonzales (Makabuhay) were agents of the Spanish Government and that, before you came here, the Spaniards gave you a large amount of money. Therefore you were to be watched carefully; and should your actions warrant it, you were to be arrested and not be allowed to escape.

"But now I am convinced that you are not the traitor described in the letter. It is plain from what I have observed of your character that the writer of that letter was wrong, and that it was he who was the evil one who wanted to destroy another. As a proof of our faith in your integrity, my comrades and I surrender to you this."

Pitong handed me the letter. It was written in pencil on a piece of paper that had become soiled and crumpled. I read it; and when I was through, I lifted my eyes to heaven to thank God for my deliverance. Then I bowed my head to reflect on the terrible scheme which could have destroyed me. Was it what I deserved in exchange for my loyalty to the Motherland? Then I tore the letter to pieces. What gross treachery it bore! I fixed a look at Pitong and he in turn looked at me.

"What, sir, do you propose to do about the matter?" Pitong asked.

"Jesus Christ asked His Father to forgive His enemies because they did not know what they were doing. In the same way, let us forgive Sergeant Lucino Lozada, for he was not aware that he was committing a transgression. I am very grateful to you, my brethren, for your confidence in an innocent comrade. Had you been misled, you would have considered him an evil enemy deserving of blows on the head."

When I had said my piece, I approached Pitong and embraced him. Then I took him to my other brother-officer, who received him with a fraternal embrace. Misty-eyed, all of us were thankful that things had turned out the way they did.

As I reflected on the dreadful fate that could have been mine, I recalled that the Supremo Andres Bonifacio used to say: "One who truly loves his country must be prepared to risk not only his blood and life itself, but also an ignominious death. However, the light of history will certainly set things right so that those who formerly failed to perceive the truth will be able to see things in their proper perspective. Then they themselves will realize how glorious it was to love one's Motherland. Moreover, they will in the end repudiate the traitors."

I used to disavow these thoughts, because then I believed in the saying, "The cassock is useless to a dead priest."

At about midnight on Tuesday, September 22, 1896, a group led by a Katipunero known as Lieutenant Andres came to our headquarters in Masuyod. In the group were the Lieutenant's brother, Jose, and seven others, all of whom were deserting the Spanish civil guards to join our forces. They had escaped from their garrison at Binangonan, Rizal, with fourteen Remington guns and plenty of ammunition.

Katipunero Hermogenes Bautista, whom I assigned as head soldier of the troops in Masuyod, arrived at about nine o'clock in the morning of the next day, September 23. He organized the troops and chose the ones who had to be given unallocated guns. At that time, news reached us that two convoys bearing food for Spanish troops were leaving San Mateo and Manila, respectively. The information also said that only a few soldiers were guarding the convoys. I decided that this was an excellent opportunity for ambush operations. I planned for the Balara troops to set upon the convoy from San Mateo and Masuyod contingent to take care of the convoy from Manila.

I left Masuyod for Balara the next morning at eight in order to apprise them of the ambush plan. But when I reached the site called Payong, I met Lieutenant Isyong, a Katipunero from Diliman, who said that General Lucino de la Cruz and Luis of the Balara contingent, along with their troops, had gone with Captain Mariano Llanera to Nueva Ecija. This news shattered my plan to ambush the enemy convoys. I went back to Masuyod accompanied by Lieutenant Isyong to stop the troops there from carrying out the ambush, since their Balara counterparts would not be able to participate in the operation.

LIII

So that this account of the Katipunan and the Revolution will be cohesive, let us at this point consider the narrative of Katipunero Lucino de la Cruz (Ipo-Ipo) before resuming the story of General Ramon Bernardo (Salogo).

Memoirs of General Lucino de la Cruz (alias Ipo-Ipo)[37]

After meeting with General Salogo, I left him in the village of Bilog at past ten o'clock on that Monday morning, September 14, 1896. Then I proceeded to Kamias, where I was to meet Captain Mariano Llanera, his son Eduardo, and their troops. They arrived in Kamias in the afternoon of Wednesday, September 16, 1896.

---

[37]For the sake of consistency with the preceding account, the following narrative was changed from the original third person to the first person.

The following day, the 17th, I returned to Bilog, to take General Ramon Bernardo to Balara, where Captain Mariano Llanera, Luis Malinis, Licerio Geronimo, and others were waiting for him. We did not find General Salogo at Balara, because he had gone with two Katipunan brethren from Marikina to visit his troops in Pantayanin. He wanted to transfer his men to Balara if the conditions in Pantayanin became critical.

We waited for General Salogo to come back to Balara, but after a week of waiting and still he did not arrive, we accepted the invitation of Captain Mariano Llanera to go with him to Nueva Ecija. We left Balara September 23. We were more than four hundred in that group. I carried a gun with a double barrel; Luis Malinis had a Remington; Captain Mariano Llanera had a rifle, while his son Eduardo had a revolver. In addition, Captain Llanera's men had another Remington, two piston rifles, and two small guns fashioned from iron tubes. These were all our firearms. The rest had only bolos, daggers, and lances.

We entered the town of San Jose (in Bulacan province) without any resistance at six o'clock in the evening of the same day. We battered the church door, but we encountered no enemy inside. We broke into the parish house and still saw no enemy. But we did see a long, wide table in the dining room loaded with all kinds of delicious food—roasted pigs, ham, several meat dishes, stuffed chicken, big loaves of bread, butter, pickles, vegetables cooked in various ways, sweetmeats and wines of different kinds and taste. Obviously this sumptuous fare had been prepared for many guests.

Many among the Sons of the People were tempted to partake of that bountiful spread, but the stern warning of Luis Malinis stopped them. He forbade everyone from eating or drinking anything in the parish house, for fear that food and drink there were all poisoned and were intended as bait for us. Nobody touched any food, not even water to drink.

In that town we did not see any adult male. According to a few women we saw, the civil guards and the priests had rounded up all the males and fled with them to the town of Santa Maria.

That same night, we left San Jose just after the church bell pealed the hour of ten. We walked to a village near Garay,[38] where we ate supper and retired for the night. Very early in the morning of the following day, September 24, we began to march towards Garay. At about six o'clock, when we were nearing the town, we were suddenly attacked by civil guards

---

[38]The popular name of the town of Norzagaray in Bulakan Province.

and infantrymen who rained bullets on us. A Katipunan comrade from Caloocan, Rizal, was hit on the right thigh.

Luis Malinis quickly deployed the men. He ordered those of us with bladed weapons to conceal ourselves behind a hill and those with firearms to form the first line of defense. We were positioned on top of a hill, while the enemy troops were on a ridge facing us. The enemy and we were within shouting distance and the only reason we could not hear each other was because of the continuous gunfire. Our standard bearer was Lorenzo,[39] whose Katipunan *nom-de-guerre* was Lupa. He rode a horse back and forth our line, waving the red Katipunan banner and shouting, "Long live the Motherland!"

The fighting continued until about one in the afternoon, when the enemy suddenly stopped firing and retreated, carrying their wounded with them. There were no deaths on either side, however. On our side we had only one wounded, the one hit in the thigh at the beginning of the encounter.

After we had reorganized our forces, we discovered that Captain Llanera's contingent was missing. They had slipped out of our ranks during the battle without our being aware of it. Because of this situation, we thought it prudent to go back to Balara. But just as we were leaving, we saw a group of volunteers led by Captain Jose[40] of Santa Maria rushing towards us. They had come to aid the retreating enemy.

But our troops—Luis's and mine—quickly confronted them; and after two stages of heavy fighting, Captain Jose and his volunteers withdrew. When we saw that they had retreated to a safe distance from us, we began our trek back to Balara. But we lost our way, and for two days we just walked and walked, hoping to find the right trail. Worse, we had nothing to eat, so we decided to slaughter two horses each morning. We cut the meat into equal portions, each measuring three inches square and one inch thick. The bones with meat were similarly allocated, with a piece being shared by three to five people, depending on the size of the bone to be divided. These were all the rations we had. While desperately wandering about trying to find our way, we swore that if we saw Captain Mariano Llanera and the "guide" who had deserted us, we would kill the two without mercy.

---

[39]The original typescript has a question mark after the name.
[40]The original typescript has a question mark after this name.

It was Saturday, September 26, 1896. At about five in the afternoon, General Luis and I came upon a hut. As we approached it, we saw three men jump out and run for cover into a thick clump of tall grass. We went close to the house and fired shots in the air. An old woman came out and implored us to spare the men in hiding. She explained that they were her husband and two sons and that they fled because of fear.

I placated her by saying that we were not bandits, and all that we wanted was a guide who could show us to the pasture lands of the Spaniards in Karitas. The old woman was reassured and quickly summoned her two sons from their hiding place. The two brothers readily agreed to take us to Karitas. When we reached the cattle path leading to the villa known as the "Spanish house," the brothers refused to go any farther. They feared that the enemy was lurking there since the house was used as a resthouse by Spanish civil guards.

General Luis and I told our men to stay behind while we reconnoitered the place. We went up to the house, and luckily we did not encounter anyone except the caretaker. While General Luis spoke to the caretaker, I left the house to call the troops.

It was nearly eleven that night when all our men were accommodated at Karitas as guests of the caretaker of the Spanish house. We cooked rice in five pots—a regular-sized iron pot, a large clay one, and three ordinary-sized clay pots. As soon as the rice pots began to boil, General Luis called the troops to form a queue. Each man moving up the line, after some time of waiting for the rice to cook, was given a ration of one scoop from a half-coconut shell used as a spoon. The line moved continuously to the other side, so that it was easy to tell who had gotten his ration and who had not. The ration consisted of nothing else but plain boiled rice; there was not even any salt to flavor it. The sun was already up when the last man was served, and that was after having cooked rice many times over and scooping spoonfuls for each one.

After an early breakfast on Sunday, September 27, we prepared to march back to Balara. Before we left, we asked the caretaker of the estate to give us a cow. The request was readily granted. When we reached Balara we found twenty-three men from the First Spanish Infantry waiting for us so that they could defect to our camp. They had escaped from the powder arsenal at San Juan del Monte and each brought a Remington gun and a cartridge belt full of bullets, aside from three boxes of ammunition they commonly carried.

This defection to our ranks boosted our morale. We prepared for an offensive against the enemy in the town of Montalban that we carried out in the afternoon of Tuesday, September 30. We expected to encounter a large enemy detachment, but all we battled with were the civil guards from whom we captured twelve guns. We lay in wait for the enemy until the following morning; when still they did not arrive, we went back to our base in Balara.

At three o'clock in the afternoon of Thursday, October 1, the day following our return to Balara, we received a message from General Ramon Bernardo (Salogo) sent from his headquarters at Mt. Masuyod in Marikina. The message instructed us from Balara to ambush the food convoy of the Spaniards coming from San Mateo. The Masuyod troops, on the other hand, were to waylay the convoy coming from Manila. We were to meet at the Langka River to coordinate the operations; and after the ambush we were to retreat to the same place on Sunday, October 4, 1896.

LIV

Let us put aside the account of General Lucino de la Cruz (alias *Ipo-Ipo*) and resume the story of General Ramon Bernardo (alias *Salogo*) in order to maintain a proper chronology of the whole narrative.

It was Sunday, October 4, 1896, the day set for the ambush of the food convoys for the Spanish troops. Stationed at their respective places, waiting for the convoys from San Mateo and Manila respectively, were General Luis and Lucino with the Balara troops and General Hermogenes Bautista, alias General Menes, together with Pitong and Onyong[41] with the Masuyod detachment. From where he was lying in wait, General Menes saw a *calesa* [a horse-drawn rig] coming down the road with two Spaniards, Mores and Chufre, as passengers. General Menes intended to let the Spaniards pass unmolested since they were not objects of the ambush. Moreover, only two of the enemy did not seem worth the bother. However, Chufre must have detected their presence, for he began shooting as the vehicle approached their hiding place.

"They're enemies!" the bladed weapons detachment shouted.

The Katipunan gun-bearing group responded with a volley of shots.

---

[41] They must have been the same "Pitong and Polonio from Marikina" mentioned earlier; Onyong and Polonio are nicknames for the Christian-given name Apolonio.

Chufre and Mores jumped out of the rig and tried to flee backwards. Facing the Katipuneros, they alternately fired shots as one covered the other in his flight. By protecting each other in that manner, the Spaniards hoped to retreat and return to Manila. But Mores was caught in an unguarded moment and was hacked down by General Menes with a strong swing of his bolo.

His courage shaken by the sight of his fallen comrade, Chufre began to flee in earnest to the nearest house he saw. This house was in the village of Malanday. Its owner, a sick old man over seventy years old, was alone, helpless and in bed. Chufre shot him dead and then ran to a window from where he continued shooting at the Katipuneros who pursued him.

Katipunero Lorenzo (Lupa) wanted to besiege the house to capture Chufre, but General Lucino and others prevailed upon him to desist. They came to believe that the Spaniard possessed a talisman that had the power to deflect bullets, or else how was it that he was never hit, nor even grazed at all, after so many shots fired at him? They also came to admire openly his cool courage in battle. This led General Luis Malinis to remark that Chufre's gallantry was misplaced; had it been given to a Tagalog, they would have profited no end from it in their struggle. This kind of talk praising the present enemy irritated Lorenzo Lupa. Refusing to believe that Chufre was invulnerable, Lupa set fire to the part of the house which served as its kitchen.

The fire easily spread throughout the whole house. When Chufre was cornered, he threw his gun and ammunition to the flames, jumped out of the window, and fell on both knees before the Katipuneros. Folding his hands in the manner of the Sons of the People, he cried out in all humility, "Brother! Brother!"

"You have killed two of us aside from the very sick old man whom you shot in cold blood. How dare you call us 'brother'? Now you will get your just deserts!"

General Lucino was shaking with anger as he fired two shots at Chufre. One pierced his right thigh and the other his chest. Chufre fell then and there in the burning wreckage of the house. The fire all but consumed the body, and all that was left afterwards were its charred remains.

Mores, Chufre's companion who had been killed earlier, was buried in a bank of the Langka River. General Luis Malinis took possession of his rifle and a cartridge belt filled with about 200 bullets, while General Lucino de la Cruz took his revolver. I do not recall what happened to his personal belongings like his watch, pocketbook, etc.; they could have been buried with the body.

General Luis and Lucino insisted that I accompany them back to Balara. We reached Balara at about two o'clock in the afternoon and found a message from the Supremo Andres Bonifacio waiting for us. He asked to be fetched from Tulyahan, where he was staying, so that he could join us at Balara. After we had eaten lunch, General Lucino chose eight among the gun-carrying troops and a few others among the bolo detachment to escort him to Tulyahan. General Luis assigned sentinels atop a tall tree to keep watch over the departing contingent and be ready to aid them should they encounter the enemy.

Following a trail through fields and woodland, General Luis and his troops arrived at Tulyahan at about four the same afternoon. They paid their respects to the Supremo Andres Bonifacio, who happily received them with fraternal embraces. After they had exchanged greetings, the Supremo talked privately with General Lucino, who reported on his activities since their last meeting. At the end of their interview, the Supremo gave General Lucino the authority to use the revolver and ammunition captured from Mores, Chufre's companion. He also asked who among the elder brethren were with them at Balara.

"Do you have with you Brother Andres Soriano, chairman of the San Juan del Monte Council, Brother Laureano Gonzales, chairman of the Mandaluyong Council, or Brother Romualdo Vicencio, chairman of the Patriotic Committee?"

"No, sir. None of them are there. The only elder with us, and who organizes us, is General Ramon Bernardo (alias *Salogo*)."

"That's fine. I have been wanting to talk to him," the Supremo said.

After our talk, the Supremo prepared to go with us to Balara. He asked his secretary, Emilio Jacinto, and his brother, Procopio, to get ready to join us. We all walked back to Balara, arriving there at about seven in the evening. Two long rows of gun-bearing and bolo-bearing troops lined both sides of the road leading to the camp to welcome the Supremo. After the fraternal embraces, the Supremo happily shouted over and over (with everyone repeating after him), "Long live the native land for whom we Sons of the People offer our blood and life!"

The next day was a Monday, October 5, 1896. The Supremo inspected the Balara defenses and made an inventory of guns and other weapons. He saw that while Balara was not impregnable, still it would be difficult for the enemy to penetrate it. Moreover, it had the advantage of an easy egress and, therefore, they need not fear being trapped.

They had thirty-two guns of various makes, among them Remingtons and firelocks of one or two shots. These firearms, however, would be inadequate should a great number of the enemy descend on us. We had more than 300 troops, most of whom were armed only with bolos, daggers, and lances. Those with bladed weapons were assigned to aid their gun-bearing comrades and to penetrate the enemy lines to engage them in hand-to-hand combat.

The inspections over, the Supremo invited all to a general assembly. He presided over the meeting with Secretary Emilio Jacinto at his side. He told the troops of the need to elect a commanding officer and his deputy, who were to be in charge of the Balara camp. He reminded them that the men on whom such authority would devolve should enjoy the respect and confidence of everyone. Spontaneously and in unison the men shouted, "We're all for Luis Malinis as General and Chief, and Lucino de la Cruz also as General and second in command!"

This was followed by shouts of "Long live the newly-elected generals!"

The Supremo Andres Bonifacio nodded his approval of the unanimous choices. Thus began the careers of Messrs. Luis Malinis and Lucino de la Cruz as Katipunan Generals.

The meeting and election were conducted expeditiously and were over before noon. The Supremo scheduled another meeting, this time in the afternoon, with the detachment that was defending Mt. Tungko. More than a hundred men, nearly all of whom were armed only with bladed weapons like bolos, daggers, and lances, attended the meeting. The only firearms they had were one revolver and fourteen Remington rifles. The rifles were acquisitions from civil guards who had defected from their garrison in Tinajeros, Malabon, Rizal to join the Katipuneros at Mt. Tungko. General Juan de la Cruz (alias *Palamara*) had led the defectors in their escape from the Tinajeros garrison, which was then under the command of General Mariano Gutierrez and Pedro Giron.

The Supremo authorized the men to elect their own chief officers. He admonished them to be circumspect in their choices; they should pick those who could be expected to serve faithfully and well. They should never choose anyone out of gratitude or because of friendship or kinship; they should choose only those who were able and deserving.

After a brief exchange of views and impressions, the men unanimously elected Katipunero Mariano Gutierrez to be their General and Katipunero Juan de la Cruz to be second in command. The Supremo heartily approved of their choices.

On Tuesday, October 5, 1896, the Supremo Bonifacio sent a letter to the Masuyod camp to ask them to elect their own officers also. The letter contained instructions and guidelines in the choice of leaders similar to those he gave to the detachment at Mt. Tungko.

The Supremo received a reply from the Masuyod camp reporting the results of their election. A certain Francisco (alias *Kikong Labe*) was chosen Brigadier General, and Hermogenes Bautista, his assistant. The Supremo immediately dispatched a letter to let them know that he approved their choices.

Mulling over the problems that faced the Resistance during his stay in Balara, the Supremo Bonifacio asked me (General Ramon Bernardo; alias *Salogo*) and Major Juan Reyesa (alias *Baging*) to confer with him. He asked us about the possibility of making our own weapons. After some reflection, I volunteered to relate my boyhood experience on the matter.

"We were marking the nine-day celebration preceding the feast day of our patron saint in Pandacan," I began. "Our contribution to the festivities was to make a lot of noise. This we did by exploding firecrackers and improvising with gunpowder. We searched everywhere for iron and cooper pipes which we fashioned into toy cannons. Those who could not find any iron or copper tubes made do with stout bamboo sections, which were then girdled with strong wire. This contraption was pitted against those made of iron or copper, and the explosions they produced were just as strong, if not stronger. We did have a lot of fun drowning out the noise of the firecrackers with those from our homemade cannons."

"Well, then. Let us look for ways by which we could make those mini-cannons," the Supremo declared.

"That's easy, sir," Major Juan Reyesa volunteered. This Katipunan member had had some expertise in the task, for he was a carpenter, a tinsmith, and also a mechanic. "All we have to do is look for iron or copper pipes and reinforcement in the form of coarse wire. Then we shall improvise artillery to the satisfaction of those who will use them."

The Supremo saw how zealously Major Baging and I were setting ourselves to the task of assembling the materials for the artillery we were going to produce. On his part, the Supremo instructed all milkmen who were members of the Katipunan to buy some saltpeter and sulphur each time they came home from their daily trips to Manila. He gave the same instructions to other Katipuneros who regularly commuted to and from the city as vendors. Buying only a little quantity at a time from the Chinese stores in the city that sold these chemicals, the Katipuneros were able to smuggle enough of the critical materials to accumulate a sizable supply in only a few days.

We tested the first cannons we made in the afternoons of Tuesday, October 13. We produced four, which Major Baging and I proudly presented to our assembled brethren. In front of the Supremo and all the Balara troops, I announced the auspicious event thus: "Two o'clock in the afternoon of Tuesday, October 13, 1896. For the Sons of the People ... one, two, three!"

When I let fall my upraised hand, immediately four volleys rent the air.

"Long life and liberty to the Motherland!" the Supremo cried out in joy. We all repeated the cry after him. Then he added, "Balara, you have seen and heard for the first time the sight and sound of the people's struggle for freedom!"

Having demonstrated that we could make our own ordinance, we proceeded to make more.

LV

The Supremo Bonifacio prepared for an offensive in San Mateo, which he scheduled for November 7, 1896. He planned the tactics and instructed the People's troops accordingly. Troops at Antipolo and Uyungan were to combine with the Masuyod contingent and all together were to be under the command of General Kiko (alias *Labe*). They were to guard and defend the Langka River. The Antipolo and Uyungan detachments numbered more than a hundred armed men, of whom thirty-two had firearms. They also had two small cannons.

The Mt. Tungko troops, under Brigadier General Mariano Gutierrez, he assigned along the periphery of San Mateo town. The main army that the Supremo himself would lead was to consist of the Balara detachment, under Generals Luis Malinis and Lucino de la Cruz, and whatever contingents might arrive to join them in the attack and seizure of the garrison of San Mateo. Each group prepared to carry out its assignment accordingly.

At ten o'clock in the morning of the day of the siege, all contingents were in their assigned positions. Katipunan troops were guarding the Langka

River and the other entrances to the town. Inside the town itself, the Supremo had his men deployed 250 yards from the church yard and parish house where the Spanish troops and civil guards were quartered. They had six cannons poised in readiness against the enemy position. Meanwhile, the hundred-strong Balara troops led by Generals Luis Malinis and Lucino de la Cruz surrounded the town hall.

Suddenly guns and cannons unleashed angry, hissing bullets. Figures stampeded and scampered away in all directions. With every bullet fired, the Sons of the People were spilling life-giving blood on the hot and parched earth of the Motherland to coax it to bloom and give fruition to the freedom for which they most devoutly wished. Let it never be said that the cry for freedom was an empty one, bereft of flower and fruit like the cypress of the lonely graveyards.

After a whole day of fighting, the Katipunan troops failed to make any headway. On the side of the Spanish forces, they fired fewer and fewer shots as evening fell; obviously this was a tactic to save ammunition.

Katipunero Lorenzo (alias *Lupa*) thought of a plan to exhaust the enemy's ammunition. One of the newly-elected lieutenants, he volunteered to be a decoy to sally back and forth in front of the parish house for the enemy to shoot at. But when he asked the Supremo Bonifacio to permit him to carry out his plan, the latter refused. The Supremo would not allow such bravado. He said that they could not afford to risk a life through such foolhardy daring. He said that to lose a life in battle was the honorable way to die, not in such a show-off manner.

Then suddenly the Spanish forces began to fire furiously once more at the People's troops. The Katipuneros returned the fire, but intermittently. With each flash of light from the bullets, they discerned a shadowy figure walking back and forth in front of the enemy line. The Supremo ordered a halt to the firing in order to find out who was exposing himself so foolishly. Out of curiosity, several crawled in the darkness to see who it was. Finally they recognized him to be Lieutenant Lorenzo (alias *Sianong Lupa*), who obstinately carried out his scheme despite the Supremo's disapproval. The Supremo then called for the recalcitrant Lieutenant to report to him at once.

After reprimanding Lupa, the Supremo ordered his troops to make as fast as they could ten effigies the size of the average male. The men quickly made these from banana trunks and straw, and on the heads they put their own headgear. He asked Lupa to put up the effigies in front of the church and parish house. The whole night the Spaniards vented their fire and spent their ammunition on the effigies. Their expected troop reinforcements from Marikina failed to arrive, because that afternoon they had been repulsed by the advance guards of the People's Army under General Kiko (alias *Labe*) at the Langka River approach to the town.

The next day, November 8, the Supremo had a sled covered with *carabao* hide to be used as a protective vehicle in their approach to the holed-up enemy. However, the device proved futile, because even the layers of raw hide were not protection enough from the enemy bullets.

On the same day, more enemy troops from Marikina again tried to penetrate the Langka River approach, but General Kiko Labe's advance guards drove them back with even greater courage and heroism than in the previous encounters. Thus the Spaniards were frustrated again in the second attempt to reinforce their beleaguered troops inside the town of San Mateo.

In the afternoon, the Supremo Bonifacio called a caucus of the revolutionary leaders with him to ask their advice about the tactics they should adopt to make the enemy surrender in as short a time as possible. Meeting at the San Mateo town hall, they unanimously agreed on a blockade to starve the enemy. Meanwhile, they were to continue firing, but sparingly; and when the enemy troops weakened from hunger and ran out of ammunition, then the Sons of the People would make an all-out thrust to kill all who resisted and pardon those who surrendered. After this meeting, the Supremo distributed arms to his troops and inquired about their situation. He asked if they were getting enough food and other provisions and if they had adequate accommodations.

As the battle raged, one known in the Katipunan ranks as Colonel Bato got away with an escapade. He saw a woman walking near the barracks while he was girding his soldiers for battle. Suddenly seized by desire, he laid her down and the poor helpless woman could do nothing but weep. Tears nearly bathing her whole body and deep sighs seemed to be the only recourse she had to cover her discomfiture. Unable to get up on her feet at once, she broke into another fit of heart-broken weeping when she finally got up. Then, before quitting the scene, with trembling lips and timorous voice, she respectfully thanked the man who ravaged her!

The next day, November 9, another big contingent of Spanish forces from Marikina arrived at the Langka River defense position in a fresh attempt to rescue their comrades in the San Mateo church and parish house. The men under General Labe again demonstrated their gallantry and skill in battle. Fearlessly risking their lives, they seemed to thrive on the bursts of gunfire and melee everywhere. The leader of the Antipolo detachment, who was known as Lieutenant Abra, kept shouting to his troops to advance and attack; but not long afterwards a bullet hit him in the mouth and pierced his head. He fell dead instantaneously.

After this incident, a larger enemy force consisting of guerrillas, cavalry, infantry, artillery, and civil guards surreptitiously descended on the Langka River position. Caught unawares, the troops of General Labe were easily surrounded. The General himself fled without giving any orders; and when the rank and file realized their predicament, they fell into disarray. Each one sought his own safety; and in the flight, only the gravely wounded and the dead were left behind. Thus, without firing a single shot, the enemy was able to cross the Langka River and then negotiate the Ampid River into San Mateo town.

Meanwhile, the Katipunan forces who were quartered at the town hall continued to blockade the enemy in the church and parish house. Then suddenly they saw troops approaching whose color they could not quite make out at once. Were they friends, or were they enemies?

As the troops came nearer they saw some fifty Tagalog infantrymen with their left hands on their hips in the Katipunan manner. They had fixed bayonets on their guns which they carried upright, and little white handkerchiefs fluttered from the tips of their bayonets.

Doubt gave way to joy in the thought that their Katipunan brethren had come to their aid. Numbering about 3,000, the Katipuneros surged pell-mell towards the advancing troops. But when they were within shouting distance, the Katipuneros noticed that the troops they were happily rushing to meet were slowing down their pace. Thinking that their approaching brethren were intimidated by their great number, the Supremo sought to reassure them by shouting as loud as he could: "Long live the Katipunan! Long live the country's freedom!"

The other Katipuneros followed suit and rushed to embrace the others whom they took to be their brothers. Little did they suspect that the latter were as ready to attack them as they were to welcome the others as comrades. Hardly had their jubilant shouts died down when a sonorous Castilian voice boomed, "Fire!"

Without hesitation, the approaching infantry troops began firing at the Katipuneros. The latter dispersed as each one sought to save himself. What seemed miraculous in the face of such onslaught was that not a single one of the 3,000 men died, and only four were slightly wounded. The Supremo Bonifacio surmised that most of the troops in the enemy force were their own sympathizers, if not true Katipuneros, and that they had fired their guns upwards so that they caused only a minimum of injury to the Katipunan ranks. Had it been otherwise, many would have been wounded and killed.

As soon as General Luis Malinis saw that the incoming troops were enemies, and not Katipunan brethren whom they had mistakenly welcomed, he quickly organized a contingent to halt the enemy's advance. But because of the confusion that ensued when the troops began deserting their ranks, General Malinis was able to muster only seven infantrymen. He deployed them singly on both sides of the road, with the warning that should they attempt to desert he would shoot them at once. The chosen seven went about their task with alacrity as each one knelt on his left knee and began to shoot furiously at the enemy. On his part, General Malinis stood in the middle of the road and, with consummate heroism, fired openly at the Spanish forces. By such tactics, he was able to delay the enemy's advance and to cover the escape of the Supremo Andres Bonifacio and the other Katipunan leaders with him.

The Supremo and his companions, including Colonel Bato, retreated in the direction of Montalban. Except for the four who had guns, the troops accompanying them were armed only with bolos. They encountered a Spanish contingent, which had detached itself from the main force in San Mateo, in order to surround and subdue General Malinis's small band. But instead, this contingent chanced upon the Supremo's fleeing group. They pursued the latter without being detected until they began firing.

Despite their own lack of firepower, the Katipuneros turned around and fought back. Colonel Bato—he who had violated a woman—was hit in the head; he died on the spot. The Katipunan troops were routed once more and were forced to disperse and flee. Enemy reinforcements arrived and the Spaniards retook the town of San Mateo.

The Supremo's army reached Montalban, but the following day they had to leave again to evade the enemy who had pursued them there. They retreated to Balara where they established their base. When it became known that the Supremo was in Balara, other Katipuneros who had strayed came trooping in and congregated there.

LVI

Continuation of General Ramon Bernardo's Account

In the afternoon of November 11, 1896, the Supremo Bonifacio gave me a letter to deliver to President Emilio Aguinaldo of the Magdalo Council and President Mariano Alvarez of the Magdiwang Council. The latter contained a report of our situation and of the battles we fought. I left at six in the evening of the same day accompanied by brethren from Pasig— Katipunero Bruno of Ugong, Captain Selmo of Pineda, and a few others. After crossing Krus-na-Ligas, we took the Marikina road, the Blumadero road, the Escombre road; then we went through Mapuntod, Maliklik, and Bulak. When we reached Pineda, we ate supper and rested. At ten o'clock that same night we resumed our journey. After crossing the Pasig River, we walked to Malapad-na-Bato; then we took the Daang-hari road until we reached the village of Almanza in Zapote, Cavite.

When we arrived at the Magdalo fortifications in Zapote, it was six o'clock in the morning of the following day, November 12. The guards refused to let us in because they did not know who we were or what our business was. The situation was especially delicate since, at that precise time, the Magdalo were fighting two separate battles, one in Noveleta and the other in Cavite.[42] However, when I showed them the letter from the Supremo that I was carrying, they allowed us in and assigned a soldier to take us to General Aguinaldo. As he was then busy with the emergency at Binakayan, General Aguinaldo had little time for us. After meeting us, he dispatched a soldier to take the letter we had brought to be delivered to the Magdiwang Council. Then he told us to wait for the reply.

While we were waiting, the General had a little respite from his duties on the front. He was about to write his own reply to the Supremo's letter when the answer from the Magdiwang Council arrived. The Magdiwang letter requested General Aguinaldo to send the bearer of the Supremo's letter to their headquarters and to provide him and his party a safety pass.

Thus we reached Magdiwang territory, where we enjoyed the warm hospitality of their Captain General, Mr. Santiago V. Alvarez (alias *Apoy*). There I stayed until the Supremo Bonifacio arrived in Cavite province.

---

[42]The author must have meant Binakayan instead of Cavite. Cf., *Aguinaldo and the Revolution*, 55.

Before I end my narrative, I wish to say that while at Balara, the Supremo Bonifacio promoted me to the rank of General of a division and placed the troops at Balara, Tungko, and Masuyod under my command. However, I refused the new assignment because I knew my limitations as a military commander. I told the Supremo that I could serve the Katipunan better as a humble deputy of the Supreme Council of the Sons of the People.

LVII

Additional Accounts as Narrated by Colonel Genaro de los Reyes

[*Author's note*: Katipunero Genaro de los Reyes (alias *Bato-Balani*), of Mandaluyong, Rizal, was personal assistant of the Supremo Andres Bonifacio. He held the rank of colonel in the Katipunan army. The following is his narration of events he witnessed, heard about, or experienced in the days before the Aguinaldo government was set up at Biyak-na-Bato.]

Led by the Supremo Andres Bonifacio, General Ramon Bernardo and General Kalentong (Vicente Leyba of Mandaluyong), the Sons of the People seized the enemy's powder arsenal called "Polvorista" in San Juan del Monte on August 29, 1896. The following day, Sunday, the 30th, the Supremo asked General Lucino (de la Cruz) and me to investigate if there were battle casualties, dead or wounded, among the Katipunan ranks. He instructed us to rescue the wounded, bury the dead if possible, and try to collect firearms so that these would not fall to enemy hands. He left the means to carry out the mission to our own devices. But because the encounter was still very recent, General Lucino and I decided against any precipitate action. We agreed to go about our task separately and then we parted ways.

I began looking for General Lucino and the Supremo on a Thursday, August 3, 1896. I wanted to see the former in order to clarify certain matters with him, and the latter so that I could report on the task he had assigned me. When I reached Balara, I went to the house of the village head, Mr. Pablo Garcia, who gave me a warm fraternal welcome. Mr. Garcia's Katipunan *nom-de-guerre* was Bayog. However, he could not give me any information as to the whereabouts of the Supremo and General Malinis. (He must have meant General Lucino de la Cruz).

In Headman Garcia's house, I met Domingo Malinis and his son, Luis, who were both well-known bandits, but had become steadfast defenders of freedom during the Revolution. I met the father first and soon after we started talking, the son arrived. With the help of my host, I seized on the opportunity to enlist father and son in the Katipunan. I explained to them that the secret society had been founded by the Supremo Andres Bonifacio in order to break the strong fetters binding the Motherland to slavery. I told them that Katipunan members, bound by fraternal love and affection, identified themselves by means of secret signals. I was able to convince father and son to become Katipuneros; but due to the limited time and because I did not have all the materials for testing neophytes, all I could do was to give them counsel and to explain the principles guiding the Sons of the People.

"For three generations," I explained, "the Spaniards have been enslaving the Philippines. Now they are an irritable lot and they kill off anyone who comes out in defense of reason. They came as conquerors, and along with the members of the religious orders, they trampled upon our lives and seized our properties. Using religion as a means of deceiving the people, they appropriated our land and resources. These dastardly acts were then validated and legalized by the government they established and headed. In the three hundred years of their rule, the administrators could have learned our national language in order to have a better rapport with the people they were ruling, but they did not. On our part, we have no desire to propagate their language and use it for rapprochement with them.

"Their schools are full of the teaching of prayers, to make us Filipinos continue believing in miracles of saints and to keep us submissive to priestly authority by making us believe that priests have power over our bodies and souls. Through the confessionals, the priests have access to all our secret thoughts and activities. They use the confessional to collect information. The priests oblige us to tell them what we know, hear, and see of other people's activities. Forbidden to reveal what was told them at the confessional, they unilaterally make decisions and impose penances.

"Only one of every 10,000 Filipinos gets the opportunity to pursue higher education and become a lawyer, priest, etc. But should any of these few educated ones try to defend justice in the light of what his enlightened outlook compels him to do, he at once becomes an object of scorn and is exiled or imprisoned for life, or killed. They trample upon the life and blood of our beloved parents and plunder openly or covertly the wealth which should be our patrimony.

"Thus we see that the oppression we suffer from the Spanish Government is no trifling matter. The time has come for us to rescue our Motherland and uphold our integrity and sacred rights. It is high time that we avenge the dishonor and outrage committed by the rapacious government on our parents and brethren.

"Did you understand well all that I have said?" I asked after a brief pause.

"Yes, sir. We understood everything well," father and son answered.

"Well, then, what can you say about what I have just explained to you?"

"We agree that it is time for us to avenge the numerous outrages done to our people. We can not bear their oppression any longer."

When I heard those words from the Malinises, I jumped up and laid my hands on their shoulders and said, "Thank you, my brethren. I am so happy to know that you have been convinced about the need to rise in defense of our people's honor. But before I embrace you tight into our fold, I must read to you the sublime principles of the Katipunan so that you may decide to accept them or not."

Then I got a copy out of my pocket and read to them the following:

The Code of Ethics of The Sons of The People

A life that is not dedicated to a noble cause is like a tree without shade, or a poisonous weed.

A deed lacks nobility if it is motivated by self-interest and not by a sincere desire to help.

True piety consists of being charitable, loving one's fellowmen, and being judicious in behavior, speech, and deed.

All men are equal regardless of the color of their skin. While one could have more schooling, wealth, or beauty than another, yet all that does not make one more human than anybody else.

A person with a noble character values honor above self-interest, while a person with a base character values self-interest above honor.

To a man of honor, his word is a pledge.

Don't waste time; lost wealth can be retrieved but time lost is lost forever.

Defend the oppressed and fight the oppressor.

The wise one is careful in all he has to say and is discreet about
    things that need to be kept secret.

In the thorny path of life, the man leads the way and his wife and
    children follow. If the leader goes the way to perdition, so do
    the followers.

Never regard a woman as an object for you to trifle with; rather,
    you should consider her as a partner and a helpmate.

Give proper considerations to a woman's frailty and never forget
    that your own mother, who brought you forth and who
    nurtured you from infancy, is herself such a person.

Don't do unto others what you don't want done to your wife,
    children, and brothers and sisters.

A man's worth is not measured by his station in life, neither by the
    height of his nose nor the fairness of his skin, and certainly
    not by whether he is a priest claiming to be God's deputy.

Even if he is a tribesman from the hills and speaks only his own
    tongue, a man is truly an honorable man if he possesses a
    good character, is true to his word, has fine perceptions, and is
    loyal to his native land.

When these teachings shall have been propagated and the glorious
    sun of freedom begins to shine on these poor islands to
    enlighten a united race and people, then all the lives lost, all
    the struggle and sacrifices will not have been in vain.

"If the applicant has understood the above precepts and believes that he
can carry out the responsibilities that membership in the organization
entails, then he can be inducted subsequently. What is your reply?" I asked
finally.

"We understood everything well, sir. We respect and subscribe to the
great Katipunan ideals," the Malinis father and son answered with alacrity.

"If that is the case," I (Colonel de los Reyes) continued, "please kneel
down, fold your arms, look up to the sky and say after me the Katipunan
oath."

Father and son promptly fell on their knees and took the following
oath:

From this day forward, we pledge before the universe that we
are true brethren of the Katipunan of the Sons of the People. We

respect its teachings and ideals. We pledge all manner of sacrifice, even our blood and life itself, for the sake of freedom for the Motherland. We also pledge to love our brethren, protect and cherish their welfare, and defend them against their oppressors. May the Almighty God help us! Amen.

On a sheet of writing paper, I wrote in pencil a certification of their having been inducted into the Katipunan. This they held as they knelt to take their oath. Afterwards, father and son signed the document with their own blood. Then I embraced them tightly, calling each of them "Brother!"

I inducted the Malinis father and son into the Katipunan not in the prescribed way, but in my own fashion because I did not have the necessary paraphernalia. I improvised on the ritual and in my improvisation, Katipunero Bayog (village head Pablo Garcia), who witnessed the ceremony, was much surprised because that was not the way he himself had been inducted. I did not bother to write their Katipunan names, because I thought this was unnecessary since the times called for an open struggle and hiding behind a *nom-de-guerre* was uncalled for.

After the oath-taking, I made a little speech about what they as Katipunan members were expected to do. They should fight all evil, especially those individuals who commit injustice and violate a fellowman's peace and honor; they should continue to fight the Spanish enemy as a matter of course. I also instructed them to enlist as many troops as they could and to strengthen the Balara defense.

I performed the ceremony in my capacity as colonel and as a personal deputy and guard of honor of the Supremo Andres Bonifacio. I had two soldiers with me who were carrying thirteen Remington guns aside from ammunition; these arms I was to turn over to the Supremo. In order to bolster his enthusiasm, I entrusted the arms, along with a letter, to Luis Malinis for delivery to the Supremo. The letter contained a report of the outcome of a mission he had entrusted me with.

LVII

Colonel Genaro de los Reyes's Account Continued

After I had inducted Domingo Malinis and his son, Luis, into the Katipunan, I left Balara for Pantayanin and Masuyod. In Masuyod I met some Katipuneros, among them Sixto de la Paz, Treasurer of the Marikina

Council, and Hermogenes Bautista (alias *Bara*) who put the Pantayanin defense position in order. At Pantayanin I rested for a few days in the home of Katipunero Modesto Mangatlang; there I met other Katipuneros, among them Simeon de Jesus; Elias Leoncio Lopez (alias *Payapa)*, Simeon Lopez, and Martin Torres.

General Ramon Bernardo (alias *Salogo*) together with Katipuneros Agapito de Leon and Pablo Carpio, arrived at Pantayanin just as I was about to leave the place. I asked them where I could find the Supremo, but none of them had any idea where he was; the only information I got from them was that General Salogo had met him last at Maypajo, Caloocan. I tarried a few more days before continuing my search for the Supremo.

I went to Pasong Malapad-na-Bato, in Balara, where I saw General Lucino de la Cruz and a large number of men under the command of Luis Malinis. At that time, Mariano Lanera and his son Eduardo were visiting the camp; with them were troops they had brought over from Cabiao, Nueva Ecija. The Llaneras were also looking for the Supremo Bonifacio. They wanted to invite him and all the troops in Balara to join them in their camp in Nueva Ecija.

After resting for four days in Balara, I went to all the Katipunan emplacements in the hills in search of the Supremo, but he was nowhere to be found and neither could anyone tell me where he was. Finally I reached Pineda, where I met General Kalentong, who invited me to go to Cavite where he said he had a cache of seven Remingtons and a stock of ammunition. However, I declined his invitation, for I wanted to continue looking for the Supremo. My search took me through Diliman and on to San Francisco del Monte. At the latter place, I encountered Faustino Guillermo, who was organizing many troops on his own initiative. Seeing how busy he was, I did not have an opportunity to ask him about the whereabouts of the Supremo.

From San Francisco del Monte I proceeded to Bago Bantay. The village head, Mr. Regino Deliguado, informed me that Generals Luis Malinis and Lucino de la Cruz had been on their way to Nueva Ecija with the Llaneras when they had an encounter with the enemy at Santa Maria, Bulacan. During the battle, the Llanera group had broken away unnoticed. The rest of the Katipunan ranks dispersed with Luis and Lucino, retreating to Balara. The Katipuneros got lost in the wilderness and, fatigued from sleeplessness and hunger, they suffered untold hardships.

Soon after hearing this news, I went to Balara. There I saw Luis Malinis, who confirmed the information that his group had gone with Captain Mariano Llanera with the intention of going to Nueva Ecija, but they had been intercepted by the enemy at Santa Maria. He also told me that Lucino de la Cruz and some soldiers had gone to Tulyahan to escort the Supremo Bonifacio back to Balara. True enough, the party returned soon after, with the Supremo being accompanied by his brother, Procopio, and Secretary Emilio Jacinto. It was a poignant meeting for us as we shed tears of sadness and joy at seeing each other again.

The Supremo busied himself with matters of organization while at Balara. On Monday, October 5, 1896, he confirmed the election of generals chosen by the army. Among them were those of Katipunero Licerio Geronimo and General Ramon Bernardo. He appointed the former as Brigadier General and commissioned him to organize and command troops; the latter he promoted to General of a division. On hearing of his new appointment, General Bernardo begged the Supremo to revoke it, arguing that he could better serve the Revolution as deputy in the Supreme Council of the Sons of the People. The Supremo acceded to his request and assigned General Hermogenes Bautista instead. Then he appointed me (Colonel Bato-Balani), along with General Francisco de Asis, to command the defense position at Pantayanin and Masuyod. He also asked me to investigate at once the best routes and outposts we should take in the siege of San Mateo we were soon to undertake.

In a week's time, through the initiative of the Supremo and under the supervision of Salogo and Baging, four small cannons were made from iron tubes bound by course wires. After they had been tested and found satisfactory, everyone was pleased over the achievement. Preparations were made for the San Mateo offensive. I finished my report on the routes and outposts the troops were to take; stocks of saltpeter and sulphur for the canons were purchased by milkmen who were free to go in and out of the city of Manila; the leading troops were primed for action.

When everything was ready, the Supremo ordered me and General Francisco de Asis to deploy our troops to guard the Langka River approach. We were to have the tactical support of other detachments under their respective officers. Meanwhile, he asked Luis Malinis, Lucino de la Cruz, and Mariano Gutierrez to get their troops ready to accompany him in the siege of San Mateo on Saturday, November 7, 1896.

LIX

General Genaro de los Reyes's Account Continued

Just before the San Mateo operations were carried out, two prominent citizens of this town were identified as collaborators and spies. They were known to be responsible for the arrest and torture of anyone they suspected to be on the side of the defenders of freedom. Families of Katipuneros who had been thus tortured pleaded with the Supremo Andres Bonifacio to arrest and execute the collaborators. The two spies were duly arrested, but when they were about to be executed, I (Colonel Genaro de los Reyes) hastily dispatched a letter to the Supremo through Katipunero Mariano (alias *Bataling*). In that letter, I interceded for one of the prisoners who happened to be my cousin. I implored the Supremo to stay the execution of this relative and that I would take full responsibility for his subsequent behavior if his life were spared. My cousin's life was indeed spared, but not the other's, whose head was mounted on a stake and exhibited in the center of the town.

Before noon of that Saturday, November 7, our forces were deployed and ready for action inside the town of San Mateo and along the Langka River. Katipunan morale was high as we swaggered around the town, confident with the knowledge that the enemy had holed themselves up in the town church and parish house. Men armed with bolos freely visited us at the Langka River outposts and happily reported on the excellent situation in town. Helping me in the defense of the perimeter at Langka were General Francisco de Asis (alias *Labe*), troop chief Atilano Santa Ana, and one Luciano, who led a band of his fellow hillsmen. Later on our ranks were swelled by the contingent led by Katipunero Juan de la Cruz (alias *Palamara*). Palamara's group brought with them two small cannons and thirteen Remington guns. Later, however, Palamara decided to join forces with our comrades in town, who seemed to have more urgent need for reinforcements than we did, since the enemy was concentrated there. But before they left, I convinced them to leave their arms with us.

On Sunday afternoon, November 8, a large group of enemy forces consisting of civil guards and infantry descended on our Langka River position. We immediately opened fire and after two phases of fierce exchange of firepower, we succeeded in repulsing them. They retreated to their garrison in Marikina.

At nine o'clock that evening, Juan de la Cruz came to retrieve the arms he and his group had left with us, because they were anticipating a heated battle in the town. Shortly afterwards, Katipunero Angel de Guzman, Barrio Lieutenant of Bayan-bayan in Marikina, came to inform us of the arrival at the Marikina garrison of a large number of enemy troops from Manila. Intended to aid the beleaguered enemy inside the town, the group was made up of Spaniards as well as of Tagalog troops. They were to enter the town early the next morning, so I immediately alerted our troops for action.

"With courage and correct leadership," I reminded the officers, "we shall surely win. But if we give way to laxity and fear, we will be annihilated. Any comments?"

"If we are to die, let us die fighting!" General Francisco de Asis shouted. To this statement everyone responded with "Long live the Katipunan!"

Very early in the morning of Monday, November 9, our sentinel atop a large tree descended quickly to tell us that he had just sighted a large number of enemy troops. We immediately readied our forces. I called the troop heads Kiko,[43] Atilano, and Luciano, of the band of hillsmen, and told them: "Troops derive their courage from their superiors, so take care not to let your men down."

"Aye! We are seasoned in struggle!" they answered. To their men they said, "Be ready to collect [enemy] guns!"

I snatched a few minutes to write to the Supremo Bonifacio, to report to him that we had surrounded the enemy in town and that we were bracing for a major battle. However, as soon as I had handed my letter to the soldier who was to deliver it to the Supremo, the enemy opened fire. Soon the bullets came thick and fast.

Fazed by the advancing enemy troops, a soldier of Captain Atilano Santa Ana's contingent began shouting obscenities at the Spanish forces. When I ordered him to keep quiet, he faced me and said, "Go away if you are afraid!"

Then he aimed his gun at me, but at that precise moment he reeled and fell on his face to the ground. An enemy bullet had hit him in the mouth and pierced his head. I immediately picked up his gun.

The barrage of enemy bullets from their many guns and mountain cannon defoliated the bamboo and tamarind trees and other vegetation. It

---

[43]Nickname for Francisco—a reference to General Francisco de Asis.

plowed through and tore up the sod, and of course, it killed men and beasts. I rushed to the band of hillsmen and shouted, "Dive!"

"Aye! But we are going to die!" their chief answered me.

Once more I ordered them to dive, but instead of jumping into the water they spirited away in retreat. They did not miss seeing General Francisco de Asis (alias *Labe*) running away ahead of them and calling my attention to the spectacle. This negative example led to mass desertion from our ranks and the easy penetration of our lines by the enemy.

Left alone, I could do nothing but follow suit. I lugged with me, aside from my own rifle, the gun of the fallen one who had cursed the enemy and the revolver thrown away by Captain Atilano Santa Ana. I found a trail that made a shortcut to the hills. While following this trail, I felt a hot spot at the tip of my eyebrows above the cheek. The hand that I pressed to the spot was instantly smeared with blood. Frightened, I ran even faster. I began to feel giddy; and when I thought I had traveled a sufficient distance from where I started, I stopped to rest and probe the bleeding spot. I discovered that it was only a surface wound caused by a bullet that had grazed the skin. I continued my trek up Mt. Patiis. In the paddies that I passed, I collected twelve Remington guns that the troops had thrown away during their flight. In this way, I traced the trail of the fleeing troops to the hilltop.

There I saw a hut with some people inside. I asked if they had seen some Katipuneros passing that way, and if they had, in what direction they had gone.

"A great number of them passed this way, all of them running. They took different directions—some went down the river while others went eastward. One of them, sir, is still around. He is up in the tallest mango tree in front of you. I heard from the fleeing men that the one up the tree is a general."

I went under the particular tree pointed out to me and shouted repeatedly at the one up there to come down. But instead of coming down, he hid himself more securely among the thick foliage at the top. Finally, I decided to fire two shots in the air to scare him. That did it, for then and there I heard a voice saying he was coming down. Soon I was face to face with the erstwhile fugitive, none other than General Kiko (Francisco de Asis) himself!

"Why did you run away?" I exploded. "Most of the troops followed your example; and as a result, our defense lines were completely broken."

"I became wretchedly frightened when a cannon ball nearly hit my head. The only reason I'm still alive is because I ducked when I saw it coming."

"In that case," I said, "please go to San Mateo and report to the Supremo what happened to our Langka River position. We face a grave culpability for allowing the enemy to overrun us at Langka without warning our comrades in town about our defeat."

"Please forgive me, sir. I can no longer face the battlefield. I already told you I am scared. Ask somebody else to deliver the message."

With this confession, I decided to make the report to the Supremo myself and to send the poor fellow to return the guns I had with me to the Pantayanin post. I told him to wait for me at Pantayanin, and this he promised to do.

I was on my way to San Mateo when I luckily chanced upon a dark, fat horse in an open field. I mounted it and sped to my destination. When I was nearing the town, I saw a man running out towards the paddy fields. I stopped to ask him what was the matter. He said that the Spaniards in town were shooting in all directions, despite the fact that the Katipuneros had already fled. I then decided to go to Balara instead; I surmised that the Supremo must have retreated there. But when I reached Balara, I found the place deserted. I turned back and proceeded to Montalban, where I finally found the Supremo. I was relieved to see him safe and sound. He was then busy supervising the construction of defenses in the villages of Burgos and San Rafael. After a tearful greeting, I related to him what happened to us at Langka River.

Among the many Katipunan casualties in the battle at San Mateo were Corporal Lorenzo, whose legs were amputated up to the knees, and Captain Simeon Lopez, who lost his right hand. Both were victims of cannon fire. Natives of Rizal province, these brave Sons of the People are still alive today (1927) and impoverished like myself. Among the dead was Lieutenant Elias (alias *Payapa*).

After he had heard my report, the Supremo asked me to go to Pantayanin to collect the guns which General Kiko had brought there for safe-keeping. We needed the guns right away because the enemy had threatened to attack us at Montalban the next morning. I was very tired from the harrowing experience I had just gone through; moreover, I was bothered by sores on my buttocks, which I had gotten from riding a horse whose back was riddled with sores. But I dared not complain despite my miserable physical condition. Seeing the sorry state of my horse, the Supremo gave me his own mount, a splendid white horse. He also gave me an experienced guide to escort me in my delicate task.

I (Colonel Bato-Balani) reached Pantayanin after an uneventful ride. But I was disappointed to find neither General Kiko nor the guns I was to retrieve. Katipunero Sixto de la Cruz told me that General Kiko had gone to Mount Bulak in Antipolo for the purpose of organizing troops. I left quickly for Antipolo, but despite a whole night of riding about Mount Bulak and in and out of Antipolo town, I did not find any trace of him. I returned to Pantayanin in the morning of the following day, Tuesday, November 10. At the outpost I saw the men engrossed in listening to the hiss of crisis-crossing bullets in the battle raging at Montalban. The next day I learned that the Katipunan forces had been defeated in this battle and that they had retreated to Balara.

On Thursday, November 12, I received a letter from the Supremo that confirmed the information we had received earlier—they had retreated to Balara after their defeat at Montalban. He asked me to see him, but I could not do so at once because I was waiting for the arrival of the couriers I had assigned to look for General Kiko. The couriers arrived three days later, with thirteen guns and a letter from General Kiko to the Supremo Bonifacio.

In his letter, General Kiko asked the Supremo to relieve him of his duties as General because he felt that he was not equal to the position; consequently he was surrendering the thirteen guns in his keeping. He offered to serve instead in some non-military position. The Supremo accepted the resignation, and in his place appointed General Hermogenes Bautista (alias *Bara*).

LX

General Genaro de los Reyes's Account Continued

Those were critical times for the Most Venerable Supremo of the Katipunan, Generalissimo Andres Bonifacio of the Revolution. He came close to death on several occasions. First was the close shave he had when a bullet grazed his side while he was at the front line leading the Katipunan troops in the last big battle at San Mateo. Then there was the invitation for him to visit the Katipunan chapters in Cavite province.[44]

---

[44]It was during this visit that he was captured and killed by Magdalo.

The invitation to visit Cavite was extended to him by General Mariano M. Alvarez, President of the Magdiwang Council and gallant Father of the Revolution in that province. Because he believed that it was his duty to visit the towns and provinces where the Revolution had spread, the Supremo could not reject the invitation. Before he left Balara, he assigned Katipunero Julio Nakpil officer-in-charge at Pantayanin and appointed him deputy President Supremo of the Katipunan on a provisional basis.

He prepared to leave for Cavite and when he was ready to go, an incident soured the relations in the Katipunan ranks. General Luis Malinis suddenly came up and demanded that one of the two tin biscuit boxes filled with gold coins they had excavated while building the defenses at San Mateo be turned over to him. Many Katipuneros chided General Luis, saying that the trove should not be despoiled for private purposes, but should be used to help finance the Revolution. Individual members should not profit from it; on the other hand, they should try to augment Katipunan coffers through solicitations and contributions. This was the prevailing opinion among the rank and file, and they tried to dissuade Malinis from pursuing his demands. But just as the Supremo and his party were about to leave, General Malinis called his men to his side and grabbed a small cannon to aim at the Supremo's group.

"I was asking you to give me one of the cans of gold and you refused," Malinis shouted sternly; "now you cannot go if you do not leave both cans."

"Don't you respect anybody anymore?" I (Colonel de los Reyes) asked quickly.

"I still give my due respect, why not? But you must give us what is due us. You must acknowledge that we were the finders of the treasure and that we risked our lives doing so. And can you bear to leave us, your brethren, without any means even to buy our food?"

To avoid further trouble, Secretary Emilio Jacinto advised the Supremo to accede and leave one box of the gold coins with General Luis. I myself handed the box to the General.

"The Katipunan was not founded for money," Secretary Jacinto said by way of bringing the incident to a close.

Before leaving for Cavite, the Supremo talked to me about my responsibilities over the troops he was leaving in my care. I realized that I should not fail them in any way.

Some ten days after the Supremo and his party left Balara, Luis Malinis prepared to attack the enemy position at Novaliches. He carried out the siege towards the end of November 1896. After a pitched battle, the Sons of the People burned, at noon, the civil guard headquarters and the chapel where the enemy had entrenched themselves. Unfortunately, however, the brave General Malinis was killed by the Spaniards, and his death turned the tide of battle. The people's troops dispersed afterwards, thus making it easy for the enemy to win this engagement.

LXI

General Genaro de los Reye's Account Continued

After the battle of Novaliches, I received word from the Supremo Bonifacio that he wanted me to join him in Cavite. I quickly prepared for the trip. I started from Caloocan in the company of two convent school girls, daughters of Lieutenant Tomas, and another, a relative of Father Tuto, all of whom were from Bacoor, Cavite. Another member of our party was the wife of Pedro Camus; she wanted to join her husband who was then in Cavite.

We stopped at Pineda, where I learned that a Katipunero, Pedro Mercado, had been assigned by the chief of the civil guards to watch the Pasig River crossing at Malapad-na-Bato. I secretly summoned Katipunero Pedro Mercado to ask him to prepare a big boat for ferrying us across the river at sundown. We needed an extra big outrigger for ferrying more than twenty bolo-carrying and nine gun-bearing troops. Everything was carried out as planned; and after he had brought us safely across the river, Katipunero Pedro Mercado gave us many bullets as well as a cash contribution of 350 pesos.

My contingent and I were approaching Bacoor when we chanced upon some troops of the Spanish cavalry fast asleep, obviously from fatigue. After we had seized the enemy's seven guns that were stacked against a pile of stones, someone suggested that we should also capture the sleeping Spanish soldiers and should they resist, shoot them since they were already disarmed. When I learned about these whispered suggestions, I dissuaded my men from carrying them out with these words:

"It is neither fair nor honorable to consider someone asleep as an enemy. To attack somebody when he is not in a position to fight back is traitorous. Let us not take advantage of a defenseless foe. I will not approve it. Don't do unto others what you would not like others to do unto you! March on!"

That entire night we trekked through tangled woods and over grasslands, mud holes, and crooked paths, while the cold wind and rain whipped in spurts. We reached the Zapote defense position at about ten the following morning, and after another hour's march we were in the town of Bacoor. We were very tired, not only from lack of sleep, but also from hunger since we had not eaten any food throughout the long march.

I sought out Mariano Noriel, the town executive, for help. I thought that he was a Katipunan member, but I realized my mistake when he failed to respond to my coded greeting. Nevertheless, Noriel cooperated with us. He made arrangements for us to be accommodated at the fort near the sea and promised to send us food later.

I had some fifty troops with me when we were billeted at the seaside fort. We had sixteen guns, mostly Remingtons, and a few rifles for shooting birds. The majority had only bolos. Mine was the only revolver in our contingent.

But what a miserable hungry lot we were! Some of us were doubled up in pain from stomach cramps, others were throwing up yellowish slime from sheer hunger, while still others were slumped wordlessly with their eyes closed and their hands clutching their aching heads. When the promised food came at about five in the afternoon, it was only half a gunny sack of unhusked rice and nothing else. In our state of hunger, I felt it was an insult to send us unhusked grain since there were no facilities in the fort for pounding or unhusking the grain. I politely rejected the unhusked rice and had it returned to Noriel with many thanks. I decided that we should each look out for ourselves. Those who had money could lend to those who had none so that each one could go out and buy himself food from the stores in town. Or if they chose to, they could go up the people's houses and rely on their kindness to feed them. We ended up by dispersing and seeking the hospitality of the townspeople of Bacoor.

Sensing that we should not allow the municipal executive Noriel to manage our affairs, I prepared my troops to leave for Malabon [now called General Trias], which was the seat of the Magdiwang Government. We left after breakfast the following morning to meet with the Honorable Supremo Andres Bonifacio, who was then visiting the Magdiwang Council at Malabon.

While passing through the village of Binakayan, we met Katipunero Vicente Leyba (alias *Kalentong*), with whom I left a message for Lucino de la Cruz (alias *Ipo-Ipo*) to meet me at the house where the Supremo Bonifacio was staying in Malabon. I asked him to tell Ipo-Ipo to bring with him the sixty guns he had borrowed from me at Pantayanin.

"You'll never see him again if I tell him that you want the guns back," Kalentong laughingly said. "You see, General Lucino and I met on our way to Bacoor. He came from Balara while I came from Pineda. We crossed the Pasig River together at Malapad-na-Bato. Except for nine who had firearms, my troops were armed with bolos. On the other hand, General Lucino had seventy-one troops with guns aside from those who carried bolos. Altogether we had eighty gun-bearing soldiers between us; as we marched into Bacoor, the sight of so many guns awed the townspeople. General Ipo-Ipo especially became the center of flattery and attention. Heading the impressive gun-bearing contingent, he soon was receiving offers to buy off the guns. It did not take him long to succumb, for he readily agreed to sell them at five pesos each. When he asked me in confidence what I thought of the proposition, I told him that if I were in his place I would not sell even a single gun because I knew how important it was to have arms. Then we parted company and I led my men to Imus. One of my men, who was left behind but later caught up with us, said that he saw for himself General Lucino receiving 300 pesos for the sale of sixty Remington guns. Disheartened over this news, I parted with Kalentong to keep my appointment with the Supremo Bonifacio.

I stayed in the same house where the Supremo was temporarily residing. I reported to him what I had heard and seen. I told him about the condition of the Katipunan defenses in the eastern front where I came from. I told him the needs and wishes of the troops, and I narrated the difficulties I had encountered during my trip. I also reported the perfidious sale by General Lucino of the guns I had loaned to him. Finally, I turned over to the Supremo the remaining sixteen guns my troops and I had with us.

The Supremo Bonifacio received reports about the activities of two prominent citizens of San Mateo who were sworn enemies of the Katipunan. Known as Kapitang Matias and Kapitang Ismael, they were responsible for the sufferings of many townsmen. Grieving parents, wives, and children of the victims denounced the two as spies and collaborators of the Spanish enemy. They had their victims either tortured or summarily executed by the Spaniards. The Supremo called a meeting of leaders from

Balara for the purpose of passing judgment on the traitors. The decision as to arrest the two and bring them to Balara for execution.

I (Colonel Genaro) learned that the spies were already being held prisoners of the Katipunan at Balara. Before the execution could be carried out, I sent word to the Supremo requesting him to spare the life of one of the prisoners and that I would be responsible for his conduct afterwards. The request was granted, and only one of the prisoners were executed. The head was cut off and set on top of a bamboo stake. When the Katipuneros entered San Mateo, they planted this gory stake in the middle of the road at the center of the town.

[*Alvarez Narration Continued*]

Let us leave aside for the moment the preparations and activities of the Sons of the People in their current campaigns, to review the dark, thorny, and precipitous road to death that the Katipuneros gladly took for the sake of freedom for the Motherland.

To those who participated in the siege of the Spanish enemy's powder arsenal at San Juan del Monte, Rizal, on the morning of August 30, 1896, the thundering command of the Supremo Andres Bonifacio, "My brethren, attack!" still resounds in their ears.

As the Katipunan bolo brigade rushed towards the enemy position, they were met by a hail of bullets. The shooting intensified from their front and rear when new enemy reinforcements arrived. The latter were the same troops who earlier in the morninghad routed the army of General Salogo (Ramon Bernardo) at Santa Mesa. Among the Katipunan officers in that siege was Lieutenant Miguel Ramos (alias *Bulalakaw*).

"To each his own! Seek your own safety!" the Supremo shouted. The Katipunan ranks broke pell-mell in a frantic effort to escape. But just then Lieutenant Bulalakaw shouted, "Lie down on your bellies!"

The bolo brigade dropped to the ground, and each one tried to burrow a safe niche for himself. At first no one dared to stand because of the low-flying barrage of bullets. But they soon realized that they were easy targets in that position and that it was better if they died fighting on their feet or else fleeing to safety. This reasoning must have led one to get up on his feet in spite of the crisis-crossing bullets and run for his life. His example was quickly followed by the others and soon all the bolo brigade was fleeing aimlessly in all directions. Quite a number escaped unscathed, but many were wounded. And in their hurry to get away, the Katipuneros left their dead where they fell on enemy ground.

The enemy's cavalry troops chased the fleeing Katipuneros and tried to block their flight. At noon they overtook and arrested a group of them on top of a mountain. Among those taken prisoners were Katipunan members Manuel Castañeda, Teodorico Castañeda, Claro Casteñada, Catalino Bustamante, Victor de los Reyes, and Miguel Ramos.

LXII

Account of Miguel Ramos

[One of the Katipuneros captured and imprisoned by the Spaniards, after the Battle of San Juan on August 30, 1896, was Lieutenant Miguel Ramos (alias *Bulalakaw*; lit., Shooting Star). He wrote the following account to prove that those imprisoned by the enemy suffered no less than those who were left fighting in the battlefield.]

After our arrest by the Spanish cavalry troops, we were ordered to put down our bolos in a heap on the ground. Then with both hands up, we were lined up a yard-and-a-half away from the pole of bolos. Our captors searched our bodies thoroughly and then bound us individually at the elbows with rope as thick as a finger. They brought us thus trussed up to the civil guard garrison at Marikina.

We prisoners agreed on a common defense strategy. At any trial court in which we would be arraigned, we were to say that we had been peasants working in the fields when men with guns had pounced on us. They had forced us to produce guns; and when we could not, they had hauled us off and impressed us into their army. They had placed us in the vanguard of troops that attacked the powder arsenal at San Juan del Monte. After our ranks dispersed, the Spanish cavalry troops had chased and captured us. This was our testimony to every Spanish officer who interrogated us.

In the afternoon of September 2, 1896, we were brought to the Bilibid Prison in Manila. We were not given any supper that evening. The following day we were fed once, and at eleven o'clock that night our elbows were again tightly tied behind us. Then we were hustled off from Bilibid and brought to the pier.

Our captors put us on a steamboat called "Churruca." All sixty-five of us prisoners were so weak and hungry that if we stopped to rest for a while we found it difficult to get up and walk again. Mobility was hampered, not only because of our weakened conditions because of hunger, but also because of the discomfort from the tight binding of our elbows behind us. They herded us into a dark, windowless compartment, with a single opening on top that was covered by a piece of canvas measuring about three feet square. They surrounded us with guards, which seemed to me unnecessary if the purpose was to prevent us from escaping. Besides being hog-tied, we were all too weak from exhaustion and hunger to escape.

Suddenly, two Spanish soldiers began to beat us with canes, while two others joined by kicking and shoving around until we fell down in the keel of the boat. We fell in different positions, on our backs, bellies, sides, or on our heads. Then a big voice boomed out, "Bury the dead!"

We were packed like sardines at the bottom of the keel. To sleep, we could not even lie down horizontally. We could hardly move as we huddled close to each other, sitting on our haunches. The air was fetid since the only aperture was the door above, and even this was blocked by many guards. Since it was stifling hot, we were a grimy and stinking lot, with bedraggled and soiled clothes. And to top it all, we were still hogtied. But the will to survive did not leave us, for we ate and drank the foul food and water they gave us.

Our destination was Yap,[45] in the Caroline Islands. On reaching land, they bailed us out of the hold of the boat with rope and herded us onto the beach like cattle. They made a head-count as we landed, to make sure that no one had escaped. With sticks and kicks, they propelled us to where the governor of the island, Major Miguel Marquez, was waiting. But when we were about to be presented, the governor refused to let us come near him, perhaps because of our stench and squalor. He ordered our handcuffs removed and had us transferred to a corral on the beach. Located at the foot of a mountain, the corral was sturdily fenced for keeping captured cattle. There we bathed and washed our clothes. We were a naked lot hanging our clothes to dry when two Spaniards came to take photographs. Hustling us to pose, they took pictures, with none of us wearing any clothes.

The Spaniards used Yap Island as a prison. The military governor, Major Marquez, was extremely cruel and churlish towards us prisoners. Looking down on Filipinos as inferior to Europeans, he considered us fit only to be their slaves for all time. Our meals never varied and were very

---

[45]Iyap in the typescript.

meager; they consisted only of boiled rice of the roughest kind and plain boiled lentils.

Everyday we were assigned to do hard labor at projects that had to be finished at once. We had to carry loads of soil from one place to another and dig or fill up sites. Considering the whimsical and unplanned nature of the assignments, we often felt that the tasks were given to punish us, not necessarily to finish some specific project. However, there was one job that we detested most of all. Whenever the mailboat arrived, we were made to repair the road to the wharf and the government house. These were the only times the road was opened. In three days we had to level the humps and fill the potholes; this stretch of a road we referred to as "Hell."

As soon as the boat had docked, we prisoners were lined up at the landing to be ready to unload the ship. An officer of the boat would hand Governor Miguel Marquez the manifest; after the latter had read it, he would put his arms akimbo and then hold up and wave the document. This was the signal for us to begin unloading the cargo.

With the heavy loads on our backs, we walked down the gangplank and down the road we called Hell. For on both sides of the road were lined Spanish troops and elements of the 78th Infantry, who were armed with tough wooden planks or bamboo and rattan sticks, ready to torment us with beatings for such imagined transgressions as not carrying our loads properly, being too slow and dawdling, balking at carrying heavy loads, not walking straight, etc. And when we stumbled or fell, we also got a beating. In the interim, between the unloading and the loading of new cargo, we prisoners were made to fill up the potholes and level the road to the wharf; and as we went about our task, our tormentors inflicted the same vexations as before. It was not surprising that after each departure of the mailboat, many of us were confined in hospital, suffering from fever, bruises, muscle and nerve fatigue, and abrasions all over the body.

We were convinced that the pain we suffered was not any less than those of our brethren who fell in the night fighting for the Motherland. And should we die before we could see our dear ones again, we commended to Bathala [Supreme Being in Tagalog mythology] the care of our beloved parents, wives, children, and brothers and sisters. We also prayed that the love of country be always kept alive in their hearts.

In our desperation, we fervently wished for death. We were quite certain that it was near at hand for all of us, considering the hardships we were enduring. We were most despondent every time the mailboat arrived, and to us it became a symbol of our oppression. It became so that we came to detest its very sight and sound—seeing and hearing it made our flesh creep. After more than a year of intolerable conditions, we had all fallen ill. We were emaciated, pale and weak, and the only reason we could still do some work was because of the threat of merciless beatings we would get if we did not obey.

One Sunday, the island became agog with the news that the governor, Major Miguel Marquez, would be replaced by a colonel. And indeed, within a week a battleship arrived in port with the new governor, Colonel Salvador Cortes. Major Marquez boarded the boat to meet his successor.

The poise and physique of Colonel Cortes impressed us. With a stern visage, he looked at the person he talked to straight in the eye. This was unlike Governor Marquez, who had a comely face and who had the habit of looking down when talking to people. The fierce look in the new governor's eyes provoked the following observation:

"Well, what do you know! The one who looks as meek as a lamb made our lives unbearable. We should know what to expect from that one who looks as fierce as a lion! Instead of quibbling, let us get ready for any eventuality that should befall us."

As part of the routine in the turnover of responsibility and position, Major Marquez accompanied Colonel Cortes to the various government offices. When they came to the prison, we prisoners fell in line and saluted them. The colonel saluted back enthusiastically. Going to the kitchen to find out what the prisoners had to eat, he saw the usual fare of boiled rice of the toughest kind and boiled lentils. He stirred the pot vigorously and asked the attendant what was cooking and for whom.

"That, sir, is the prisoners' food," the attendant answered.

Taken aback, the colonel sighed and threw a glance at us. Then he kicked the pots until they broke. After a while he asked if they were keeping beasts in the place. His face was red with rage when he said, "Why do you feed your fellowmen with stuff fit only for animals!"

He called for the superintendent and lectured to him thus: "I am the new governor replacing Major Marquez. I order you to give the prisoners decent food. Procure only good fish and have tasty dishes prepared for them. The dishes shall be prepared in accordance to the prisoners' tastes. Should fresh supplies be lacking, I authorize you to open the pantry and give the prisoners meat and other good food. And give them only clean rice, not the rough kind I saw today."

He looked at his watch; and seeing that it was past eleven o'clock, he ordered the opening of the pantry. After giving instructions about feeding the prisoners not later than twelve noon, he left together with Major Marquez.

After they had left, the superintendent told us, "Now your noses are up in the air."

Major Miguel Marquez departed from East Yap after the office and responsibility of governing the island had been properly turned over to Colonel Salvador Cortes. He left aboard the same battleship that had brought his successor.

The first of the new governor's reforms that affected us was his order to the prison superintendent to feed us well. For breakfast we were to be given lots of good coffee, sugar, newly-baked bread, butter, and sardines. The bounty extended to the other meals as well—lunch, afternoon snack, and dinner. On Sundays and holidays we had special fare: for breakfast and snacks we had chocolate, bread, cheese, ham and fried eggs; for lunch and dinner, delicious dishes of pork, beef, chicken or tasty fish, cooked with abundant vegetables with or without broth, fresh fruits, a goblet of good wine for each, and sweetmeats.

We were to be free as possible, to sleep when we wanted to, to take walks, to amuse ourselves, and if we were so inclined, to work. The only restrictions imposed were that we could not leave the island and that we must be inside the compound from ten at night to seven in the morning. We were thankful for a regimen which began at six in the morning with breakfast and ended with supper at six in the evening. My companions were happy enough in our relative freedom to work when we pleased, to spend our time leisurely in promenades or other diversions, and in being well-fed besides.

"Yet," I explained to them, "we are not truly free. We are still prisoners on this island. Of course, we are better off than before, but we should realize that only when our country is free can there be real contentment. Then everything else—intellectual life, material wealth, nobility of character—will flourish and be sources of pride for us all."

On Sundays and feast days of saints, it was customary for everyone on the island to hear Mass at the Roman Catholic church on top of a hall. One such morning, we left our prison compound at seven to go to church.

Midway up the hill we saw on the horizon what looked like a *tabo*[46] bobbing about at sea. It was a black object that grew bigger the longer we looked at it. Then we discerned traces of smoke that became darker as we continued to watch. Apprehension began to sap our strength so that we could barely climb the hill. The object we saw coming towards us was the dreaded mailboat!

"Sink! Sink! Damn you, sink!" we chorused, meanwhile raising our fists.

Just then the governor, escorted by some troops, passed us on the road. He signaled for us to walk faster to the church, where he was also going. We all heard Mass together; and when it was over, the governor told our superintendent to take us prisoners to the wharf. What we had always dreaded was going to happen again: we were to unload the ship's cargo. We trembled with fright at the prospect of the suffering that awaited us. My companions' thoughts were more morbid; they suspected that the reason we had been allowed a measure of freedom and given good food was that we were being readied for execution on the island. Those fears gnawed at us as we stood waiting for the tortures to begin.

Some ten minutes passed before the boat docked. The captain greeted the governor and handed him a letter. When he had read the letter Colonel Cortes reddened and trembled in agitation. He summoned Vicente Suarez, the prison superintendent, handed him the letter and ordered him to translate it into Tagalog and to be read aloud for our benefit. The letter read as follows:

Colonel Cortes,
Honorable governor:

Here's wishing you a pleasant sojourn in Eastern Yap of the Carolines. May you triumph in the defense of the glory and honor of Spain, our Motherland, in that far-flung outpost of her empire. The religious corporations wish to remind you that the Filipino rebels now being imprisoned on the island you now administer are traitors to our government and our religion. Therefore it is your duty to starve and beat them to death!

---

[46]Polished coconut shell opened at one end and used as a water dispenser.

May God protect you and grant you a long life.

I kiss your hand,

(Signature of a friar)

After the letter had been translated into Tagalog and then read to us, the governor took it from Mr. Vicente Suarez. With a smile he reassured us:

"I am the person in authority here. No friar has the jurisdiction, much less the power, to give orders to me. I hereby repudiate all the evil elements like them. And I intend to punish them should they try to meddle in my territory. I am appealing to you to help unload the cargo intended for us; but when you do the job tomorrow morning, it will be in a manner that will not be oppressive to you. And should you get tired on the job, you are free to leave, take a walk, or return to your quarters. You don't have to worry about anything because there will not be anyone to watch you or order you about."

As he said the last sentence, he gave a meaningful look to his troops. He told them that the prisoners would police themselves. He dismissed his troops and again spoke to us.

"As far as I am concerned, you are free to do as you please on this island; you may promenade or rest in your quarters as you wish. No schedules or guards will interfere with you. The only discipline I impose is that at mealtimes you should all eat together. And don't forget my appeal for your help in unloading and loading of cargo in the mailboat tomorrow morning. You will work shoulder to shoulder with the soldiers, and nobody will wield the stick and neither will anyone be beaten. You may now walk around or rest in your quarters. You are free to do as you please...."

He smiled at us again and then saluted. We returned the salute with great pleasure.

Under the aegis of Governor Cortes, our stint as exiles on the island passed happily. And were it not for our concern for the freedom of our native land and for our families back home, our contentment would have been complete. Aside from the kindness he had already demonstrated, the governor also ordered that our rations of good food and drink be increased. Thus for lunch on Sundays and holidays we were given an extra plateful of *arroz a la*

Valenciana[47] and a cup of fine wine. Where before we were weak and pale because of lack of sleep and nourishing food and because of the merciless beatings endured, under the benign regimen of Governor Cortes we regained our health, vitality and zest for life.

One day news reached us that the Caroline Islands, East Yap, Bonaparte, and Saipan[48] were to be ceded by the Spanish Government to the Germans. True enough, two ships, the Uranus and the Alba, soon arrived on our shores to take us away. The Uranus was to take us prisoners back to the Philippines; and when we were all aboard, Governor Cortes spoke to us.

"Gentlemen," he began, "we shall now part ways. You will go back to your own country and we to ours. May God grant that we reach our destinations safely. You must realize that I am a soldier whose duty is to uphold the Spanish Government. In that role, I am a Spaniard wherever I might be, whether here, or in Spain, or anywhere else. In truth, however, I am French by birth, race, and origin. But fate had it that I should marry a Spanish woman of Cartagena. I came to love the place, and that was where we made our home until I was assigned this onerous responsibility.

"However, this assignment gave me an opportunity to meet and make friends with you. You must have been very surprised at the comradeship and leniency I showed you. But you must know, as I have already told you, that I am a Frenchman and not a Spaniard who kneels and kisses the hands of the friars. I can never work as a secret assassin for those who pretend to be holy. I feel compassion for my fellowmen because God has given me the capacity to think and to sympathize with others. I am thankful that you still had some strength remaining, although perilously close to death, when I arrived. I am also grateful that you were able to regain your strength and vitality. Thanks be to God!

"You can all go back to your own homes, for you are free from now on. You need not be ashamed of anything, for you were imprisoned only because of your love for your native land and your desire to defend her liberty. By risking your life and blood unstintedly like you did, you have earned the respect of your fellowmen. This is the highest honor a patriot could aspire for, and it should be written into our historical record as a source of inspiration for all."

---

[47]A Spanish gourmet dish of rice with stewed chicken, pork sausages, clams, and vegetables.

[48]Sepan in the typescript.

After this short speech, Governor Cortes shook hands with all of us while shouts of "Bon voyage!" filled the air. Then the good governor took his leave of us and joined his troops on the other ship, the Alba, which was to take him back to Spain. Our ship, the Uranus, on the other hand, was bound for Manila. When the two vessels were about to depart, we and the passengers on the other ship cried out to each other, "Farewell! Farewell!"

But as the distance widened between us, the last distinct sounds we heard from the other ship were shouts of "Long live Spain!"

That provoked in us a surge of patriotic fervor and we could do no less than shout back, "Long live the Philippines!"

But no sooner had we uttered the cry than we began to regret having done so. Our other companions, carried away no doubt by the heady feeling that we were finally free, echoed the cry again and again.

We had forgotten temporarily that there were Spanish troops with us on board. Already they were looking annoyed over what we had done. What if they decided not to take us to Manila but to another island where we would again be exiled? Then we would suffer the same tortures we had undergone on East Yap. However, nothing of the sort happened and we reached Manila uneventfully.

[That was the end of the brief account by Katipunero Bulalakaw, Lieutenant Miguel Ramos.]

LXIV

As soon as the news of the outbreak of the Revolution reached Nueva Ecija and Bulacan, patriots in those provinces began to mobilize men to join the uprising. Mobilization began on the first day of September, 1896. In Nueva Ecija, among the leaders were Messrs. Mariano Llanera, Eduardo Llanera, Mamerto Natividad, and Manuel Tinio, while in Bulacan, they were Messrs. Isidoro Torres, Felipe Estrella, Melecio Carlos, Simeon Tecson,[49] Bustamante, Dr. Maximo Viola, and his brother Eusebio (alias *Dimabunggo*), otherwise known as "Maestro Sebio." These patriots left their homes and properties in town and brought their whole families to the forest, where they hoped they would be out of the reach of the vicious

---

[49]The typescript has Pekson with a question mark. Cf. *Ricarte Memoirs*, 69, and *The Philippine Revolution*, 63.

Spanish enemy. After they had evacuated their families to safety, they girded for the struggle in defense of the freedom of the Motherland.

In the month of September, 1896, while the revolutionary forces were engrossed in the task of liberation, there arrived in Cavite a student by the name of Zulueta.[50] Introducing himself as a writer, he offered his services to the Magdiwang and Magdalo Councils. He volunteered to write an eyewitness account of the Revolution. After the Magdalo Council accepted his proposition, he stayed with its leaders President Baldomero Aguinaldo and General Emilio Aguinaldo.

Among others who went to Cavite to offer their services to the Revolution was a pair from Bulacan, Maestro Sebio (Dimabunggo) and Felipe Estrella. Coming soon after Zulueta, they sought out the leaders of the Revolution to inform them that General Isidoro Torres had established headquarters and was organizing troops in the village called Binakod, located between Bulacan[51] and Santa Isabel.

Maestro Sebio and Estrella traveled from one place to another in Cavite province. Wherever they went, Estrella told the people that the schoolmaster possessed the wonderful gift of making a person invulnerable to bullets of all kinds, from guns as well as from cannon balls. An amulet from the schoolmaster would do the trick, he claimed. When swallowed, the amulet would make anyone free from all sorts of enemy ammunition for a week; one could even expose himself to enemy fire, but no bullet would hit him. The people who heard Estrella believed him implicitly and were delighted to submit to the ministrations of Maestro Sebio. As a result, throngs sought him out and filled the house where they were staying.

The charm consisted of round pieces of white paper with some inscriptions of Latin. Some were the size of a half peso, while others were bigger, the size of a silver (Mexican) peso. Estrella was kept busy cutting the round pieces of white paper, while the schoolmaster did the honor of putting the talisman in the mouth of the communicant and then blessing it, in the manner of a priest serving the host. At the conclusion of the ritual, Dimabunggo collected fees ranging from twenty centavos to one peso. A special ceremony, with three such amulets swallowed separately, was supposed to produce a correspondingly higher potency and endowed the communicant with greater agility and vigor in springing away from and

---

[50]Jose Clemente Zulueta. Cf. E. Arsenio Manuel, *Dictionary of Philippine Biography*, II (Quezon City: Filipiniana Publications, 1955), 458.

[51]The provincial capital of the Province of Bulakan at the time.

escaping physical harm. But this kind was difficult to obtain, for it was seldom performed; and when it was, it required a donation commensurate to its supposed greater merit.

After spending two weeks in Bacoor, Imus, and Kawit of Magdalo territory, giving "aid" to the Revolution in the manner described above, Dimabunggo moved to the Magdiwang area. He paid his respects to the leaders and offered his services to them. The Council President, General Mariano Alvarez, admonished Dimabunggo against receiving payment for his ministrations, saying that should he need funds and provisions, the schoolmaster only had to tell him and he would be provided for. Dimabunggo's rejoinder was that he never solicited any fee but people gave their donations voluntarily to compensate him for his efforts in serving them. He accepted the amounts as tips for cigar or cigarette money.

The Minister of War of the Magdiwang Council, Mr. Ariston Villanueva, protested to General Mariano Alvarez, the Council President, against his sanction of the schoolmaster's activities. Mr. Villanueva argued that by tolerating Dimabunggo, they were in effect abetting superstition, much in the manner of the friars who used similar methods to keep for themselves political and economic power. He feared that allowing such rituals as practiced by Dimabunggo would encourage belief in the validity of the pope's blessing and such other church ceremonies that would enable the friars to regain their stranglehold on the people.

The President laughed and dismissed Mr. Villanueva's fears. He said that faith in itself was not evil, especially if professed by patriots dedicated to the welfare of the country. He cited the example of the Japanese whose belief that those who die in defense of the native land or of a superior officer would be met by angels at the heavenly gates and escorted to their deserved places in the kingdom of everlasting glory; there they would be joined by their loved ones who were to share their eternal bliss. Just as the Japanese were emboldened in battle because of this belief, so would the Filipinos gather more courage in facing the enemy if they were similarly fortified. They would fight fearlessly in defense of their freedom if they believed that Maestro Sebio's talisman had the power to deflect bullets.

Maestro Sebio and his companion, Estrella, stayed in Noveleta as houseguests of Major Pantaleon Granados. There he ministered to Magdiwang partisans who came in great numbers. The present writer, General Apoy, himself developed Dimabunggo's friendship and visited him often in order to observe more closely his wondrous feats.

The tense war situation, intensified by rumors of impending enemy attacks, drove milling crowds to Maestro Sebio. The old and young, mothers with their brood in tow, elbowed their way to partake of the "host" in the hope of becoming invulnerable to bullets. They would have no other serve it to them, for they believed that for the amulet to be truly effective, it had to be dispensed by Dimabunggo himself. For this reason, Dimabunggo became so harassed that he went about his ministry almost breathless with fatigue and in clothes soaked in sweat. His helpmate, Estrella, was just as harried, continuously cutting round pieces of paper that the crowd of men and women, old and young, fought over. It was Estrella's job, too, to collect the donations of twenty centavo and peso pieces from those who offered them. On his part, Dimabunggo wrote pencil inscriptions in Latin and drew a cross in the middle of the paper medallions.

When these were ready to be dispensed, he stood before each individual applicant whose arms were humbly folded. With each piece he intoned, "Ego ... Peravit ... Ego ... Peravit ... Ego ... Sacrificit."

Then, in the manner of a priest serving the host, he put the paper piece on the tongue of the kneeling communicant. The final touch was his blessing: "Enom ... Dre ... Enom ... Go ... Enom ... To."

General Apoy was an interested observer as Maestro Sebio served his paper amulets to admirers and believers. He said not a word either in reproach or in praise. In truth, he was elated, but he wanted to keep his feelings to himself and in so doing, shed furtive tears. He secretly approved of Dimabunggo's amulets and blessings, because through them thousands found new courage to fight the Spaniards. This was a crucial need of the Revolution; and seeing that Dimabunggo's ministrations were helping boost the people's morale, General Apoy was pleased indeed. He even brushed aside his former admonition against accepting donations; instead, he justified the collection of fees to pay for such expenditures as transportation, food, provisions, and supplies, like paper, pencils, etc.

Dimabunggo was not unappreciative of General Apoy's patronage. When he saw that the latter was about to leave, he signaled Felipe Estrella, his assistant, who forthwith handed a little box to Lieutenant Abiyog, the General's aide-de-camp. Inside the box were excellent cigars from the Insular cigar factory; these were his parting gift to the General.

After his stint with the Magdiwang, Maestro Sebio moved to Magdalo territory; and with the sanction of Magdalo leaders, he continued to practice his vaunted wonderful gifts. The Magdalo received him as enthusiastically as did the Magdiwang. One day, he and his assistant Estrella suddenly disappeared. The people looked for him everywhere, not only because they believed in his power to protect them, but also they were eager to meet him and cultivate his friendship. He was reputed to be a good man who got along famously with his fellowmen. He had such an enviable reputation that whole communities vied with each other in convincing him to stay with them, for they believed that his mere presence deflected the dreaded bullets. But he was nowhere to be found in all of Cavite province.

LXV

For some unexplained reason, Dimabunggo and Estrella left Cavite and moved to Kakarong, a hilly village in Bulacan. His adherents made a determined search and finally located them in this village where the pair had built a camp for the revolutionary forces. Once discovered, Kakarong became a center for hordes of his followers and refugees from other areas. Whole families moved in, and the population swelled to some 10,000 people, men and women, old and young.

Kakarong became a full-fledged revolutionary area, with Maestro Sebio as its head and Felipe Estrella as his deputy and secretary. The collective arms they possessed included four Remington guns, six air rifles for shooting birds, three cannons improvised from thin iron pipes bound securely with coarse wires, bolos, lances, spears, sharpened bamboos, bows and arrows, an arquebus, and one "Mohara" blow gun. They built a barrack at the center of the camp and individual houses surrounding the main structure. All were made of bamboo with grass roofing and siding.

The community resembled a well-populated resort town with varied recreation facilities. While food and other prime commodities were abundant, they were nevertheless in keeping with the revolutionary situation; food, for example, was simple but nourishing. There was gambling, but this only served to quicken the pulse of commerce. Money changed hands quickly; and since the winners shared their winnings, everyone, even children, had money to spend. Thus Kakarong became well known not only for its military strength and organization, but also for the bravery of its citizens. Their courage, of course, stemmed from their belief in the magical powers of Dimabunggo. It was often demonstrated in their fearless encounters with the Spanish enemy, from whom they confiscated the various firearms they had in their possession.

On their part, the enemy devised all means to subvert the Revolution. Spanish officers and friars induced and cajoled Filipinos to betray their country and brethren. One of those who turned traitor was a full-blooded Filipino known by many as Captain Jose Sta. Maria. He was head of the volunteer corps composed of Spaniards and Filipinos in the service of the Spanish Government. Annoyed at the repeated defeats his men suffered at Kakarong and envious of the growing prestige of this rebel outpost, Captain Sta. Maria plotted to humble Kakarong. He organized a large contingent of Filipinos and Spaniards for this purpose. Outwardly, nothing seemed to change the routine of the enemy troops; but, behind their apparent calm, their officers racked their brains and bent their energies towards the goal of attaining glory for themselves through a resounding victory over Kakarong.

In due time, three Filipinos in Captain Sta. Maria's volunteer corps disappeared from the garrison. Known by their surnames, Santos, Robles, and Dumas, they left behind their uniforms, guns and bullets, and bolos. After about three days and still they had not returned to headquarters, everyone presumed that the three had gone back to their respective hometowns. No one suspected that they would infiltrate the revolutionary ranks in order to spy on them.

The Kakarong community had been flourishing for nearly a year, and its citizens were impatient to prove their mettle in the battlefield. With Kakarong firmly established as a base of operations, they felt that the time was ripe for an offensive. They were further emboldened by the thought that Maestro Sebio's magical powers made them invulnerable, but that they should take advantage of its protection before the magic lost its potency. And since the enemy had not dared attack their outpost, they agreed that they should seize the initiative and launch an offensive against the Spanish forces in San Rafael. Everybody was in high spirits, especially when the news reached them that the few Spanish soldiers guarding the San Rafael garrison had been overpowered and disarmed.

But spies had infiltrated Kakarong, and through them the enemy learned of the plan to attack them. Infiltration by Filipino traitors was easy because the people were so trusting and naive that every Filipino who came to the community was welcomed as a comrade in the struggle to free the enchained Motherland. And because of this utter trust and love for their countrymen, the three traitors from Captain Sta. Maria's troops managed to blend with the insurgents without arousing suspicion. The rebels welcomed the three to their camp, unaware that by so doing they were digging their own graves.

Seeing the impatience of the men to initiate an attack, Estrella asked Maestro Sebio for authority to organize a contingent for the purpose. The latter assented, after a reminder about the guidelines of behavior the Sons of the People must observe. Estrella quickly called on half of the gun-bearing troops and half of the bolo brigade to join him; they were to leave camp the following morning, so early that they planned to eat breakfast at four o'clock. The night passed in fearless anticipation of the next day's adventure. The insurgents were completely at ease, happy in the thought that they were all brothers-in-arms committed to the cause of defending their freedom. It never occurred to them that three spies from Captain Jose Sta. Maria's detachment were within their ranks, and least of all, that one of them had slipped out of the camp unnoticed that very night, leaving the two others to carry out their assigned tasks.

Very early the next morning, Felipe Estrella's army began its march across open fields towards San Rafael. Perhaps due to their eagerness to fight, many who were not in the group before joined the march, leaving Kakarong with fewer men that was planned. Arriving at San Rafael in high spirits, they quickly wiped out the enemy and confiscated their arms. In the jubilation that followed their victory, the Sons of the People reveled in the praises heaped on them. They happily exchanged news and impressions with the people. Meanwhile, their commander, Felipe Estrella, and his fellow officers went about the task of soliciting and collecting food contributions they could bring back to Kakakarong.

On the very same day—it was a Monday in May 1896—when the Sons of the People captured San Rafaela, a large detachment of the volunteer corps led by Captain Sta. Maria himself invaded Kakarong. There was little doubt that the operation was carried out with the help of his three spies who had infiltrated the community. Felipe Estrella's troops had barely reached their destination when the enemy suddenly descended on Kakarong and began shooting in earnest.

Shortly after the firing started, a conflagration broke out inside the camp and gutted the headquarters and the houses surrounding it. The two spies who had remained in camp were caught in the act of starting the fires. The few troops left to guard the outpost were kept busy trying to extinguish the fire and to save the screaming old people and women and children engulfed in the flames. Meanwhile, the enemy pressed their advantage and quickly overran the camp, especially when they sensed that from the few shots fired from within, only a handful were defending the Katipunan outpost. Sparing no one, from suckling infants to doddering old people, they shot and killed everyone they saw in the camp. The only survivors were a few who managed to escape, among them Maestro Sebio himself.

News of the massacre at Kakarong swiftly reached San Rafael in the afternoon of the same day. Estrella hastened to mobilize his troops who had dispersed and were still heady over their victory. Knowing that Kakarong had only a few men left to defend it, he became impatient with his disbanded troops, whom he found difficult to mobilize at once, so he left with only a few of his men while instructing others to follow immediately.

However, they had scarcely left San Rafael when they were suddenly ambushed by the enemy. Their path was blocked, and enemy troops, who sprang at them on both sides, opened fire ferociously and without let-up. The Spanish forces were so numerous that they were able to encircle almost all of the San Rafael area. Bullets from all quarters rained on the little band of Felipe Estrella.

Estrella and his men valiantly fought back, but their puny efforts in the face of great odds could not stem the enemy onslaught. The tiny Katipunan band dispersed and sought shelter inside shops and houses and fired away at the enemy from their concealment. On their part, the townspeople began to flee. They fled with their babies and the old, and the sick in their arms or on their backs. The women with their brood in tow were led away by the hand.

Soon the Spaniards had so effectively encircled the town that the fleeing folk could find no way out. All the exits had been blocked and anyone attempting to get out would surely have been shot and killed. As a last resort the people grouped together and decided to take refuge inside the town church and parish house.

The Spanish hordes marched into town without resistance and mercilessly shot all they encountered on the way. They let loose a hail of bullets on shops and houses and on unkempt areas. But this was not the worst. They surrounded the church and parish house and forced open the bolted doors by battering them down with artillery from mountain cannons. Forcing their way in, they rounded up all the refugees who were mostly old people, women, and children. They ignored the people's gestures of surrender and pleas for mercy. Instead, they began shooting and stabbing them with bayonets. Not a single life was spared, not even those of innocent infants suckling their mothers' breasts.

What a sacrilege to the saints! The heinous acts were done right before their beloved and venerable images inside the church and parish house. And when the last person had been murdered, they turned to all other moving creatures. Only then were they satisfied and they stopped in their rampage.

The scourge of death petered out into silence on the desolate and grieving town of San Rafael. Hundreds of corpses and bodies of the seriously wounded littered the church and parish house, houses and wayside stores and streets and yards. Young and old, women and patriotic men, lay lifeless, while a few wounded managed to crawl and conceal themselves in the underbrush and in bamboo clumps, albeit bathed in their own blood. Some two thousand people were killed, among them the patriot and hero Felipe Estrella and his assistant Ato Kingwa. Fighting to the last, they commanded their troops neither to surrender nor to retreat. They fell with a smile on their lips, knowing that only over their dead bodies would the enemy pass to snatch away the freedom they were committed to defend.

After overwhelming the Sons of the People, the Spaniards shouted, "Long live Spain!"

One of the few who escaped the debacle was Dimabunggo. Disappointed over the easy fall of Kakarong, he dedicated himself once more to looking for and preparing new bases in order to continue the fight against the Spaniards. But he was overcome with fatigue and he fell ill. While recuperating in the village of Sili, in the municipality of Angat, he began preparations for a renewed struggle. In his impatience to strike back against the enemy, he went ahead with his preparations despite some uneasiness over security. His apprehensions were not unfounded, for one day he found himself being pounced upon by Spanish troops who then bound his elbows behind him. He was brought to the town of Bulacan and was detained in an open-air enclosure where a Spanish officer interrogated him.

"Are you the rebel chief, Maestro Sebio, who is posing as king of this province of Bulacan?"

"Yes, I am Maestro Sebio, but I am not king of the Tagalogs in Bulacan. I am one of the leaders of the Sons of the People who have committed ourselves to the defense of justice and to uphold our rights and our way of life," Dimabunggo answered sternly and fearlessly.

On hearing Maestro Sebio's answer, the Spanish officer signaled his firing squad to shoot. Simultaneous shots felled the patriotic schoolmaster Sebio, the Dimabunggo of the Katipunan.

LXVI

General Isidoro Torres and His Army

After the death of Maestro Sebio and Felipe Estrella, the survivors among their troops joined the army of General Isidoro Torres in its outposts at Masukal and Binakod. Thousands of men joined General Torres in these camps; and under the leadership of this patriot and hero, Masukal and Binakod became as formidable as Kakarong before its fall. One day at a large meeting of the Katipunan of the Sons of the People called for the purpose of evaluating the abilities as well as the rights of each member, General Torres was unanimously elected to the position of First General of the Revolution.

The security of the camps became the most worrisome problem for General Torres as men continued to pour in to join his army. Although the fortifications were strengthened and the camps were guarded at all times, still there was the fear of infiltration by spies from the enemy ranks. The Kakarong experience made General Torres most circumspect. Once, when he had to leave camp in order to look for more secure defense areas, he instructed his deputy to observe strict security measures and be on alert at all times against enemy attack.

General Torres and the few aides who accompanied him returned to their camp after two days. After being sufficiently rested from the trip, General Torres ordered a general mobilization of the troops to a new site he had discovered near the Pacific Ocean. This was in a mountain called Biyak-na-Bato, but it was not to be confused with the place of the same name to which General Emilio Aguinaldo had retreated. The mountain was more popularly known as "Biyak-na-Bato of the Pacific Ocean," but according to those who saw it, it should have been called the "magic mountain" because of the many wondrous things they saw the whole night they were there.

The Biyak-na-Bato by the Pacific Ocean was a mountain lair for nocturnal birds. All night long these birds brought food they had gathered elsewhere and deposited them in hidden nooks and crannies. Then when the rainy season set in, they would draw upon these stored provisions to last them until they could replenish them again. Compared with the other Biyak-na-Bato, which was the venue of the peace pact,[52] this one discovered by

---

[52]The Pact of Biyak-na-Bato concluded late in 1897 suspended hostilities between the rebel forces and the Spanish government. Located some ten kilometers

General Torres along the Pacific offered a far better defense position than the other. Thus it was that when they moved to the new location, thousands of Katipunan members composing the army of General Torres found the place more congenial than the camps they had left.

Meanwhile, the Spaniards were planning to attack Masukol and Binakod, but they had to call it off when they learned that the outposts had been abandoned. The offensive was later carried out when they eventually came to know of the new Katipunan mountain retreat. The battle was as bloody as the previous encounters. The Sons of the People fought valiantly against the ferocious onslaught of the Spanish army; and despite the increases in casualties in their ranks, their courage did not fail them but instead they became more determined to win.

When the river fronting the stronghold was strewn with bodies of their dead and wounded, the Spaniards had no recourse but to withdraw. The Sons of the People chased them back to San Miguel de Mayumo. This important victory of the Katipunan was due to the brilliant tactics of General Isidoro Torres and his deputies, Tekson [Simeon Tekson] and Kabling [Tomas Kabling].[53]

LXVII

The Philippine Republic at Biyak-na-Bato

The Government of the Philippine Republic established headquarters at Biyak-na-Bato in San Miguel de Mayumo in Bulacan. There it awaited battle reports from scattered units of the Katipunan army.

Simultaneously, the Spanish administration circulated a bulletin announcing their new strategy of concentration of troops and all-out war. Within a stipulated period of time, all relatives and friends of rebels were to be rounded up and concentrated in designated camps in open fields or exiled in distant places. This was to cut them off from contacts and involvement with the rebellion, so that they could not give aid to their kith and kin in the planned intensive campaign of the Spanish army.

---

from the town of San Miguel de Mayumo in Bulacan, this Biyak-na-Bato was a mountain stronghold of the revolutionary government led by Emilio Aguinaldo.

[53]Cf., *The Philippine Revolution*, 59.

In the face of such intimidation, there arrived at Biyak-na-Bato the Spanish Governor-General's[54] emissary to negotiate a truce with the rebel government. He was Pedro Paterno, a full-blooded Filipino educated in Spain and a recipient of the *Cross of Isabel the Catholic*, a decoration conferred by the King of Spain. Because of these credentials, he was received warmly by President Aguinaldo and other officers of the Revolutionary Government. At first Mr. Paterno was timorous that his overtures might be rejected, but his apprehension was dispelled by the evident esteem and affection with which he was welcomed at Biyak-na-Bato. He was accompanied by Mr. Emiliano Riego de Dios, Secretary of War of the Philippine Republic.

The same day that Mr. Paterno arrived at Biyak-na-Bato, Lieutenant General Mamerto Natividad, with some soldiers, went on a mission to survey the areas under Spanish control. But before departure, he promised to work for the acceptance of Mr. Paterno's proposals as soon as he returned from his mission. However, he was not to fulfill his promise because he died before he could come back.

His band was ambushed by an enemy detachment while he was talking to his troops on a small bridge in the village of Kalaba in San Isidro, Nueva Ecija. They returned the enemy fire, but General Natividad was felled by a bullet that hit him on the forehead and came out at the back of the head. Fortunately, despite the difficult situation, his troops were able to take his body to Biyak-na-Bato, where he was given a hero's burial. At the funeral, President Emilio Aguinaldo and other high officials of the Government of the Philippine Republic delivered eulogies that inspired the Sons of the People to resolutely fight for freedom and to emulate General Natividad's praiseworthy example of service to his country. The rebel government also decreed a period of mourning.

Mr. Pedro A. Paterno spoke at the funeral services, but he departed from the theme of the other speakers. Instead of inspiring his audience to greater efforts in defense of his country's freedom, he spoke of an end to the armed struggle by agreeing to his truce proposals. Sensing that the leadership of the Revolution was not enthusiastic about his proposition, he and his

---

[54]Governor-General was the title of the chief administrator of the Philippines during the American colonial period. During the Spanish period, the title was Governor and Captain General, but some writers tend to confuse the two titles and use the American title even when they refer to this official during the Spanish period.

companion, Secretary of War Emiliano Riego de Dios, left for home three days afterwards.

But because of the warm welcome and high regard shown him by the leaders of the Philippine Republic, Mr. Paterno became confident that he would triumph eventually. Using all means to reach his goal as quickly as he could, he sought an audience with Governor Primo de Rivera, with whom he had a serious talk. Within a few days after the interview, in the same month of October 1897, he returned to Biyak-na-Bato full of optimism about his mission. He was accompanied by some patriots whom he had retrieved from exile or prison; among them were Isabelo Artacho, Felix Ferrer, Vicente Lukban, and Doroteo Lopez. That he was able to have these detainees released proved once more that he was influential with the Spanish authorities. After giving his companions some secret instructions, he left quickly for Manila.

Soon after Mr. Paterno's departure, his proteges asked for permission to talk with President Emilio Aguinaldo. They offered to serve in the Revolutionary Government, and forthwith President Aguinaldo and the cabinet members who were present acceded. Messrs. Isabelo Artacho and Felix Ferrer were assigned to write the constitution, while Messrs. Vicente Lukban and Doroteo Lopez were given the task of fortifying the defenses and of procuring materials for the manufacture of weapons.

Mr. Paterno returned once more to Biyak-na-Bato on November 1, 1897, with Messrs. Celestino Aragon and Agustin de la Rosa, two rebels released from prison because of his intercession with the Spanish authorities. Mr. Paterno stayed on for a few days after until the constitution written by Artacho and Ferrer was ratified.

The constitution was finally approved, despite many who objected on the ground that it was bodily lifted from the revolutionary constitution of Cuba. As a result of the approval of the constitution, the departmental system of government was abolished. Other matters taken up at the assembly that approved the constitution were the elections of new Ministers of State and Interior, respectively. Mr. Antonio Montenegro, the incumbent Governor of Manila, was elected to succeed the late Mr. Jacinto Lumbreras as Minister of State, while Mr. Isabelo Artacho was chosen Minister of Interior, Vice General Pascual Alvarez, who was appointed Intendent General of the army.

After the assembly was adjourned, Mr. Pedro Paterno voluntarily joined the Revolution. President Aguinaldo took the occasion to rebuke Mr.

Paterno for not attending the deliberations of the assembly despite his repeated invitation.

"I did not wish to interfere in the affairs of the Revolution that was leading the country to ruin," Paterno replied.

Stung by Paterno's statement, President Aguinaldo accused him thus: "You people with higher education should have led those of us who were blind. You could do better than be the thorn on the side of the freedom fighters of our Motherland! You are the more vicious enemies and traitors to the people's will, to reason and justice."

Hurt by President Aguinaldo's accusation, Paterno answered back, "We thought of those matters much earlier than you did. We took up arms before you did. And if we had failed, you, too, will fail if you proceed in the way you are now doing."

Had third parties not intervened, the heated exchange of words would have led to a bloody affray. After the incident, many speculated that Mr. Paterno's truce mission would fail. Mr. Paterno soon sought a reconciliation with President Aguinaldo at the latter's Biyak-na-Bato residence. After this rapprochement, Mr. Paterno presented to President Aguinaldo his draft of the truce agreement. The Supreme Council of the Government of the Philippine Republic approved the terms of the peace proposal after some discussion and analysis. Finally Mr. Paterno took the approved draft to the Governor-General in Manila for his consideration and approval.

According to General Artemio Ricarte, who participated in the proceedings at Biyak-na-Bato, the following were some of the terms of the peace pact:

1) Indemnity of one million pesos to be paid by the Spanish
   Government to the rebels for giving up the arms used in the
   Revolution.

2) General amnesty for all political prisoners.

3) Abolition of civil guards and their replacement by municipal
   police.

4) Expulsion of friars from the country.

5) Immediate establishment of an autonomous nationalist
   government.

6) Underwriting of the travel expenses of any Filipino rebel who chose to live abroad.

General Ricarte asserted that the ones who had signed the peace pact and worked for its approval were the same persons Mr. Paterno had brought along with him to Biyak-na-Bato. As Mr. Paterno's proteges, they had exerted all effort to promote his mission.

Meanwhile, just when Mr. Antonio Montenegro had assumed the position of Minister of State at the temporary headquarters in Biyak-na-Bato, President Aguinaldo received a letter denouncing Mr. Montenegro. Written by the Secretary of War of the Philippine Republic[55] and presented to the President by Mr. Feliciano Jocson, Minister of the Interior in the former Departmental Government, the latter accused Mr. Montenegro and his clique of ordering the assassination of General Julian Santos.

General Santos was cornered and shot; and when he was lying prostrate on the ground although still alive, he was beaten to death until his body was a mangled mass. The letter asked for an investigation of the case in order to punish the guilty parties, but the matter was suddenly dropped in the flurry of preparations for the peace treaty.

Toward the end of December 1897, Pedro Paterno returned to Biyak-na-Bato with good news for the rebel government. This was in the form of the following changes in the truce terms:

1) The Spanish Government would not be able to pay more than 800,000 pesos in indemnity. This amount they promised to pay in three installments in the following manner.

a) 400,000 pesos to be paid on arrival in Hongkong of rebel leaders who wished to reside in that city after the truce agreement.

b) 200,000 pesos to be paid after 1,500 guns were surrendered to the Spanish Government; and

c) 200,000 pesos to be paid after a thanksgiving Mass (the *Te Deum*) was celebrated.

2) As regards the demands for expulsion of the friars, the abolition of the civil guards, and the establishment of an autonomous

---

[55]Kalaw lists Emiliano Riego de Dios as this official in the Biyak-na-Bato Government (*The Philippine Revolution*, 64).

government, Governor Fernando Primo de Rivera at first was reluctant to accede, but later on was prevailed upon to do so in view of the granting of amnesty to all rebels and the exile of those of their leaders who might wish to live abroad.

After a careful study of the amended truce terms, President Aguinaldo and his cabinet ministers approved the peace proposal, on condition that two generals of the Spanish Government were to stay in Biyak-na-Bato as hostages while he and his party were to be escorted to Hongkong by Mr. Pedro Paterno and a Spanish colonel. Mr. Paterno happily returned to Manila with his mission accomplished.

President Aguinaldo called a meeting of the leaders of the Revolutionary Government after Mr. Paterno's departure. At this meeting, Mr. Isabelo Artacho's appointment as Director of Commerce was approved. Mr. Artacho was also authorized to be the custodian of the money the Spaniards were to pay for the surrender of arms. This money was to be used to capitalize certain business enterprises and to underwrite the studies of some Filipino students abroad. General Vibora was assigned the task of collecting the stipulated 1,500 guns to be surrendered to the Spanish Government.

Soon after this meeting, Mr. Paterno arrived once more in Biyak-na-Bato from Manila, so eager was he to conclude the negotiations for the peace pact successfully. He was accompanied by a Spaniard, Mr. Miguel Primo de Rivera, a colonel in the Spanish army. The colonel asked President Aguinaldo to give him custody of the Spanish friars being held prisoners by the Revolutionary Government. President Aguinaldo readily agreed, and the friars were taken to Manila by Mr. Paterno and Colonel Primo de Rivera.

Subsequent to these events, a complaint was filed with the Council of War of the Philippine Republic against a major of the Katipunan contingent at Irulong in Baler. Director Isabelo Artacho stopped the investigation of the case on the ground that after the truce agreements had been signed, such matters became irrelevant.

Artacho insisted that they should devote their efforts instead towards an information campaign to implement the armistice. He also instructed all armed units of the Katipunan to send to the government headquarters at Biyak-na-Bato statements signed by their respective leaders of their whole-hearted support to the peace agreement approved by President Aguinaldo and the Supreme Council. Although bitterly opposed by General Mariano Noriel and Colonel Agapito Bonzon in this matter, Artacho's opinions nevertheless prevailed. A related incident was President Aguinaldo's confrontation with General Vibora, Captain General of the Philippine Republic. Aguinaldo accused Vibora of holding secret meetings in order to conspire against him. The matter ended amicably, with the latter offering a satisfactory explanation which dispelled the other's suspicions.

Following these incidents, General Tomas Mascardo arrived at Biyak-na-Bato accompanied by a relative of President Aguinaldo and the widow of Candido Tirona, the patriot and late Minister of War in the Magdalo Council. They came to bid good-bye to the President and his party who were leaving for Hongkong.

Next to arrive at Biyak-na-Bato was Mr. Feliciano Jocson, who had boycotted the signing of the truce agreement. He had come to explain his reasons for objecting to the pact, but Aguinaldo paid little attention to him. Undaunted, Mr. Jocson returned to his outpost at Pugad Baboy in Kalookan and persuaded many to take up arms again by raising the issue of the assassination of Andres Bonifacio. He argued that the great Father of the Katipunan had been betrayed by his own brethren and that it was now their duty to avenge his death and carry on the unfinished task. He was able to convince many officers of the revolutionary army of the righteousness of his objections to the truce. This resulted in their setting up a number of resistance units in different areas, foremost among them Malabon and Kalookan in Rizal province, and in Tondo, Binondo, and Sampaloc in the city of Manila.

Meanwhile, in fulfillment of one of the conditions of the peace agreement, Messrs. Pedro Paterno and Maximo Paterno brought two Spanish officers as hostages to Biyak-na-Bato. They were General Tejeiro and Brigadier General Monet of the Spanish army.

The hostages were lodged in a room in the building that housed the Biyak-na-Bato Government and were heavily guarded by the People's troops. In order to provide maximum security to the hostages, the guards were instructed not to let anyone except the ranking officials and generals of the Revolution communicate with them.

The Paternos also brought along several photographers to Biyak-na-Bato.

LXVII

President Emilio Aguinaldo left Biyak-na-Bato in the afternoon of Friday, December 24, 1897. After lunch and a short rest, he mounted a splendid-looking horse and bade farewell to the throng that gathered to see him off. Among those watching his departure were the two Spanish generals, hostages from their government. Shouts of "Long live Spain!" filled the air as he rode away. What a dashing military figure he cut! A crowd followed him to Baliwag, Bulacan, where he rested and spent the night.

Very early the following day, December 25, President Aguinaldo and his party, along with others who wanted to see him off, left Baliwag and proceeded to the railroad station at Barasoain in Malolos, Bulacan. There they boarded a train from Manila that took them to Dagupan, Pangasinan.

On the train, he sat with Mr. Pedro Paterno and Lieutenant Colonel Miguel Primo de Rivera. A boat that was to take the party to Hongkong awaited them at Dagupan. Among those composing the party were Generals Vito Belarmino, Mariano Llaerna, Tomas Mascardo, Salvador Estrella; Colonels Lazaro Makapagal, Agapito Bonzon, Wenceslao Viniegra, Benito Natividad, Gregorio del Pilar, Ignacio Pawa; Minister of State Antonio Montenegro, Treasurer Silvestre Legaspi, Dr. Maximo Viola, Messrs. Vicente Lukban, Anastacio Francisco, Celestino Aragon, Agustin de la Rosa, and Primitivo Artacho.

On December 29, President Aguinaldo's cable telling of their safe arrival in Hongkong reached Biyak-na-Bato. The cable also relayed the information that he had received the 400,000 pesos initial payment stipulated in the peace pact.

Upon receipt of the communication from Hongkong, the leaders left at Biyak-na-Bato, among whom were Baldomero Aguinaldo and Isabelo Artacho, convened a meeting wherein they approved the unconditional release of the two Spanish hostages, Tejeiro and Monet. Thus they were relieved of the heavy responsibility entailed in keeping the hostages in custody.

The following day, December 30, as the Katipunan flag fluttered in the cool morning breeze at Biyak-na-Bato, General Vibora called his troops for presentation of arms. He made a little speech about the need to accept the peace terms—the war-weary could at last find time to rest, and their comrades who had fallen in defense of freedom could finally be fittingly honored. Hoping to bolster the morale of the troops and to make the acceptance of the truce more palatable, Mr. Isabelo Artacho, the Director of Commerce, also spoke in similar vein. When the speeches were over, General Vibora ordered the troops to lay down their arms on the ground in front of the two Spanish generals. This done, he ordered them to march ten paces backwards. Then he had the Katipunan flag hauled down. Never before had this flag ever been vanquished or forcibly lowered by the enemy. A heroic symbol, it stood for loyalty to all those who struggled under its aegis.

A chorus of stifled sobs rose from the crowd. Those who fell in the night would have wept, too, like their living but wretched brethren. General Vibora himself could not hold back his tears. How he must have wished he did not have to carry out this bitter task!

It was as if the guns were shrouded with a mantel of grief and drenched in the tears of those who laid them down. Then suddenly everyone was hushed. It must be that each one heard a voice reminding him to look after the loved ones left behind by his departed comrades. Indeed, it must be so, for in parting the voice said, "May the all-powerful God bless you!"

As soon the as Katipunan flag was lowered, the Spanish flag was hoisted in its place to the tune of the royal anthem of Spain. Then the surrendered guns were turned over to Generals Tejeiro and Monet, in accordance with the terms of the peace agreement.

The Spanish officers immediately took over the administration of government. They ordered safe-conduct passes to all the rebels so that the Spanish troops would allow them to travel freely to their hometowns. General Pio del Pilar was assigned the task of issuing the passes, and because he was also in charge of transporting the many livestock—cows, carabaos and horses—he was among the last to leave Biyak-na-Bato.

Soon after these events, General Vibora presented a petition to the Spanish governor, General Primo de Rivera. Signed by Vibora himself and by Messrs. Artacho and Natividad, the petition asked the Spanish Government to release the sum of 100,000 pesos. The amount was to pay for the guns surrendered by the troops of Mariano Trias and Baldomero Aguinaldo at the price of fifteen pesos per gun. As provided for in the truce agreement, the sum was intended for distribution to those who suffered in the Revolution.

Governor Primo de Rivera immediately called a meeting of his aides to deliberate on the petition. They approved the 100,000 peso disbursement, which was paid to the petitioners. However, no money reached the hands of those who surrendered their guns nor those who had suffered during the Revolution. No one seemed to know if the officers even visited their men after their units were disbanded. When some soldiers deserted the Spanish army and joined the revolutionary forces, only then did the intended beneficiaries learn that their chiefs, along with Mr. Isabelo Artacho, had boarded a boat bound for Hongkong.

A rumor spread to the effect that the 100,000 pesos was to have gone to those who surrendered their guns and to the victims of the war was never paid at all. This was because, according to the talk, General Tejeiro was angered, despite his release along with another hostage, because the guns turned over to him were old and broken-down and that only a few bullets were surrendered. His ire was directed against Messrs. Baldomero Aguinaldo, Mariano Trias, Lucas Camerino, General Vibora, Esteban San Juan, Pascual Alvarez, and Wenceslao Diwa. Because of General Tejeiro's objections, the Spanish Government did not release the 100,000 pesos, so the story went.

Shortly afterwards, Mr. Mariano Trias, Vice President of the Philippine Republic, took a bride. He married Maria Ferrer, a belle from San Francisco de Malabon, now General Trias, Cavite, in a joyous and well-attended ceremony.

Vice President Trias, accompanied by General Vibora and other leaders of the Revolution, called at Malacañang Palace in Manila to pay their respects to the Spanish governor, General Primo de Rivera. After an exchange of amenities, the latter was probably so pleased with the goodwill of his callers that he gave them 12,000 pesos. He said that half of that amount was for General Vibora and the other half for Vice President Trias. The other members of the delegation wondered why they had been left out of the largesse when they also had risked their lives in no less measure than the two singled out. On the same occasion, the two beneficiaries, Trias and Vibora, asked General Primo de Rivera to release two Filipino priests, Manuel Trias and Esteban del Rosario. The priests had been detained by Spanish friars at the San Carlos Seminary for their revolutionary activities.

The exiled Filipino community in Hongkong was racked with dissension upon the arrival of Isabelo Artacho. Artacho demanded that he be given custody of the 400,000 pesos paid by the Spanish Government, but General Aguinaldo refused, saying that Artacho's position as Director of Commerce in the Revolutionary Government was only temporary in nature. The feud worsened as the Spaniards and a few Filipinos supported Artacho, while all of the President Aguinaldo's companions sided with him. Each time they met, the two glared at each other and their bodies shook with rage. They would have come to blows if their partisans had not intervened each time. Sandiko mollified Artacho by convincing him to let the Hongkong courts decide the case. But Aguinaldo was adamant despite the mediation of his comrades. Underlying all these tensions was Aguinaldo's plan to use the money for buying arms and to conceal this intention from Artacho and his group. Such was the state of affairs in the exile community when an American warship arrived in Hongkong to take Aguinaldo back to Cavite.

President Aguinaldo soon established a dictatorial government to continue the Revolution against Spain. Shortly afterwards, the American warship that had fetched Mr. Sandiko and the brothers Isabelo and Primitivo Artacho from Hongkong arrived in Cavite. Mr. Sandiko disembarked to call on President Aguinaldo. When he learned that the Artachos were on board the same ship that had brought Sandiko home, President Aguinaldo ordered General Mascardo to arrest the brothers. Aguinaldo was determined to resolve in Cavite their feud that had been left unresolved in Hongkong. He had Isabelo and Primitivo Artacho imprisoned and deprived of all comforts and privileges, even food. On the intercession of General Vibora, they were released after about a year of detention.

The *Te Deum*, the Thanksgiving Mass stipulated in the truce agreement, was held on a Sunday, March 2, 1897. The Spanish Government decreed that it be sung in churches to celebrate the end of hostilities between the Filipinos and the Spaniards. The Catholic churches were not as sumptuously decorated as on other occasions when the *Te Deum* had been sung, but this lack was compensated by the lifting of bans on all games of chance played in private homes and a proliferation of games of skill in public places enjoyed by many people.

The following day, Vice President Mariano Trias, Director Baldomero Aguinaldo, General Vibora, and a few other leaders of the Revolution went to Manila to see Mr. Pedro Paterno. The latter was to take them to Governor Primo de Rivera to collect the remaining 200,000 pesos that was, according to the terms of the Biyak-na-Bato Pact, to be paid after the *Te Deum* had been celebrated. However, it was not known whether they collected the amount or not.

LXIX

Meanwhile, Feliciano Jocson continued his resistance to the peace treaty. He opposed it because he had not been present when the truce discussions were held and because there was no document affirming its approval by the Revolutionary Government. Establishing headquarters at Pugad Baboy, Kalookan, Rizal, he gained supporters by issuing leaflets denouncing President Aguinaldo and urging the people not to accept the truce with Spain. In thirty days, he was able to organize Katipunan units for continued resistance in the following municipalities: Polo and Bulacan in the province of Bulacan; Malabon, Kalookan, San Juan del Monte, Pasig, and Mandaluyong in Rizal province; Tondo, Binondo, Sampaloc, Santa Mesa, and Pandacan in the Manila area. Among those he picked to lead this army were Modesto Ritual, whom he appointed General, and Nicomedes Carreon, appointed as Lieutenant Colonel. Most of his recruits were Katipuneros whose courage and will to defend their freedom remained undimmed. Others were young men who were eager to fight the Spaniards to avenge the death of their fathers.

The structure of the new organization that could properly be called the Jocson Katipunan, consisted of two regional chapters and one central council. Although it was essentially an underground movement, its leaders were able to recruit members quite openly and establish branches in the areas mentioned above. This was due, no doubt, to the zeal and enthusiasm of the organizers. On their part, the Spaniard's main concern was the pursuit of peace as delineated in the Biyak-na-Bato document.

Before President Aguinaldo left the Philippines, he had instructed his followers to end hostilities and carefully abide by the truce terms. When these loyal Lieutenants learned that Katipunero Jocson was mobilizing men for continued resistance in violation of the peace agreement, they kept a secret watch on his every move.

Jocson set a general meeting on a Saturday, November 20, 1897, for the purpose of approving a plan to attack the Spanish enemy inside the Walled City of Manila. The meeting was to be held at a house in Camba Street (in Binondo, Manila) that was the residence of Cenon Nicdao, Council Chairman and Brigadier General in Jocson's army.

Invitations to this meeting were duly sent out, but some of them fell into the hands of Aguinaldo's agents and eventually fell into the hands of the

Spanish enemy. The Spaniards quickly plotted to nip the planned attack against them.

Very early in the morning of the day of the meeting, enemy agents began to surround the house on Camba Street and all the passageways leading to it. When more than forty persons had arrived and Jocson was about to convene the assembly, the Spanish enemy suddenly opened fire. Caught off-guard, many fell dead or wounded. Aside from the intended victims, innocent neighbors, women, children, and old people were hit by bullets. As they lay prostrate and helpless, they were bayonetted to death, hit with the butt of guns, hacked with bolos, and kicked in the bellies. It is a terrible experience, indeed, even to recall that horrendous outrage.

Because of this debacle, the partisans of Katipunero Jocson were convinced that Aguinaldo's agents were out to persecute them. They lost heart and dispersed until they were regrouped by General Modesto Ritual and Lieutenant Colonel Nicomedes Carreon of Jocson's army. They went to Matikaw (in Pangil), Laguna, where they established new headquarters. They organized troops with the help of a certain Antonio, a Matikaw townsman; General Ritual appointed Antonio as secretary.

Aguinaldo's agents were determined to harass Jocson. They indicted him in the courts of the Spanish Government for being "in the pay of friars in order to sabotage the peace agreements of Biyak-na-Bato."

Jocson's plans seemed to evoke no further response from his followers. Feeling desperate over this turn of events, he decided to move to a more favorable place for reviving his resistance movement. Jocson left the lowlands of Rizal province with a few loyal colleagues and boarded a boat for Santa Cruz, Laguna. They arrived at Santa Cruz in happy anticipation of the task before them, with no premonition whatsoever of the trap that had been laid for their leaders.

While walking about the town soon after his arrival, Jocson was arrested by troops of (municipal President Venancio Cueto). He was easily identified because of a description of his facial and physical characteristics, which was contained in a circular letter sent by General Pio del Pilar to many municipal heads. The letter instructed the local functionaries to arrest Jocson, whom, it was said, was wanted by the Government of the Philippine Revolution for allegedly being an agent provocateur of the friars. The letter said that the friars wanted the hostilities to continue and had designated Jocson to carry out the job in violation of the truce agreement.

To understand the role of General Pio del Pilar in this affair, it is necessary to relate a previous event. It will explain why he assumed the unpleasant responsibility of having a brother-in-arms arrested.

On the initiative of General Vibora, a meeting of the leaders of the Revolutionary Government was held in the Manila home of Mr. Pedro Paterno. Those who attended were Vice President Mariano Trias, Director of Welfare Mariano Alvarez, General Vibora, General Apoy, General Pio del Pilar, and Majors Julian Montalban and Antero Reyes. At this meeting, Mr. Paterno prepared a statement accusing Feliciano Jocson of sabotaging the peace treaty of Biyak-na-Bato and assigning General Pio del Pilar the grave task of arresting Jocson. Paterno asked those present to sign the statement, but the two Alvarezes refused to do so because they objected to giving General del Pilar an assignment of such serious implications.

When the meeting was over, General Vibora asked the group to join him in paying a courtesy call on General (Basilio) Augustin at Malacañang Palace.[56]

All but Mr. Pedro Paterno joined General Vibora in paying their respects and offering their services to the new Spanish Governor and Captain General. When he saw General Augustin, General Apoy immediately nicknamed him Abot-kilay, ("He who has joined eyebrows") because his brows were unbreached between the eyes. After General Augustin had thanked them profusely for their visit, each one went his own way.

At the same time that he had Jocson under custody, Cueto was also providing sanctuary at his house for the honorable and "Sublime Paralytic," Apolinario Mabini. A frequent visitor of Mabini was General Paciano.[57] Having read General Pio del Pilar's circular letter against Jocson, General Rizal was aware of the circumstances behind the detention of Jocson and his companions.

At first the prisoners were treated harshly, but as they awaited General del Pilar's final decision and as the days wore on, Cueto's attitude towards Jocson changed. Eventually he gave the prisoner as much freedom around the house and showed him as much cordiality as he did towards Mabini. Cueto's changed attitude was the result of a long and intimate exchange of

---

[56]General Augustin was successor to General Primo de Rivera, who resigned his position as governor and captain general. Cf., *The Philippine Revolution*, 84. The typescript spells the name Augusti consistently.

[57]The typescript has Ponciano, which is clearly in error. General Paciano Rizal was the elder brother to the national hero, Dr. Jose Rizal.

views with the Sublime Paralytic. Inevitably, Mabini and Cueto developed a warm and sincere relationship with Jocson.

Soon afterwards, General Pio del Pilar came to Laguna in response to Cueto's letter saying that Jocson had been arrested and was in his custody. He brought along his beautiful (wife) Monica, and the couple was hospitably accommodated by Mr. Cueto in his home. Also on hand to give them a warm welcome were Jocson, Mabini, and General Paciano Rizal.

When they settled down to the business at hand and General del Pilar wanted to take custody of Jocson, President Venancio Cueto refused to surrender the prisoner without General del Pilar's solemn promise not to allow any harm to come to Jocson. Cueto's defense of Jocson came from a conviction that Jocson was not a tool of the friars. With Mabini and General Rizal likewise vouching for Jocson, General del Pilar was finally convinced that the charge against the prisoner was false. Nevertheless, he took Jocson under custody, saying that the latter could be of help to him in his work.

On his word of honor, General del Pilar promised to take good care of Jocson, not to turn him over the Spanish authorities, and not to allow anyone to do him harm. Despite all these protestations, the Great Paralytic Mabini, President Cueto, and General P. Rizal were against Jocson's leaving with General del Pilar. But Jocson went on his own volition after General del Pilar made personal assurances for his safety.

President Cueto asked Jocson to write to them at once should he need their help. But from the time Jocson left with General del Pilar, his friends in Santa Cruz, Laguna, never received word from him. For a long time, they received no news at all about Jocson. Finally a sad rumor reached them that a body had been discovered near the cemetery of the Catholic church in Mandaluyong, Rizal. People who knew him identified the dead man to be Feliciano Jocson.

LXX

It will be recalled that Jocson's men were nearly decimated in a surprise attack at a meeting on Camba Street in Binondo, Manila, and that the stragglers regrouped at Matikaw in Laguna. There they built fortifications under the direction of Brigadier General Modesto Ritual and were aided by Lieutenant Colonel Nicomedes Carreon and the former's bosom friend, a certain Antonio from Pasig.

General Ritual established himself as lord of the domain in the style of a Muslim sultan. Like the absolute ruler he fancied himself to be, he had the habit of aiming the barrel of his gun on any of his troops who happened to displease him. Also, he let it be known to all that he did not believe in the priests' dictum that a man should have only one wife.

One day he asked an aide and some troops to go to town to ask for contributions of food for the camp. This aide had a comely daughter who had attracted the chief's roving eye. However, the young woman spurned his suit despite his ardent wooing. Taking advantage of the father's absence and seized by a dark passion, Ritual forced his attentions on the girl. Despite her screams for help, nobody dared to come to her rescue because Ritual, invoking his authority as chief, threatened to shoot anyone who would attempt to come to her aid.

When the father returned to camp, he at once learned of the dishonor done to his daughter. He received the news in silent anguish as tears rolled down his cheeks and a deep sigh heaved his chest. Then he bore down a heavy fist on his seat and walked away from his companions. He ignored General Ritual's summons for talking things over. Ritual countered this rebuff with a threat of arrest for insubordination, but this was not carried out because father and daughter disappeared and could not be located.

Believing that the girl was hiding somewhere in the vicinity, he planned to mobilize his men to find her. But his approach would be honorable and amicable this time. He would offer her love and marriage and security for the father. Ostensibly for the purpose, Antonio, his trusted friend from Pasig, arranged for the preparation of a sumptuous luncheon.

The fare consisted of boiled and fried chicken, *pesang kanduli* and *adobong hito*,[58] a flask of La Campana gin, two bottles of dry red wine, and other appetizers. General Ritual and Lieutenant Colonel Carreon sat down at the table pleasantly surprised at the festive spread.

"Where did all the food come from?"

"From town, sir, solicited by our troops," Antonio answered.

"Goodness!" General Ritual exclaimed. "Is this special fare only for the two of us?"

"No, sir," Antonio answered quickly. "There is plenty more of it. The soldiers have their own shares."

---

[58]*Kanduli* and *hito* are freshwater catfish. A *pesa* recipe calls for fish and vegetables dropped in boiling rice water spiced with ginger and onion.

The two who sat across each other at the table poured their drinks; they mixed red wine with gin and then toasted each other. After drinking broth, they started eating, each one intent on the plate before him and without any presentiment of any untoward happening.

Suddenly Ritual was hit on the head by a blow so hard that it smashed his skull and killed him instantly. Carreon made a move to retaliate, but the attackers of Ritual lunged at him. Carreon eluded the blows, jumped out of the house, and tried to negotiate the fence to the next houseyard. But a concealed guard felled him with a fatal blow on the head.

Lieutenant Antonio, the former loyal aide and confidant of Ritual, had planned the revenge. He had eighteen men armed with guns ready to shoot at Ritual should the plan to kill him instantly with a blow on the head fail. He had not intended to kill Lieutenant Colonel Nicomedes Carreon, but when the latter made a move to fight back, Lieutenant Antonio was forced to say, "Kill Nicomedes also!"

When the bodies of the two men had been laid out properly, Lieutenant Antonio's men continued the banquet begun by the two who now lay dead.

This is the story of a revenge carried out on behalf of a father and his daughter who had been wronged. Thanks to the cooperation of his men, Lieutenant Antonio was able to carry it through successfully.

LXXI

At this stage of the narrative, let us go back to the time when Spanish and Katipunan forces were fighting in the town of San Mateo, Rizal province.

The Katipuneros rounded up some residents denounced as traitors to the Motherland. Among them were prominent citizens, two of whom were known as Kapitan Israel and Kapitan Matias. At the instigation of the Sons of the People, they were arraigned before the Supremo Bonifacio who was about to sentence them to death. Just then, Katipunero Mariano (alias *Bakleng*) came in breathless from running. He handed the Supremo a letter from Colonel Genaro de los Reyes which more or less read as follows:

Most Honorable Supremo:

Allow me, sir, to vouch for the sincere patriotism of Mr. Matias and to attest hereby that he is no enemy of our sublime goal. As a matter of fact, he has been contributing to the support of our troops.

I believe that he was incriminated by his enemies who were themselves exposed as traitors to the Motherland. For the above reasons, I beg of you, sir, to set Kapitan Matias free and to keep him from all harm.

Your brother who embraces you with all his love,

[Sgd.] *Bato-Balani*

After reading the letter, the Supremo Bonifacio set free Katipan Matias. Katipunero Mariano escorted Kapitan Matias to his house and afterwards went to report the good news to Colonel Genero de los Reyes. Needless to say, the latter was very happy to hear the news brought to him by Katipunero Bakleng.

LXXII

Because a good historical account must record the important events during the period it encompasses, we must not overlook the emergence of a religious sect that spread all over Cavite province during the height of the Revolution in 1896.

Known as "Kolorum," the sect was involved in the bloody struggle against the Spaniards for the freedom of the Motherland. But before we describe their participation in the Revolution, let us attempt to answer the following questions: How were they organized? Who was their leader? What was their credo?

It all started when the Spanish army seemed certain to overrun a community east of the lands owned by one named Sebastian Carres of Taal, Batangas. The people in the community fled to a large forest in Alfonso, Cavite. There, under the leadership of Sebastian, otherwise known as Ka Baste, they organized themselves to pray to God and ask for protection in the imminent dangerous situation they were facing. They promised to help and cherish one another, especially in times of need, and to share the food that one had with those who were without.

Water was very difficult to get in the forest that had become the refuge of so many people. The only source of water they knew was a stream, but to get to it, one had to negotiate very steep slopes. To fill four or five bamboo tubes required more than one man-hour of labor, for going up the steep slopes was as tortuous as the descent.

The prayer-and-mutual-aid society that evolved from the difficult existence in the forest spread quickly to include everyone in the community. Helping one another somehow made life more bearable and led to personal relationships very much like those obtaining in the Society of the Sons of the People, at a time when the spirit of brotherly love had not yet been eroded.

Then a wonderful thing happened. On the mountain top near the refugees' camp, there suddenly spurted from a break in the ground a stream of clear water. Several persons who claimed to have witnessed the appearance of the stream reported that Ka Baste was there himself, and that when the water issued forth, he fell on his knees before the spring. After straightening his frame, Ka Baste lifted his eyes to heaven and said aloud the Lord's Prayer.

Some witnesses who were at first some distance from the praying man moved closer cautiously. And when they saw for themselves the spring gushing forth on the mountain top, they also fell on their knees and began to pray. Others ran to tell the rest of the community, and soon a crowd of young and old, men and women, gathered around the kneeling group. Everyone was struck with awe and some trepidation. They were sure that what they saw was no less than a miracle. They believed that it was an act of God to reward Ka Baste's saintliness and to heed his prayers for a source of water other than the stream below the deep and difficult gorge.

From that time on, the sect grew in number. Many believed in Ka Baste's holiness and were, moreover, attracted to his humble and kindly ways. In his characteristic humility, Ka Baste denied that he was the highest leader of the sect. He said that their chief was a hermit who lived in a cave in Mount Banahaw in Tayabas [now Quezon province].

The hermit's name was Rufino Luntok, but was more popularly known as Tatang Pinong.[59] Inside his cave, he was always on his knees, praying and communing with God the Father. He was reputed to be able to hear the Holy Voice, the voice of God.

According to Ka Baste, God had transferred the Holy Land, Jerusalem and Calvary, and all other things having to do with the sufferings of Christ, to Mount Banahaw and had entrusted their care to Tatang Pinong. The

---

[59]Tatang means "father" but is interchangeably used to mean "uncle." "Pinong" is a nickname for the Christian name, Rufino.

passion of Jesus Christ took too long to recount, but one had only to visit Mount Banahaw to make him a true believer.

Mount Banahaw became a shrine for over 20,000 believers. Below Tatang Pinong in the sect's hierarchy were numerous pastors who were in charge of propagating their faith. Among these were Sebastian Carres (or Ka Baste), Juan Magdalo, and one named Eligio (who was better known as *Diyos-Diyosan* [One Who Imitated God]).

On the purported assurance of the Holy Voice that they could make the Spanish enemy capitulate without a fight, Ka Baste ordered his aides to begin mobilizing men to help fight for the country's freedom. They did not need to carry any weapon; all they had to have was a yard's length of rope for each man. The Spaniards would surrender voluntarily, and the rope would come in handy for trussing up their hands. Ka Baste instructed Juan Magdalo and Eligio (alias *Diyos-Diyosan*) to organize troops accordingly. Tatang Pinong himself approved of the plans and said that they should indeed do everything they could to defend the freedom of the Motherland. On his part, he would pray for their victory.

Juan Magdalo, Ka Baste's deputy, carried out his assignment with zeal. He wrote to all the leading pastors to organize their brethren, men and women alike, but not the weak and the old, and mass them at the foot of Mount Banahaw. The pastors responded as zealously; and altogether they were able to gather an army of about 5,000 men and women at the appointed time and place. Pastor Juan Magdalo briefed them as follows:

"We are carrying out this plan to defend our country's freedom on instructions of the Holy Voice. Our strength lies in our abiding faith, and all each one of us needs to bring as weapon is a yard's length of rope. We shall walk into town as in a huge procession. We shall carry candles and the image of a saint who will have the power to make the enemy surrender; and we shall pray all the while, for prayer is our real weapon.

"We shall be dressed like we would for a procession. The older brethren will wear long robes like those of the apostles. Around our waists we shall wear like a belt our piece of rope. At our approach, the enemy will be stunned and immobilized. We shall hurl our ropes at them, and these, as if by magic, will tie the hands of the motionless Spanish troops. Then we shall collect their guns and bullets which we shall need for future battles."

This talk was given shortly before that fateful day of June 24, 1897.[60]

At six o'clock in the evening of that date, a multitude of men and women, old and young, had gathered outside the town and were getting ready for a procession. Some were dressed in long white robes. As they walked towards town, they carried torches and chanted prayers. In the middle of the procession was a figure dressed as St. John the Baptist.

Standing on a low table carried on the shoulders of four men, "St. John" was none other than Juan Magdalo himself. The procession was intended to take their St. John into the church inside Tayabas town, so that they could be as close as possible to the parish house where the enemy was entrenched. When within striking distance of the parish house, they would undo the ropes around their waists and hurl them at the Spanish troops and civil guards inside the house.

But the enemy was awaiting their approach, ready for attack, for they already had suspicions about what ostensibly was a pious procession. Getting alarmed when they saw the marchers undoing their belts at the same time, the enemy suddenly opened fire on the advancing *Kolorum* lines.

After some sustained shooting, many bodies lay dead or seriously wounded. St. John's platform bobbed up and down as the bearers tried to duck the bullets. Finally St. John himself jumped and landed flat on his face on the ground. Then he rose on his feet and fled.

"There goes St. John! There goes St. John!"

His followers, shouting and pointing their fingers at him, also began to flee and pursue their St. John.

In the wake of what we could rightly call a self-inflicted debacle were the bodies of the dead and wounded, some with their lengths of rope still fastened around their waists while others had them clutched in their hands.

Ka Baste communed with the Holy Voice for enlightenment about the disaster. He wanted to know why their operation had ended so calamitously. The Holy Voice boomed back, "Lack of faith! Why, the dying and the wounded did not even remember to invoke me!"

Those who heard the voice were awe-struck, especially since they could not tell where it came from. On his part, Ka Baste closed his eyes, put up his hands and intoned as loudly as he could, "Have faith, have faith, my brethren!"

---

[60]June 24 is the feast day of St. John the Baptist. Apparently it was chosen by Juan Magdalo as a propitious day. His Christian name was Juan and his patron saint, therefore, was St. John.

The believers' faith was manifestly reinforced. They showed almost no concern anymore for their dead and wounded kin; instead, they set about buying many candles and lighting them on the site they called Gate of Souls. This was on a bank of the deep river called Santa Lucia in Mount Banahaw, Tayabas province. The Kolorums believed that the souls of all dead people pass through this place in their journey to the other life.

From that time on, the Kolorums desisted from participating in any form of overt rebellion, but they always aided the rebels each time their help was asked. They were victimized many times by unscrupulous persons who used the name of the Katipunan for their own personal gain.

LXXIII

Similar to the Kolorum misadventure narrated above is another that happened earlier. In early October 1896, a native of Pagsanjan, Laguna, by the name of Severino Taeniyo,[61] with the help of a few others, began to gather men at a site called Talong.

At a large meeting, Mr. Taeniyo was chosen to head this army to fight the Spaniards, while a certain Mr. Abad Roldan was elected as his deputy. After electing other officers, they took an oath of allegiance to the Katipunan and affirmed their avowed aim of upholding the freedom of the native land, even at the risk of spilling blood and losing life itself.

Being a pious man, Severino Taeniyo immediately sought out the Tagalog priest of Pagsanjan to ask him to offer a Mass for the success of his army. The priest graciously consented. On the morning of October 11, 1896, the Catholic church of Pagsanjan was filled to overflowing. But it was a strange crowd of worshippers that was assembled there. They were armed with all sorts of sharp-bladed knives and spears. Chief Taeniyo and his assistant, Abad Roldan, watched solemnly as the Tagalog priest at the altar offered his prayers for the country and the Katipunan.

After the Mass, Chief Taeniyo divided his troops into three contingents. Then he instructed them on the tactics they would take in attacking the enemy that was entrenched in the town of Santa Cruz, Laguna.

---

[61]This surname is written as Teano in *The Revolt of the Masses*, 188; as Taeno in the *Ricarte Memoirs*, 50; as Taino in Gregoria F. Zaide, *The Philippine Revolution* (rev. ed., Manila: Modern Book Co., 1968), 227. In the typescript itself, the name appears as Taenio in succeeding paragraphs.

With Taeniyo and Roldan in the middle of the last contingent, they entered the town stealthily. They approached the center of the town where the town hall, church, and parish house were located close to each other. At the appropriate moment Chief Taeniyo shouted as loud as he could, "Advance! Advance!"

Alerted by the repeated shouts of "Advance!," the Spaniards readily took up defense positions and began to fire on the attacking Sons of the People. A short while afterwards, the ground was littered with fallen Katipuneros. However, the courage and determination of the remaining able ones did not falter. Instead, they tightened their grip on their short but sharp-bladed bolos and with utmost bravery crept forward to concealed positions. Some moved towards the stone wall surrounding the Spanish defenses, other towards the front of the cemetery nearby. They wanted to prevent the escape of the enemy or to waylay them in case they had already done so.

Chief Taeniyo ordered the burning of surrounding houses so that they could easily see the approach of enemy reinforcements. The sound of continuing gunfire and the sight of flames devouring houses and bamboo trees that crackled as they burned caught the attention and alarmed the citizens of the neighboring areas. Thousands of patriotic townsmen went to the aid of their beleaguered people; among them was a big group of peasants, also converts to Taeniyo's religious group, and a band of well-known outlaws.

Claiming supernatural powers of immunity to bullets and ability to jump to great heights, the outlaw leaders proposed an improbable scheme. They were to negotiate a single leap from the ground to the top of the church and its bell tower or to the rooftop of the parish house. From these vantage positions, they could descend on and encircle their trapped enemies.

Awestruck, the credulous audience thought that this was an easy way to vanquish the enemy. Chief Taeniyo assented to the plan.

The Spaniards, meanwhile, were lulled into believing that they had repulsed the attackers. This was because they saw that only a handful of men were up and about, while the bodies of the dead and severely wounded lay strewn on the ground. Unaware that many of the besiegers were well hidden in temporary shelters, the Spaniards ceased their barrage of gunfire despite occasional shots from the invisible Katipunan ranks.

In their impatience to win victory and to test the powers claimed by those who had come to their aid, the Katipuneros prodded the outlaw leaders to demonstrate their powers. So infected were their spellbound spectators with their audacity that they also came to believe that they, too, would be immune from bullets. They were led to believe that no matter how much the Spaniards fired at them, none of them would be hit, for the bullets would deflect from their bodies.

It was not a difficult task to so convince the audience, for they were themselves members of the same religious sect that believed in such supernatural phenomenon.

Everyone was made to kneel on the ground, fold his arms, lift his face, and fix his eyes to the sky. Then they were all asked to pray intently to ask for divine mercy and help to attain victory. And finally they were to leap at the enemy.

All this spectacle was in full view of the Spaniards, who were keeping a close watch on their movements. The amazed Spaniards must have thought that the people on their knees suddenly had had a change of heart and, instead of attacking them, had now turned into their worshippers, so suppliant were their attitudes in prayer as they knelt facing them. Nevertheless, the Spaniards opened fire from their carefully calculated positions. In a short while, the kneeling crowd was nearly decimated. Those who were still able suddenly came to their senses and ran for their lives.

After this disastrous event, Chief Taeniyo ordered a search for the outlaw leaders, but they were nowhere to be found and neither were they among the dead and the wounded. Despite two successive debacles suffered by his army and the consequent horrors caused by the shedding of blood and the loss of lives, Chief Taeniyo never lost courage or energy in pursuing the dangerous path to freedom of the Motherland. He never gave up the hope of eventually routing the Spaniards. To this end, he ordered his deputy, Abad Roldan, to supervise the building of a fort in the site called Sambal. Surrounded by the municipalities of Pagsanjan, Magdalena, and Santa Cruz in Laguna province, the Sambal fort was ideally located for ambushing Spanish reinforcements from Cavite and Batangas.

One day there suddenly appeared at Sambal an infantry detachment composed of Filipinos. With guns on their shoulders and their heads bowed, they slowly approached the fort. When they were within shouting distance, they asked where the commander of the fort was to be found. On hearing this, Abad Roldan thought that the troops were deserters from the Spanish army who wanted to defect to the Katipunan. Elated, he emerged from his place of concealment and shouted back, "I am the chief. What do you want?"

A burst of gunfire was the reply. A hubbub of voices filled the air as more Spanish troops materialized as if from nowhere. Outnumbered, the Katipuneros once more went through a bloodbath and a depletion in their ranks. Among those who fled was a head soldier named Nicolas Gilil. In his flight he was heard to implore St. Joseph tearfully to save him and to offer the good saint ten pesos for the bother. There was no mention about the wounded, but talk had it that among the wounded was the deputy chief Mr. Francisco Abad Roldan.

Seemingly unconcerned about their fallen comrades, the survivors had no other preoccupation than to flee the scene of the debacle. Each one was concerned only with his own survival. Only three escaped unscathed, and they included Chief Taeniyo himself. The regrouped at Bainan, a site within the municipality of Liliw, Laguna.

Taeniyo never lost heart despite repeated setbacks. Probably motivated by a strong conviction and a singular dedication to his goal, he took each defeat as a challenge that made him more determined than ever to succeed. At Bainan he was able to mobilize a great number of men for an offensive against the Spanish position at San Antonio. The new army fought heatedly a whole day, shedding much blood and losing many lives. But despite his dedication and iron will, Chief Taeniyo was thwarted again. His troops dispersed, and he retreated to Balubad in Pagsanjan to recover and nurture his dream of either redeeming the freedom of the Motherland or dying for her sake. Once again, he was able to form a contingent, albeit small and armed only with shotguns for hunting birds.

Taeniyo decided to go to Biyak-na-Bato to report his encounters with the Spaniards to President Emilio Aguinaldo. In order to bolster his forces in future engagements, he asked for authority to augment his army with gun-carrying troops from various Katipunan camps. The request was granted, and Taeniyo returned to his bailiwick ready to raise a new army to operate in the Laguna de Bay area.

No one could doubt General Severino Taeniyo's patriotism and heroism. Always ready to risk blood and life itself in defense of his country's freedom, he was, however, hounded by defeats and setbacks everywhere he engaged the enemy.

LXXIV

At about the time that Taeniyo was suffering from his reverses, a brilliant youth by the name of Gregorio del Pilar was rising in Bulacan. At the age of twenty, he had already demonstrated his great love for the freedom of the Motherland.

Returning from his studies at the University of Santo Tomas in Manila, del Pilar established himself at the site called Lati in Malolos, Bulacan. There he organized a secret meeting of his childhood friends, colleagues, and friends. This meeting awakened their incipient patriotic feelings, so that after some preliminary discussions, they agreed to launch a movement to defend the freedom of the native land.

Lati became a miniature fort and arsenal of the Katipunan. There they collected various weapons—bolos, spears, lances and others—all with blades so sharp as to make them effective both for self-defense and offensive operations. Equipped with only bladed weapons, Gregorio del Pilar's army was not unlike the army of King David of ancient times. But this young people's army was a happy lot; it sang joyously even as it invoked God's help in the battlefield.

One day del Pilar received the information that a Spanish priest would come to Malolos with some infantrymen and civil guards as escorts. This event they regarded as a propitious one with which to start their offensive against the enemy. Del Pilar made careful preparations for an ambush in the village of Atlag where the party was sure to pass. He planned a strategic deployment of his troops to ensure victory.

They were not waiting for long in the designated place when they spied the still-distant enemy. They quickly took to their pre-determined places of concealment behind bamboo groves, clumps of trees, tall grasses, and other likely places. The road suddenly became deserted and peaceful, foreboding no evil or obstacle for the approaching party. The carefree and animated march of the Spanish troops was soon disrupted by del Pilar's shout of "Charge!"

With their bladed weapons, the People's troops pounded on the Spanish soldiers and hacked and stabbed with such lightening swiftness that the surprised enemy did not have a chance to use their guns. Not having fired a single shot, the Spaniards were quickly subdued and stripped of their arms. Those who were able managed to run for their lives, but most of them fell dead and wounded. As they fell they screamed, "Jesus!", "Maria!" or "Lord, forgive me!"

"Long live the people!" was the triumphant shout of the Katipuneros as they surveyed the prostrate bodies of the dead and the wounded. Then they confiscated the guns and ammunition and took the survivors as prisoners.

The Spanish priest survived unscathed by embracing a Katipunero and asking for his protection. He would not have been spared had it not been for his invocation of the Christian charity preached by priests like him and friars alike. Ironically, however, they were the first ones to trample upon such teachings.

A second encounter with the enemy bolstered del Pilar's growing reputation for brilliant strategy and heroism in battle. He chose the occasion of a Mass for the welfare and benefit of Spanish troops said at the church in Paombong, Bulacan. With an enlarged army, he divided his forces into several contingents and assigned them to specific places. One unit he assigned to the churchyard, another at the doors of the church and the parish house, another on the ground floor of the parish house, and still another to be dispersed in town, so that they could easily come to the aid of those in the church premises or waylay enemy reinforcements from other areas. Finally, a last group composed of men and women was to mix with the Spanish worshippers inside the church.

The fateful day arrived. It was a Sunday, May 23, 1897. Inside and outside the church were crowds of people, but this was not very strange since Sundays were traditionally a day of Christian worship. But that Sunday the crowd was bigger than usual, for very early that morning the Sons of the People led by Gregorio del Pilar had already positioned themselves at designated places. Inside the church they were pious worshippers who looked no different from those others who regularly went to confession and took communion. The women were in kneeling positions, many of them carrying babes in their arms, while the men were standing with their arms meekly folded.

The Spanish officers arrived heavily armed and escorted by many troops. Seeing the great number of people inside the church, they must have thought it prudent to leave most of their escorts outside the church doors. The Spaniards had to pick their way in the main aisle in the crowd, among whom were kneeling women with babes in their arms. Outside the church the men stood in pious postures, their arms folded, their heads bent and eyes closed as in prayer. In that stance, they were able to inch closer to the Spanish troops without arousing their suspicions.

When the bell sounded to signal the offering of the host, everyone fell on his knees and bowed his head and struck his breast in all humility and penance. All of these gestures were in accordance with traditional Catholic practice at this stage of the Mass.

The signal for the simultaneous attack was the ringing of the bell for the second time. The men who had looked like weepy worshippers a while before were suddenly transformed into ferocious creatures. The pregnant women lost their big bellies and women cradling babies rose as one and threw their babies into other arms. Big bellies and babies had only been covers for weapons concealed on their bodies, and "women" were actually Katipuneros disguised as such. Pandemonium broke loose inside and outside the church, and shouts mingled with sobs as Spanish blood was spilled by the sharp blades of Katipunan weapons. When the assault was over, bodies of dead Spaniards were strewn about, while the living were captured and taken prisoners and their guns and ammunition confiscated.

After this encounter, del Pilar's army met to elect their officers. Those chose were Gregorio del Pilar, Colonel; Juan H. del Pilar, Lieutenant Colonel; Juan Pugo, Major; Inocencio Tolentino and Teniyong Kastia, Captains; Juan Fernando, Secretary to the Colonel.[62]

LXXV

At the time when revolutionary feeling against the Spaniards was highest, the Spanish friars, who were its main targets, hit back at the revolutionary leaders by branding them as Masons. In the year 1896, in the town of Bay, Laguna, for example, the friar warned against joining the Masonic fraternity that the Spanish authorities believed was growing in numbers and influence. Thus, every Sunday when many people attended Mass, the friar never failed to picture the Masons as the very incarnation of the Devil who did not acknowledge God. It was in this manner that the credulous and ignorant people were led to attribute the most abominable and horrid deeds imaginable to Masons. So pervasive was their fear of Masons

---

[62]Gregorio H. Del Pilar is better known today as the "Hero of Tirad Pass." Promoted to general in the army, he died on December 2, 1899, at the age of twenty-two while defending Tirad Pass against the Americans, who were in pursuit of Aguinaldo, who was retreating to the mountain fastnesses of Northern Luzon. See *The Philippine Revolution*, 223.

that these creatures figured in their nightmares and waking hours as subjects of speculation in street conversations.

At the start of the Katipunan uprising against the Spaniards, a certain Mateo Andas left Pasig for his hometown of Bay, in Laguna, for the purpose of raising an army to fight the Spaniards. Andas realized that the townspeople, due to the influence of the friars, regarded the Masons with dread and contempt. By a clever ruse, however, he utilized the situation to outwit the friars.

He spread the rumor that in Manila the Masons had joined forces with the Sons of the People in an uprising against the Spanish soldiers and priests. The Masons were fearless and fierce, so the story went, and they would kill anyone who refused to respect them. They were readily recognizable in battle because they wore gala uniforms and royal trappings. A great number of them were Filipinos who had joined the Revolution to assert Philippine independence and freedom. At every encounter, the story continued, the Spanish side suffered great losses; thousands were felled by the razor-sharp weapons of the People's troops.

In their desire to picture the Masons as despicable characters to be shunned, the friars themselves encouraged the spread of such stories. They described Masons as nonbelievers who were the tormentors of Christ as he carried the Cross, etc. These talks gained credence among the people, and privately they came to question how Masons could be expected to respect their fellow men if indeed they did not respect God Himself. These bits of hearsay fixed in the people's mind the idea that Masons were evil creatures who should be feared and abhorred; and this obsession occupied their thoughts and common talk next only in importance to the rumor of a Revolution led by the Katipunan. They even speculated that the Katipunan and the masonic brotherhood were one and the same.

Such were the preoccupations of the people when Modesto Andas retreated to the village called Tranka in order to rally under-cover popular support for the rebellion. Andas worked fast and gained more followers to the movement in a shorter time than Kapitan Agustin (alias *Putol*). The latter, who was municipal head of Bay, was supposed to be taking orders from the Spanish priest, but was secretly working for the Revolution.

On the morning of Monday, September 21, 1896, Andas rode a horse into Bay town in the get-up of a Christian prince in a *moro-moro*.[63] With

---

[63] A melodrama popular in the nineteenth century in the Christianized areas in the Philippines. The plot revolves around a rivalry between two princes, a Christian

sword in hand, he galloped ahead of his bolo-carrying troops; and when he reached the center of the town he began shouting as loud as he could, "Mason! Mason! Mason!"

The townspeople fled to their homes in fear, bolted their doors, and closed the windows. Instead of getting ready to face the crises with their guns, the *cuadrilleros* (local police) shut the windows of the town hall and hid themselves inside the building.

Surrounded by his men, Andas stopped in front of the town hall and in his most authoritarian voice announced, "We are Masons! Masons! Hand over your guns and bullets, quick! You people inside the *tribunal* (town hall), do as we say if you don't want to die!"

On hearing these words, the panic stricken cuadrilleros quickly surrendered. They reopened the windows and threw out their firearms and ammunition. After gathering the arms, "Prince" Andas and his entourage went around the town to collect more guns concealed by the townspeople in their homes.

Their mission accomplished, they left Bay without plundering or confiscating anything for their personal use; neither did they abuse anybody in word or in deed. No one could accuse them of being common bandits. They returned to their Baranka headquarters with a clean conscience and a sense of accomplishment for having secured guns to be used in the service of the Motherland.

Convinced that his actuations were never for self-interest, but solely in defense of Freedom, the townsfolk accepted "Prince" Andas as a true patriot.

Still half-dazed over the events of the previous day, the people of Bay were in for another discomfiture when the governor of Laguna province arrived with an escort of artillerymen. The party went straight to see the priest at the parish house. Sensing that somehow they would be held accountable for the previous day's occurrence, many townsfolk fled and hid from the authorities. True enough, all the local functionaries and the leading personalities of the gentry and the peasantry alike were summoned to appear before the governor. Of the many who were called, only a few strong-hearted ones appeared. They were individually interrogated by the governor, who asked them about the identity of the marauding "prince," where he came

---

and a Muslim, over the love of a beautiful Christian princess. The contest is resolved by a sword-play in which the Christian prince invariably wins. Of a distinctly Filipino genre, it was more formally known as the *comedia de capa y espada*, from the cap and sword that the hero always wore.

from, where his bailiwick was, and who were his confederates inside the town.

After being interrogated, all except three were detained inside a massively built room in the parish house. Those released were local officials who were charged with the duty of maintaining peace and order inside the town. They were Municipal Captain or President, Mr. Agustin (alias *Putol*) and Messrs. Alejandro Kidayan and Venancio Cueto.

Among those detained were Pascual Estrada, Juan Hernandez, Andres Baria, and Eugenio Carillo. Their elbows were pulled back behind them and tied together with a coarse rattan rope and then they were tortured by the artillery troops. What transpired at this stage should not be told at all, for if it were, it would only cause vicarious torment needlessly. The bound prisoners were sent to Manila, and from there they were exiled to the Saparinas mountains in Africa where they might languish to their dying day.

LXXVI

In the course of writing the main body of *The Katipunan and the Revolution*, some significant details were inadvertently omitted. This chapter is an attempt to correct that shortcoming, lest insights be distorted in the interpretation of some events in which the Katipunan played a pervasive part. The present chapter also deals with the peace agreements of Biyak-na-Bato in which, in a manner of speaking, the Katipunan flag was hauled down.

For the sake of greater clarity, perhaps it is best if historical accounts of a nationalist nature be written by persons who lived in the same era as the events they write about, as is the case, for example, with *The Katipunan and the Revolution*.

For convenience, the story of the Philippine Revolution may be divided into the following episodes:

1. The Katipunan of the Sons of the People up to August 29, 1896.

2. The Revolution up to the peace agreements when the Katipunan flag was hauled down at Biyak-na-Bato.

3. The Revolutionary Government under the leadership of the President, the Ministers, and the Generals; the return of the exile government from Hongkong; and the establishment of a dictatorial government in Cavite.

4. The dictatorial regimes of Filipinos and Americans against the Spanish Government until the establishment of the Philippine Republic at Malolos, Bulacan.

5. The Philippine Republic and the Philippine-American War until the capture of President Emilio Aguinaldo by the Americans. In addition, there are the reminiscences written by Vibora and Sakay. The former was imprisoned for a long period; the latter was executed.

The following is an account of the rivalry and test of strength and courage of two colonels in the Revolution.

A large army accompanied General Magdalo, Emilio Aguinaldo, in his trek to Biyak-na-Bato.[64] The army of nearly two thousand men was under the joint command of Brigadier Generals Pio del Pilar and Mariano Noriel. They encamped in the field of Minuyan, in Norzagaray, Bulacan for some six weeks. This must have been their last major stop before finally settling in Biyak-na-Bato. With their food supply running short, they wrote to Colonel Genaro de los Reyes to ask his help in soliciting food donations.

Colonel de los Reyes was one of the Supremo Andres Bonifacio's dependable aides whose loyalty to duty and ability to rally support for the Sons of the People had already been demonstrated. With the love of freedom for his country burning bright inside him, Colonel de los Reyes responded readily to the appeals of his comrades in the field and began mobilizing his friends to look for rice for the needy army.

He assigned Katipuneros Francisco Aquino and Leocadio Garcia the task of collecting the food donations. A house-to-house campaign yielded 125

---

[64]After Cavite was retaken by the Spanish forces in May 1897, Aguinaldo was forced to abandon his location at that time and look for a suitable site where he could establish his government. The search took him first to the nearby mountains of Batangas Province, and from thence northwards to the Sierra Madre foothills at Biyak-na-Bato, east of the town of San Miguel de Mayumo in Bulakan Province. His party arrived there in early August, two-and-a-half months after leaving Cavite. Cf., *Aguinaldo and the Revolution*, 422-423.

cavans of rice, which a convoy of 139 men delivered to Minuyan. Colonel de los Reyes himself headed the convoy that had thirteen men armed with guns. Among the Katipuneros in the party were Tomas de la Cruz, Fermin Cordillero and Hipolito Marcelo (alias *Sargento*). After walking one and a half days, they reached Minuyan where they were accorded a very warm welcome by grateful comrades.

The leaders were settled in an agreeable exchange of news and experiences when a soldier arrived with the message that his superior officer, Colonel Agapito Bonzon (alias *Intong*) wanted to talk to Colonel Vicente Leyba (alias *Kalentong*). Without hesitation, Kalentong accepted the invitation and excused himself from the others to go to the house where Colonel Intong was staying.

It turned out that Colonel Intong was nursing a grudge against Lieutenant Colonel Kalentong for the latter's refusal to join him in an ambush operation against a Spanish food convoy. The ambush had been successfully carried out in the Garay[65] open fields.

Still resentful of Kalentong's rebuff, Colonel Intong thought of inviting the other as a scheme for squaring up matters between them. Lying in wait behind the door at the top of the stairs of his temporary residence, Colonel Intong hit Kalentong on the face as soon as the latter was within striking distance. Colonel Kalentong, however, was able to retaliate fast; and in quick fury, he pummeled Intong with punches and would have killed him were it not for third parties who separated them.

This incident alarmed the community because it portended a rift within the camp. As a matter of fact, the Rizal-Manila troops had already parted from the Cavite troops led by General Noriel, a partisan of Colonel Intong. This information was whispered to Colonel de los Reyes by General del Pilar, head of the Rizal-Manila unit and who counted Lieutenant Colonel Kalentong among his loyal aides.

The resulting factions were unequal in strength. While the Manila-Rizal troops had only 400 men with guns, the Cavite faction counted more than 1,000 with firearms. Both sides, of course, had more men armed with bolos than with guns. The situation was so tense that the men were ready to jump at each other at a signal from their officers. The contending generals sought to resolve the matter by presenting the case to President Aguinaldo, and it

---

[65]Common name for the town of Norzagaray, Bulakan.

was for this purpose that they went up to the hill headquarters of the commander-in-chief.

After due investigation, President Aguinaldo upheld Colonel Kalentong. He said that had the latter killed Intong ten times over, he would still believe in the integrity of Kalentong; he would still keep him as his right-hand man.

This opinion of President Aguinaldo was hailed by the Rizal-Manila troops as a demonstration of their commander-in-chief's impartiality and sense of justice. Although Colonel Intong was Cavite-born like himself, Aguinaldo did not allow such parochial considerations to influence his decision. Tensions within the rank and file eased considerably after General Noriel emerged from the consultation with President Aguinaldo and exclaimed, "Long live Colonel Kalentong!"

LXXVII

The last part of this historical account will be some vignettes about Katipunan leaders from both the Magdiwang and Magdalo factions. It is hoped that insights gained here will illuminate significant situations described in this work.

* * * * *

The establishment of the Magdiwang and the Magdalo Revolutionary Councils moved some intellectuals from Manila and the neighboring areas to go to Cavite to offer their services to the Revolution. Among them was Antonio Montenegro, an intelligent young man from Manila who spoke English. In the year 1896 this was indeed a rare accomplishment among Filipinos, and his joining the Magdalo forces to work for the Revolution was a cause of much favorable comment.

Another arrival in Cavite was Teodoro Gonzales, who was the very picture of ill health and poverty when he came.[66] Clothed in tatters, he was exhausted from lack of sleep and hunger after a journey that had taken several days. This journey was especially trying because he was

---

[66]This statement was disputed by Gonzales in a letter he wrote to the editor of *Sampagita* magazine, where these memoirs were originally published in the Tagalog language. The letter was widely circulated and was perhaps responsible in no small way in impugning the credibility of the present work as an historical document. See the Appendix for a translation of this letter.

accompanied by his wife and several small children. Identifying himself as a member of the Katipunan, he offered his services to the Magdiwang Government.

The Magdiwang leaders heard the family's narration of the extreme privations they had experienced. They were so moved with compassion that General Mariano Alvarez Malia offered them hospitality and protection and bade his son, General Apoy (the author), to do the same. Not long afterwards, however, despite the solicitous care of his Magdiwang brethren, Teodoro Gonzales left their fold to join the Magdalo Government.

LXXVIII

The Magdiwang Council was holding a secret meeting to find out the circumstances under which the Spanish friars of Tanza, together with their entourage, were able to escape from town without being detected. Rumor had it that some conspirators escorted the friars to a waiting outrigger and rowed them out to sea and that the conspirators swam back to shore afterwards.

It was at this stage of the meeting that General Vibora arrived at the Magdiwang headquarters accompanied by a friend, Juan G. Cailles. Mr. Cailles was a teacher at the same public school in San Francisco de Malabon where Vibora was teaching. Cailles made a favorable impression on the Magdiwang leaders, President Mariano Alvarez, Minister General Pascual Alvarez, and General Apoy himself. He became a frequent visitor to the revolutionary headquarters and so captured the confidence of the leaders that he was chosen to be a colonel of the Magdiwang army.

Not long afterwards, General Apoy announced the launching of an offensive against the Spanish enemy, which was defending the town of Lian in Batangas province. The operation was carried out as scheduled, but it ended dismally. The blame for the miserable failure was laid on Colonel Cailles, who did not put up a fight at the Talipusngo fort that was under his command. He had avoided the opportunity to attack the enemy reinforcements that had passed that way on their way to aid their encircled companions at Lian.

After this debacle, the Minister of War, Mr. Ariston Villanueva, stripped Cailles of his rank and expelled him from the army. Cailles was tried in court, but was pardoned despite inexcusable reasons he gave for his failure. He should have been held accountable for the loss of lives and the spilling of blood resulting from his negligence. Later joining the army of General Emilio Aguinaldo, he became a favorite and was given the rank of Brigadier General. He became a secret enemy of the Magdiwang.

General Vibora called the attention of General Apoy to what he believed to be an anomalous situation in the revolutionary ranks. Some leaders, like Mr. Mariano Trias, Minister of Justice, had their own private armies whose troops recognized no authority other than that of their own founder and chief. They refused to recognize the authority of other high officials in the Revolutionary Government, saying that these did not have jurisdiction over them.

The War President criticized the Minister of War and said that if they were to uphold the honor and respectability of their fighting forces, they had to integrate all units under one army that must be the single military instrument to serve the Revolutionary Government. This army alone would have the discipline and vested authority to defend the honor and integrity of the people. Fragmented bands outside this army of the Revolutionary Government could never maintain peace and honor in the country. Instead, they would engender disunity and discord not only among the troops themselves but also among the policy makers.

This bit of homily probably displeased the Minister of Justice, Mr. Mariano Trias, who remained silent afterwards. He did not say a word in answer to General Apoy's arguments against private armies. When the issue was elevated to the Magdiwang Council, Minister of War Ariston Villanueva and Minister of Finance Diego Mojica upheld General Apoy in his contention that there should be only one integrated army for the Revolution.

Embarrassed and hurt, Mr. Mariano Trias took this opinion as a rebuke to him as a high official in the administration. Being no less than the Minister of Justice, he thought that he had as much right as the others to head his own army. Not only did the disappointed Trias defect to the Magdalo camp with his troops, but he also secretly persuaded others to do the same. Among those he influenced to join the rival Magdalo faction was the Magdiwang Minister of Welfare, Mr. Emiliano Riego de Dios, who did not bother to resign his position in the Magdiwang Council.

LXXIX

When the Supreme President of the Katipunan, Mr. Andres Bonifacio, arrived in San Francisco de Malabon in Cavite, he stayed at the home of Ginang Paneng.[67] One evening many visitors came to Ginang Paneng's house to meet the Supremo. These are some of the incidents he narrated to his callers:

On August 29, 1896, when the Revolution started, among those who agreed to take part in the siege of Manila was General Vicente Fernandez. While the other generals carried out their respective assignments, Fernandez reneged on his commitment. He did not bring his troops to participate in the operation as agreed upon.

When the Supremo and Fernandez crossed paths again, the Supremo ordered the latter's arrest and trial. But the Magdalo leaders ignored his order of arrest and let Fernandez go free.

For various offenses, some twenty-nine individuals were expelled from the Katipunan. They subsequently established their own organization that they called *Katipunan Separatista* (of the Sons of the People). Among those who led this new group were Teodoro Gonzales and Antonio Montenegro.

The Magdiwang leaders approached well-to-do citizens in all the towns within its jurisdiction in Cavite to solicit donations for the support of its armed forces. This was also practiced by the Magdalo Council. But the Magdiwang appeal for help was rebuffed by many. In reprisal, the Magdiwang resorted to detaining those who refused to cooperate and having them guarded by troops in their fortified positions. In one enemy attack, some of these well-to-do individuals were among the casualties. The families of those who survived were frightened by this turn of events and pulled their sons and husbands out of the Magdiwang army. While they made an effort to appear like they continued to be supporters, actually they had become Magdiwang enemies.

A deplorable incident happened one moonlit night in February 1896 in San Francisco de Malabon, Cavite. Four of the highest leaders of the Revolution, each with a gun in hand, stood face to face. They stood ready to

---

[67]Ginang Paneng was Mrs. Estefania Potente. "Ginang" is the Tagalog word for Mrs.; "Paneng" is a nickname for Estefania. At San Francisco de Malabon, the Supremo and his party were housed at the home of Santos Nocon, but later they moved to the Potente home until the Spanish captured the town in early April 1897 (*Ricarte Memoirs*, 24).

duel to death to vindicate their honor and to put an end to the idle talk that tended to sully their reputation. In a lonely and narrow alley were the four men—the Supremo Andres Bonifacio, General Emilio Aguinaldo, Minister of Justice Mariano Trias, and Procopio Bonifacio. Just when they were about to shoot it out, General Apoy rushed in and threw himself in their midst. What a hair-raising experience!

By a propitious circumstance, General Vibora arrived on the scene and helped General Apoy in soothing the men's ruffled feelings. The two of them guided the protagonists up the house of Minister of Finance Diego Mojica.

Mr. Mojica immediately called for Fr. Manuel Trias, a Filipino priest, to act as mediator. After mollifying them and giving them spiritual advice, the priest commended the men to God, kissed each one of them on the cheeks, and blessed them. The feuding parties brushed aside their differences to be united by brotherly love once again.

About a month after this incident, the leaders of the Magdalo Government called a general meeting to which they also invited the Magdiwang leaders. Purportedly, the purpose was to plan a strategy for the Revolution. Those who made the arrangements were Magdalo men, President Baldomero Aguinaldo, Secretary Emiliano Riego de Dios, Deputy Santiago Rillo of Batangas, Minister of War Daniel Tirona, Secretary Severino de las Alas, and Katipunan members Teodoro Gonzales, Antonio Montenegro, and others.

In the belief that only revolutionary strategy would be discussed, the Magdiwang men paid little attention to the preparations; their only participation in the arrangements was to negotiate for the use of the friar estate house at Tejeros in San Francisco de Malabon. This assembly at Tejeros and the oath-taking at the Tanza parish house that was officiated by the Tagalog priest, Fr. Simeon [Cenon] Villafranca, have already been narrated earlier in these memoirs.

From what transpired in these two events, anybody could foretell what was in store for the Katipunan of the Sons of the People under the leadership of the hero, Andres Bonifacio.

In the period of about ten months when the rebel forces were engrossed in the inevitable task of repulsing enemy thrusts into their defense positions, the people could not make out which government was the legitimate one. Was it the Magdalo and the Philippine Republic, or the Magdiwang and the Supreme Council of the Katipunan?

One day towards the end of April 1897, General Apoy was at the house of Magdiwang Treasurer Blas Arenas, who was at the same time a colonel under President Mariano Alvarez Malia. At two o'clock in the afternoon of that day, Colonel Luciano San Miguel suddenly appeared to report to General Apoy that the troops of General Pio del Pilar were raiding the house where Magdalo Secretary Cayetano Topacio was staying. The raid had been ordered by the Supremo Andres Bonifacio for the purpose of arresting Topacio and a Spanish woman prisoner who was with him.

General Apoy at once went with General del Pilar to the scene of the raid. They saw Secretary Topacio and the Spanish woman already in the street, bound tightly and surrounded by the raiding party. Topacio was the father-in-law of General Tomas Mascardo. General Apoy went through the cordon of troops and ordered that the prisoners be unbound. Then he escorted the prisoners to the Supremo Bonifacio. But because the Supremo was very busy at the time, he scheduled the trial for six or seven that evening. General Apoy left the estate house after giving instructions to a soldier to call him when the trial was about to begin.

It was twilight when the soldier came to notify General Apoy about the trial of Topacio. General Apoy dismissed the soldier and went alone to the friar estate house that at the time was being used as the Magdiwang headquarters. When he was entering the big and ordinarily-used door at the foot of the stairs near the stone wall, he heard two guards call out, "Halt! Who are you?"

This was followed by the sound of a gun being cocked. For an instant General Apoy was taken aback as his heart pounded hard against his chest. But the next moment he resumed his steps, and when he reached the first rung of the stairs he ordered in a loud voice, "Sheath your guns!"

Two men were climbing the stairs ahead of him, and at the fourth rung he overtook them. The two were feeling their way upstairs and were warily observing the reaction of the guards who stopped them. On coming closer General Apoy recognized the two as General Emilio Aguinaldo and Secretary Baldomero Aguinaldo. It seemed to him strange why the incident he had just witnessed should have happened. He laid both his hands on the shoulders of the Aguinaldos and ascended the stairs with them. When they reached the top of the stairs, he asked the guards for an explanation of their behavior.

"Those were the strict orders from the Supremo and ..." the guards cut themselves short. We waited for the rest of the sentence, but the guards refused to say anything more. Perhaps they would have said more if there had been no other parties present.

The Supremo had received confidential information that if Secretary Topacio were not set free, he would be forcibly taken by Magdalo armed men. This was the reason the Magdiwang troops were on alert and had to be extra careful. This was also what the guards left unsaid.

In January 1897, the Magdiwang army had 3,400 men with guns while the Magdalo had 2,000. Aside from these, there were some 500 other guns which the owners were concealing and intending for their own use. The loose firearms were owned by men who could not be counted on by government, since they were not under the discipline of its army. As it happened, an individual could raise his own private army by collecting men and guns outside the ken of any higher authority, or a leader would secede from the duly organized revolutionary forces and take with him not only men but also their guns.

This inventory of armed strength did not include the fifty small bronze cannons made in the arms foundries established at (San Francisco de) Malabon and Imus. But on August 31, 1896, the only arms the three Alvarezes[68] had when they captured the town of Noveleta, Cavite, from Spanish control were one broken-down revolver, one shotgun for birds, and an old bolo.

Altogether, the Magdiwang and Magdalo armies numbered about 20,000 troops. They had a great number of armed men, but only a few were in the fortifications at any given time. The men took turns in leading quite normal lives outside the camp to provide for the livelihood of their families. However they were always ready, and a single call from their leaders was all they needed to take up arms again.

A secret and treacherous disease crept in to vitiate the Supreme Council of the Sons of the People (the Magdiwang) headed by the Supremo Andres Bonifacio. Had the malady surfaced and attacked violently, perhaps it would have been better for the Magdiwang since they would have been alerted and could have taken proper steps to cure it. And were it not for their dedication to the cause of freedom of the Motherland, it could be said of the Magdiwang that their organization declined because of stupidity or lack of ability. Their army became weaker and weaker vis-à-vis that of the Magdalo.

---

[68]That is: Mariano Alvarez, President of the Magdiwang Council; Pascual Alvarez (Mariano's brother), General Secretary; and Santiago Alvarez (Mariano's son), Captain General and General-in-Chief.

As the Magdalo armed forces began to expand and incorporate Magdiwang units, the number of men with guns left in the Magdiwang ranks dwindled to only 400, while their officers remained the only ones without Magdalo commissions.

Some hot-headed officers of the Magdiwang army threatened to attack the Magdalo camp several times, but General Mariano Alvarez, President of the Magdiwang Council, prevailed upon them to desist. He said that it was bad policy for Filipinos to fight Filipinos; to do so would only lead the country to perdition. The Revolution was against Spaniards, not Filipinos.

This state of affairs called for a general meeting of all leaders of the Revolution. Arrangements for such an assembly were made by Messrs. Mariano Trias, Baldomero Aguinaldo, Emiliano Riego de Dios, Santiago Rillo, Jose Koronel, Severino de las Alas, the Generals, and other Council leaders and troops. Held at the friar estate house at Naic, Cavite, the assembly agreed to the establishment of a Philippine Republic. This agreement accorded with many of the decisions previously made at the Tejeros Assembly. The newly elected officers took their oath in Tanza, it will be remembered, and news to that effect was disseminated.

General Mariano Alvarez believed that rivalry over positions would harm the cause of the Revolution. Thus he deemed it wiser to stay away from positions of authority, to keep quiet and take a watch-and-wait posture, but at the same time be ready always to defend the Motherland.

In the tempest that broke out at the Tejeros Assembly, the Supremo Bonifacio did not at once take precautions to guide his craft in such a way as to shield it from the storm; and when he realized that he was losing grip, he was already far adrift. Only then did he try to steer his craft to a sheltered place. But alas, he chose the village of Limbon (in Indang, Cavite) where the rocks against which his boat could be smashed were bigger....

History tells us of the sad and bitter end of the Supremo Bonifacio's odyssey in Cavite. Justice was not served and the sacrifices of life and blood not only by the Supremo himself but also by other patriotic brethren—were they in vain?

Having read so far, it is hoped that the reader will by now have an understanding of how the Katipunan and the Revolution started, how the uprising unfolded and how it ended. This saga in Philippine history spanned the years from 1896 to 1897.

Subsequent episodes like the ones listed below should also be written about: the resistance of the combined Philippine and American armies against the Spaniards; the Philippine insurrection against the Americans; the heroic resistance of Macario Sakay and Vibora against the Americans; and the other valiant, if puny, efforts in the defense of the native land. But because of the present writer's shortcomings, he could do no more than what is covered in this present work.

LXXX

This chapter deals with a few more relevant details of some events included in the scope of the present work. The account which follows is from the lucid testimony made by Katipunero Bernabe Sunga, who was Secretary and Prosecutor of the Magwagi ("To be victorious") chapter in San Juan del Monte, Rizal. Sunga was married to Francisca Angeles. A well-known Lieutenant in the Revolution, he fought in the first battle against the Spaniards on August 29, 1896, at San Juan del Monte. In this battle, Sunga confiscated a gun from a Spanish soldier and gave it to the Supremo Andres Bonifacio.

According to Sunga, the one recollection that remained vivid in his mind, despite the intervening years, was about a certain Colonel Manglonso who was in the army of General Isidoro Torres at the Binakod fortification. Famous for his strength and bravery, this colonel had a flushed face and eyes that glared menacingly at the enemy. He was steadfast in battle and feared neither enemy bullets nor knives. His reputation as a fearless warrior grew with successive encounters with the Spanish forces at Kalumpit, Pulilan, Quingwa (now Plaridel), and other places where his contingent under the command of General Torres won victories.

Aside from his belligerent visage and stance, there was something else about Colonel Manglonso that made him an object of fear. It was whispered that he ate human flesh.

After their string of victories in different places in Bulacan province, the army of General Torres rested in the town of San Rafael. The Sons of the People were enjoying their fourth day of respite when a great number of Spanish troops unexpectedly swooped down on them. Because the Katipunan ranks were dispersed, they could not fight back effectively. The suddenness of the attack did not give them time to regroup, so that they were easily overwhelmed.

Blood flowed on the streets as the dead and wounded lay prostrate. The victims were not only the combatants, but also townspeople, old and young, men and women. After a whole day of fighting, the Katipunan survivors fled in disarray, some to their hometowns and others to their Binakod fortified camp. Others tried to escape the clutches of their Colonel Manglonso, but were thwarted in their attempt.

The troops collected by Colonel Manglonso were chafing against the authority of their officer for whom they had an intense dislike and fear. Though they wanted to escape, fear of reprisal deterred them. He was known to open up the body of a dead enemy for the liver, which he roasted and ate. Even when he wore a smile, his look inspired terror in the beholder. Thus his men came to believe that he was an *aswang*.[69]

Colonel Manglonso believed that they should not go back to their Binakod camp because that would be the first place the enemy would go to in search of them. He led his troops in search of a better campsite, intending to look for General Torres afterwards to notify him about his find.

The colonel rode ahead of his troops, who fell to talking among themselves about their plight. They all hated and feared him, but they dared not escape or say they were quitting, for fear that he would do to them what he was wont to do with his enemies. They knew that when angry, he turned murderous; thus they dared not incur his wrath. Knowing that he was undaunted by bullets and knives and that he had gone through many battles unscathed, they believed that he must indeed be formidable!

At the end of such whispered talk, the men vowed to end their virtual slavery. They decided to kill him. They conspired to hit him on the head when he least expected it. The opportunity came after a long trek that lasted the whole morning.

Feeling hungry and tired, Colonel Manglonso ordered his men to cook lunch under a big tree deep inside a wooded area. After a midday meal, he slumped under the tree and rested his head against the trunk. Soon he fell in deep sleep.

Moving on the sly, the men had ready three pieces of hardwood planks with which to hit him on the head. Twice, a group tried to attack their colonel, but each time they were prevailed upon by the others to desist. What if Manglonso were really an aswang, and therefore invulnerable? They shuddered to think of the consequences should he survive the attempt on his life.

---

[69] A person who was believed to have the power to transform himself into an animal form, usually a dog, for the purpose of inflicting harm on people, especially pregnant women.

Still, there were some who were determined to do away with him. Seeing that he did not seem to be bothered by all the stirrings around him, three were emboldened to carry out the bloody deed. They hit him on the head so hard that they broke his skull to pieces. When they were sure he was dead, they gathered all his personal belongings and buried these with the body. Over the grave they wrote what to them was a fitting epitaph: "Here lies an Aswang."

Their job finished, they abandoned the site and agreed not to let General Torres know about the matter to avoid prosecution and responsibility for the deed.

LXXXI

In addition to what has already been recounted before about the leadership of the Magdiwang army, it should be noted that some old officers were commissioned as colonels. But in the time that their troops had not yet been organized, the following were given temporary positions in the bureaucracy:

Isidoro Alvarez:	Personal Advisor to the President
Dionisio Alvarez:	Personal Treasurer
Emiterio Malia:	Deputy Personal Treasurer
Adriano Guinto:	Presidential Assistant

On the other hand, the following civilian functionaries were given commissions as majors in the army:

Andres Diaz:	Justice of the People's Council
Nicolas Ricafrente:	President of the People's Council
Benito Alix:	Treasurer
Valentin Salud:	Prosecutor

Messrs. Alix and Salud refused to accept their commissions as majors in the army. They contended that if they did so, they would be betraying the Katipunan oath wherein they had pledged to serve the cause of the Motherland as Treasurer and Prosecutor, respectively. They were not disposed to break that oath, especially since it was signed in their own blood and stipulated that they were to perform specific tasks and not any others.

All the persons in the above list were Katipunan members, of legal age, and natives of Noveleta, Cavite.

The Magdiwang army likewise offered two exemplary citizens of Naic, Messrs. Blas Arenas and Ponciano Papa, appointments as colonel; but like their Noveleta counterparts mentioned above, they also declined military commissions. They gave unstinting moral and material support to the Revolution without any thought of personal gain. Arguing that they could be of greater help if they were allowed to continue in the task of procuring food for the army, they convinced the Magdiwang leadership about the soundness of their proposition.

Historical accounts tell of the heroic deed of those who truly love freedom. This is as it should be so that their memory will be cherished forever.

It is gratifying to know that the patriots, "Old Melchora" and Lieutenant Plonio[70] received due credit and recognition. Also mentioned in the accounts of *The Katipunan and the Revolution* for his whole-hearted cooperation in providing for the needs of the Katipunan in Rizal province, was Francisco Ferrer of Malabon, Rizal.

In Cavite province, two women rendered exemplary service to the cause of freedom. They were Mrs. Estefania Potente and the Widow Nocon (called "Old Anday" [for Alejandra] by the Noveleta townsfolk). Aside from offering her home as residence and as headquarters for the Supreme Council of the Katipunan, Mrs. Potente threw open her big storehouse of grain for the defenders of the people.

Old Anday, mother of Santos Nocon, also gave generously to the Katipunan. Although over fifty years old at the outbreak of the Revolution, Old Anday was at every battle in which her son, then a Katipunan colonel, was fighting. She would suddenly appear among the troops ready with provisions and weapons. Her skirts were loaded with rocks ready to be hurled at the enemy, and tied around her waist was a sash in which she tucked a bolo and a sharp-bladed dagger. As part of her accoutrement, she always carried a flour sack filled with bread for distribution to the soldiers. During

---

[70]"Old Melchora" was Melchora Aquino, popularly known as Tandang Sora. "Lt. Plonio" was Katipunero Apolonio Samson. Both provided food and lodging to hundreds of Katipuneros when they gathered first at Kangkong, Samson's village, and later at Pugad Lawin, Tandang Sora's domain, just before the outbreak of the Revolution.

battles, her son often had to leave his duties temporarily so that he could take his mother to some safer place.

LXXXII

Philippine history is replete with stories about the role of friars in awakening the Filipinos' nationalist feelings. When finally they became fully aware of the oppression by a power that should have protected them, the Filipinos sat up to watch with wide-open eyes and then rose in rebellion to avenge the life and property that were violated.

Through the instrumentality of the friars, many Filipinos were arrested, tortured, and put to death, or were exiled in distant places and their properties confiscated. But when the Revolution broke out, these self-same friars who had belittled Filipinos begged the latter's mercy so that their lives would be spared.

In the towns of San Francisco de Malabon and Tanza in Cavite, the first shots ushering in the Revolution brought the Spanish friars scurrying to curry the favor of men like Francisco Valencia, Jose and Victoriano del Rosario, and Juan Cailles. Francisco Valencia, who was municipal head of Tanza, led a group that escorted some friars out in the sea to escape. In the dark of the night, they spirited away the friars to a waiting rowboat. All the Filipinos except Valencia jumped into the water to swim back, hoping that in the dark nobody would witness their perfidy.

The municipal head of Naic, a certain Telesforo, also helped the friars in the town to escape to the sea in the same manner. He asked a trusted Lieutenant to organize a posse to take the friars to a boat at Kawit. The two town heads of Tanza and Naic who collaborated with the friars were said to be royally treated and rewarded in the big convents in Manila; and when the Revolution was over, they returned to their hometowns as wealthy men.

In the town of Guiguinto, Bulacan, on the other hand, the Spanish friar still had the upper hand. The parish priest in the town was a Father Leocadio Sanchez. Through his mistress and the municipal head, Captain Gatchalian, he learned of Katipunan activity in his parish. He immediately notified the chief of the Spanish garrison and had all suspected Katipunan members arrested, tortured, and put to death. Among the victims were Mariano Antanda, Espiridion Fernando, Basilio Mojica, Jose Kapulong, and Francisco Palipat. When they denied that they were Katipunan members, they were brought to the cemetery where they were executed and afterwards buried in one common grave.

Another of Father Sanchez's victims was Cesareo Galagaw, a young man from Guiguinto who had a bachelor's degree in arts and who was in Manila at the time for further studies. Well regarded by many, he was indicted before the municipal court for *filibusterism*. In those times a *filibustero* was synonymous with being an enemy of the church. The excuse for his arrest was his refusal to kiss the hand of this Father Sanchez when the two met as suitors in the home of a beautiful girl named Jacoba. As to be expected, the young man was pronounced guilty, imprisoned, and tortured.

In another instance, the same Father Sanchez took advantage of a frightened and helpless young girl named Bernardina. Upon learning that her father, Jose, and brother, Veronico, had fled and left Bernardina alone in the house, Father Sanchez went to the helpless girl with evil intent. Her father and brother hid in the fields to escape from being arrested and shot by Spanish troops garrisoned in the village of Tabang. The friar threatened her with arrest if she did not reveal where her father and brother were hiding. He intimidated and abused the poor girl, who subsequently bore a child.

This Father Leocadio Sanchez and some of his companions got their punishment one day while they were waiting for the train to Manila at the railroad station of Guiguinto. He was with a crowd of Spanish priests and a Spanish doctor, all well armed, when a group of bolo-wielding Sons of the People surprised them. A sharp blade thrust in the chest felled Father Sanchez. All the Spaniards were killed except one who, already seriously wounded, managed to clutch at and hold on to the Manila train that did not stop at the station. The crew must have thought it the better part of valor to speed on upon seeing the bloodbath at the station.

With great forbearance, the Sons of the People in Bulacan endured the abuses of the enemy before finally taking their righteous revenge. Indeed, the Katipunan as a whole exercised much restraint, as they did in Cavite when they saved from death even those who helped the traitorous enemy escape.

Before ending this historical account of the Katipunan and the Revolution, this writer wishes to thank everyone who has read through it all.

And as a fitting finale, allow me to quote the motto on the personal seal of Mr. Santiago Rillo, deputy of the Revolutionary Government from the province of Batangas. Approved by the Magdiwang Council, it read: *DEUS OMNIPOTENS.*

END

APPENDIX I

Comments on *The Katipunan and the Revolution*[1]
by Teodoro Gonzales

The Editor
Sampagita Weekly Magazine

Dear Sir:

In the April 1st (1932)[2] issue of *Sampagita*, I read Mr. Santiago Alvarez's account entitled *The Katipunan and the Revolution*. On page 14 of the same issue, he wrote that I arrived in Cavite province the very picture of ill-health and poverty: fatigued from lack of sleep and hunger, and wearing clothes torn to shreds, etc., etc.

He also said that although I was shown the warmest hospitality by order of President Mariano Alvarez to General Apoy, I soon quit the Magdiwang Government in favor of the Magdalo.

Mr. Editor, although I feel honored by Mr. Santiago Alvarez's inclusion of my story in his memoirs, I feel that I must set the record straight, for I find that many of the things that he said [about me] are far from the truth. What I have to say here Mr. Alvarez cannot deny because there are some witnesses still alive who can vouch for me. Among them are Dr. Agaton Cecilio (the pharmacist), Don Maximo Cecilio, Don Simeon Papa, and Don Faustino Eloriaga.[3]

The truth is that Mr. Edilberto Evangelista invited me to join the revolutionary effort in Cavite. This he did through Mr. Feliciano Jocson, who came to see me in Novaliches where I was engaged in revolutionary work. I accepted the invitation and together we journeyed through a large wooded area that is now known as Fort McKinley. We arrived in Bacoor the following day. After breakfast we took a *carromata* [a two-wheeled horse-drawn vehicle] to go the Binakayan house of General Baldomero Aguinaldo. There we met the said General Aguinaldo and Mr. Edilberto Evangelista. After I had reported about the situation in the area where I came from, I

---

[1]The following letter also appears as an appendix in the original typescript.
[2]1932? 1928?
[3] The honorific title "Don" is bestowed on men of wealth and prominence in the community.

begged to be excused so that I could visit Mr. Andres Bonifacio, who was then staying at San Francisco de Malabon.

When Mr. Bonifacio learned that I went to Cavite to resume my work in the Revolution, he asked if I would join him because he was in need of aides. I returned to Binakayan to tell Messrs. Aguinaldo and Evangelista about Mr. Bonifacio's request. The two gentlemen did not see any reason to object to my helping Mr. Andres Bonifacio. Forthwith I returned to the latter's temporary residence to be on his staff.

When I was staying with Mr. Bonifacio, a visitor who introduced himself to me as Mr. Mariano Alvarez came to visit the Supremo. A great patriot, Mr. Alvarez was also known for his kindness and nobility of character.

When I had been in Cavite for more than a month, my wife and six children arrived in Cavite from Novaliches. They paid twenty pesos to porters, who carried them in hammocks and who also toted a big *tampipi* [clothes basket] that contained clothes for all my family. From Bacoor, Mr. Evangelista put them in two horse-drawn rigs to San Francisco de Malabon.

When my wife and children arrived, we put up residence in a house near where the Supremo was staying. I was with the Supremo up to the time of the congress at Tejeros where the Revolutionary Government—not the Philippine Republic as Mr. Alvarez reported it—was established.

Mr. Andres Bonifacio and I parted ways after the Tejeros Assembly. I joined Mr. Emilio Aguinaldo, who was then elected President of the Revolutionary Government. On his behest, I went back to the Manila area to establish a government of the departmental type in Central Luzon. This organ was to direct the Revolution in seven provinces—Manila and Morong [now Rizal province], Bulacan, Tarlac, Bataan, Pampanga, Laguna and Tayabas—under the aegis of the Revolutionary Government established in Cavite and headed by Mr. Emilio Aguinaldo.

Now, Mr. Santiago Alvarez should know that except for the time when I stayed with Mr. Andres Bonifacio, my family and I had to spend our own money throughout the time we were residing at San Francisco de Malabon. It was only when we moved to Maragondon that we accepted the hospitality of others in the person of my dear friend General Mariano Riego de Dios. My children and I, as did my late wife, will never forget the kindness and care he bestowed on us. Mr. Santiago Alvarez should also know that when my family joined me in Cavite, my wife brought with her a sum of money that she had intended for capital in a business venture. However, she was constrained to sell some jewelry so that we would not have to dig into this amount. We paid for all that we needed except during our sojourn in Maragondon, when Mr. Mariano Riego de Dios refused to accept any payment from us. We brought three big baskets of clothes with us to Maragondon. We gave away some of the clothes to the kind people who sheltered us and left the remaining ones in the care of Mr. Santiago Rillo when we returned to Manila.

But most of all, Mr. Santiago Alvarez should know that I did not go to Cavite as a fugitive. I had nothing to fear in Novaliches.... I did not go begging for food from the Magdiwang Council because I did not have to do that in the first place. I had friends and townsmen in that Council who would readily and gladly help me if I needed help. They were Dr. Anastacio Francisco, Dr. Agaton Cecilio, Mr. Braulio Eloriaga, and others who could vouch for me as a person of means before the outbreak of the Revolution.

I refer to my family's solvent condition not to boast about it, but to correct Mr. Santiago Alvarez's statement that when I arrived in Cavite I was poverty-stricken and that I was in tatters, aside from being fatigued, sleepless, and hungry because of the trip. I must say that I am grateful for the kindness shown to us, but still I insist that the person who was escorted to Cavite by no less than Mr. Feliciano Jocson on the invitation of Mr. Edilberto Evangelista, a General and friend of the leaders of the Magdalo Council, could not have been the tattered and hungry wretch Mr. Alvarez pictured. As for Mr. Jocson, he was not a simple refugee in Cavite, but a valued friend, colleague, and confidant of the Magdalo leaders; a pharmacist, he was a man of means in his own right.

If *The Katipunan and the Revolution* written by Mr. Santiago Alvarez, which is currently being published by the *Sampagita* seeks to tell the truth, I wish to contribute my bit in furtherance of the same objective by setting aright some of his statements. This, I hope, I accomplished with this letter.

[Sgd.] Teodoro Gonzales

INDEX